Early Islamic Homes

Uncovering Jordan-Palestine's Early Islamic Architecture

Samihah Wi'am Baz

Table of Contents

List of Figures

17. Umayyad Citadel comparative house plans (from Northedge, *Roman and Islamic 'Amman*, fig. 166).

18. Geographical extent and major towns of the *jund* of al-Urdunn in the early Islamic period (from Walmsley, "Friday Mosque," fig. 2).

19. Typical Pre-Reform (Arab-Byzantine) issue from Jarash (from Walmsley, "Friday Mosque," fig. 3).

20. General plan of Jarash (from Walmsley, "Friday Mosque," fig. 1).

21. South Decumanus area, general plan (from Gawlikowski, "Residential Area," fig. 1).

22. The cistern loc. 43, SE corner; to the right, the stylobate foundation (from Gawlikowski, "Residential Area," pl. IIA).

23. The cistern loc. 43, seen from the east (from Gawlikowski, "Residential Area," pl. IIB).

24. The north-west house, with the Umayyad House in the foreground (from Gawlikowski, "Residential Area," pl. IVB).

25. Umayyad House, view of existing restoration by A. Ostrasz (from Gawlikowski, "Jerash in Early Islamic Times," fig. 2).

26. The staircase of the Umayyad House (from Gawlikowski, "Residential Area," pl. VA).

27. Entrance to a shop above cistern loc. 43, on Umayyad foundations (from Gawlikowski, "Residential Area," pl. VB).

28. The Umayyad Period House (from Gawlikowski, "Residential Area," fig. 2).

29. Entrance to the Umayyad House, above the sewer (loc. 12) (from Gawlikowski, "Residential Area," pl. VIA).

30. Room 7 as seen from its window-sill (from Gawlikowski, "Residential Area," pl. VIIB).

31. Room 10/20 looking from inside the door (from Gawlikowski, "Residential Area," pl. VIIIA).

32. Loc. 20 from the west; to the left, the late wall between the arch piers (from Gawlikowski, "Residential Area," pl. VIIIB).

33. The underground Room 26 seen from the east (from Gawlikowski, "Residential Area," pl. VIB).

54. Early channel-nozzle oil lamp (from Magness, *Jerusalem Ceramic Chronology*, 257).

55. The borders and administrative centers of Umayyad *jund* of al-Urdunn (from Walmsley, "Pella/Fiḥl after the Islamic Conquest," ill. 1).

56. Map of archaeological areas at Pella (from Walmsley, "Households at Pella," fig. 1).

57. Area IV. Schematic plan of Byzantine Phases I-II (from Watson, "Byzantine Period," fig. 26).

58. Area IV. Schematic plan of Byzantine Phases III-V (from Watson, "Byzantine Period," fig. 27).

59. View east showing walls of Byzantine Phases III-IV (from Watson, "Byzantine Period," Pl. 118a).

60. View east showing walls of Byzantine Phases IV-V and intrusive graves (from Watson, "Byzantine Period," Pl. 118b).

61. Schematic plan of Area IV in the Byzantine period (from McNicoll, et al., "Preliminary Report," fig. 3).

62. General plan of mid-8th century housing at the east end of the main mound at Pella (from Walmsley, "Households at Pella," fig. 3).

63. The central internal courtyard and western flanking rooms in House G (from Walmsley, "Economic Developments," fig. 10.

64. Detailed plan of House G (from Walmsley, "Households at Pella," fig. 12).

65. Marble panel and columns recovered from House G (from Walmsley, "Pella/Fiḥl after the Islamic Conquest," ill. 4).

66. Coins recovered from Pella (from Walmsley, "Islamic Coins," pl. 14).

67. Occurrence of pottery wares at Pella, *c.* 600-900 C.E. (from Walmsley, "Tradition, Innovation, and Imitation," fig. 4).

68. Pella pottery wares 6-7, 9 (from Walmsley, "Tradition, Innovation, and Imitation," fig. 5).

69. Pella pottery ware 8 (from Walmsley, "Tradition, Innovation, and Imitation," fig. 6).

70. Pella pottery wares 16, 17, 18, and 19 (from Walmsley, "Tradition, Innovation, and Imitation," fig. 9).

89. Doorway and manger in Stable A (from De Vries, "Umm el-Jimal Project, 1993 and 1994," fig. 6).

90. Doorstep of entry into Stable A (from De Vries, *Umm el-Jimal*, fig. 72).

91. View toward south wall of Room C in House 119 with flagstone paving and cement flooring in foreground and under meter stick (from De Vries, "Umm el-Jimal Project, 1993 and 1994," fig. 8).

92. Jarash lamp fragments no. 1 (from Lapp, "Byzantine and Early Islamic Oil Lamp Fragments," fig. 1).

93. Jarash lamp fragments nos. 2, 3 and 4 (from Lapp, "Byzantine and Early Islamic Oil Lamp Fragments," fig. 2).

94. Late Byzantine to early Islamic Lamps (from Kehrberg, "Selected Lamps and Pottery," fig. 5).

95. Schematic rendering of wall construction (from De Vries, *Umm el-Jimal*, fig. 64).

96. House at Il Medjdel, Syria: plan and elevation (from Ellis, *Roman Housing*, fig. 17).

97. House at Karanis, Egypt: plan and elevation (from Ellis, *Roman Housing*, fig. 19).

98. „Palace" at Boṣrā, Syria: plan and elevation (from Butler and Prentice, *Princeton Archaeological Expeditions*, ill. 229).

99. Sequence of Syrian *bayts* (from Creswell, *Early Muslim Architecture*, fig. 565).

100. Reconstruction of the housing in the Forum of Nerva in the ninth and tenth centuries (from Valenzani, "Residential Building," fig. 11).

101. Jarash (from Zeyadeh, "Urban Transformation," fig. 2).

102. The central and north area of the citadel in Umayyad times (from Almagro and Arce, "Umayyad Town Planning," fig. 2).

103. „Anjar, plan (from Hillenbrand, "„Anjar and Early Islamic Urbanism," fig. 1).

104. Civic Complex Church in the 7th century C.E. (from Walmsley, "Social and Economic Regime," fig. 5).

105. View of the Civic Complex at Pella from the north, showing the church atrium (rear) and adjacent markets (foreground) (from Walmsley, "Economic Developments," fig. 9).

106. Plan of central Jarash in the mid-eighth century, showing the inserted mosque and related commercial structures, including new shops abutting the mosque"s east wall (from Walmsley, "Economic Developments," fig. 20).

107. Aerial photograph of Jarash taken in the late 1920s and in the possession of Walmsley (from Walmsley, "Friday Mosque," fig. 5).

108. Preliminary schematic representation of the principal features of Islamic Jarash (from Walmsley, "Friday Mosque," fig. 7).

109. Plan of a private house at Ur (from Woolley, *Excavations at Ur*, fig. 13).

110. Reconstruction of a private house at Ur (from Woolley, *Excavations at Ur*, fig. 14).

111. Plans and section of typical Islamic house in Ṣan,ā" (from Lewcock and Serjeant, "Houses of Ṣan,ā"," fig. 22.1).

112. Prophet"s house-mosque, Medina (from Creswell, *Early Muslim Architecture*, fig. 7). (a) Before change of qibla; (b) After change of qibla.

Chapter 1

Historical Introduction and Overview of Islamic Archaeology

Introduction:

With the explosion of new material emerging from a branch of archaeology that focuses specifically on Islamic periods and Islamic lands since the 1980s, it is most pertinent to consider its origin, its development, and its potential in reconstructing and interpreting past ways of life.[1] Islam has been a literate culture since its inception; thus, academic inquiry has focused on written texts.[2] While documentary evidence provides a wealth of information on many aspects of life, material derived from archaeology can supplement and contextualize the written record. The material record can serve as an independent arbitrator, separate from historical sources, which were often written with an agenda.[3] While the interpretation of the material evidence may be disputed, the data cannot be denied, as it offers a first-hand record of what had existed.

The archaeology of Islam, according to Northedge, should be understood not as the archaeology of a religion, but rather of a diffuse culture comprising many different geographical regions.[4] The introduction of Islam, with its variable characteristics, and its contact with an antecedent culture resulted in changes in identity.[5] Islamic archaeology,[6] or the archaeology in the *dār al-Islam*, is enormously appealing because it is concerned with the recent past of a region"s present culture, and thus, touches on practical problems and susceptibilities that are not

---

[1] Walmsley, *Early Islamic Syria*, 9.
[2] Petersen, "What is Islamic Archaeology," 102.
[3] Walmsley, "Archaeology and Islamic Studies," 327.
[4] Northedge, "Archaeology and Islam," 1101.
[5] Whitcomb, "Spread of Islam," 3.
[6] Islamic archaeology is a term of convenience found in scholarly literature, though it is more appropriate to use the term archaeology in the *dār al-Islam*.

at issue in more ancient archaeology.[7] Islam is still a living, vibrant religious and cultural entity in the region.

This MA thesis proposes to examine the archaeological material to reconstruct and interpret houses and domestic architecture in the geographical region of Jordan-Palestine during the early Islamic period, primarily the Umayyad period. The term Jordan-Palestine is used to describe the modern states of Jordan, Israel, and the Palestinian territories. The early Islamic period represents the transition from late Byzantine culture through the formative period of Islamic culture. Archaeological discoveries at southwest Asian sites during the past century, particularly the last thirty years, have made this a viable topic.[8]

Historical Overview:

The Islamic conquest of Jordan-Palestine commenced with the initial invasion in 634 C.E. and continued through the decisive battle of the Yarmūk in 636 and the fall of Qayṣariyya (Caesarea) in 640.[9] The Islamic conquest did not create extensive destruction or long-lasting disruption, as most of the cities surrendered on terms to the Muslims, with or without undergoing sieges. While accounts recorded by Arabic sources concerning the capitulation agreements may not always be reliable, the archaeological evidence corroborates the absence of destruction.

Many sites reveal continuity of occupation from the Late Antique period; as such, the arrival of Islam in the towns and countryside of Jordan-Palestine does not represent a break in the archaeological data.[10] For instance, in the village of Rihab, in northern Jordan, the ruins of 10 churches have been identified.[11] A church dedicated to Saint Menas, an Egyptian martyr, lies on the eastern side of the northern part of Rihab. The mosaic floor of the church bears an

---

[7] Grabar, "Islamic Art and Archaeology," 239.

[8] Foote, *Umayyad Markets*, 7-8.

[9] Schick, "Archaeological Sources," 75-76.

[10] Walmsley, *Early Islamic Syria*, 21.

[11] Piccirillo, *Mosaics of Jordan*, 310.

inscription dating to 635, coinciding with the precise year of the Muslim conquest.[12] Moreover, at Khirbat al-Samrā", the mosaic floor in the Church of Saint John the Baptist bears an inscription dated to 639, while the mosaic floor in the Church of Saint George dates to 637.[13] Again, these dates are concurrent with the conquest.[14] The continued construction and completion of the churches suggest that inhabitants of Jordan-Palestine were left undisturbed in the midst of the conquest.

Following the conquest, the situation stabilized under the rule of Mu„āwiya b. Abī Sufyān, the founder of the Umayyad dynasty in 661.[15] Palestine-Jordan generally lay outside the areas of conflict during the first civil war between „Alī b. Abī Ṭālib and Mu„āwiya (656-661) and the subsequent civil war between Yazīd b. Mu„āwiya and „Abd al-Malik b. Marwān and the rival caliph „Abd Allāh b. al-Zubayr (681-692). However, the fighting during the second civil war afforded the Byzantines an opening to raid and capture some of the coastal cities, such as Caesarea and „Āṣkalān, which were subsequently regained by „Abd al-Malik.[16]

An Islamic state existed from the time of „Abd al-Malik (685-705), and probably as early as the reign of Mu„āwiya b. Abī Sufyān (661-680).[17] Donner defines the Islamic state as having an ideology of law, in addition to certain definable institutions intrinsic to establishing its law and maintaining the political order.[18] Such institutions can be considered the following: "(1) a governing group; (2) the means for preserving the position of the governing group in the political hierarchy against both external and internal threats, i.e. an army and police; (3) means for providing for the adjudication of disputes in the society, i.e., a judiciary; (4) means for paying for

---

[12] Ibid., 313.
[13] Ibid., 304-306.
[14] Schick, "Archaeological Sources," 76.
[15] Ibid., 76.
[16] Al-Balâdhuri, *Origins of the Islamic State*, 219-220.
[17] Donner, "Formation of the Islamic State," 293.
[18] Ibid., 284.

state operations, i.e., a tax administration; (5) institutions to perform other aspects of policy implicitly in the legal and ideological foundations of the state." There is evidence that „Abd al-Malik attempted to establish a more systematic state organization, such as coinage reform.[19] As well, weights were reformed by „Abd al-Malik to conform to measures concurrent in al-Ḥijāz.[20] The very act of issuing coins by the new regime may be considered a pronouncement of its autonomy and independence, even in the case of the earliest coins, which were merely slightly-modified Sasanian or Byzantine issues.[21]

As in the Byzantine period, Syria-Palestine under Muslim administration was divided into self-regulating provinces, each consisting of principal and several secondary centers.[22] These five military provinces (*jund*, pl. *ajnād*) consisted of Filasṭīn, al-Urdunn, and Dimashq in the south and Ḥimṣ and Qinnasrīn in the north (fig. 1).[23] The capital of each province was an already existing town, with the exception of that of Filasṭīn, where a new foundation named al-Ramla was established by Caliph Sulaymān b. „Abd al-Malik in about 715. In its initial form, these provinces may have been modeled after the emergency military system instituted by the Byzantine authorities during the 630s and subsequently modified under the first caliphs.[24] As the first Trans-Arabian group of provinces to be governed by Arabs, they endured well into the Ayyubid period, although they lost much of their significance with the advent of the Abbasids.[25]

Expanding rural settlement in the early Islamic period can be attributed to the deliberate development of unproductive lands, such as the Negev, through the formation of new

---

[19] Ibid., 293.
[20] Ibid., 289.
[21] Ibid., 290.
[22] Walmsley, *Early Islamic Syria*, 73.
[23] Northedge, *Roman and Islamic ʿAmman*, 48.
[24] Walmsley, *Early Islamic Syria*, 73.
[25] Shahid, "Jund System," 45.

infrastructure.[26] In particular, the digging of long irrigation canals to supply large elite-owned farm estates and new settlements contributed to growth in rural settlement.[27] Since the seminal works of Sauvaget and Grabar, it has been well known that expansive agricultural estates were associated with the *quṣūr* of the Jordanian and Syrian steppe lands.[28]

The provision of water on a major scale was an important part of these establishments, as evinced by dams, aqueducts, canals, reservoirs, sluices, wells and cisterns identified near many *quṣūr*.[29] Water not only supplied the buildings, but it was directed to field systems, usually enclosed, where agriculture and possibly animal breeding took place. For example, at Qaṣr al-Hallābāt, there is an agricultural enclosure associated with the site with an elaborate system of sluices regulating the distribution of water to its plots.[30] Schlumberger has attributed the hydraulic works at Qaṣr al-Ḥayr al-Gharbī to the Umayyad period, as well as the restoration of a Roman dam.[31] According to Schlumberger, the site is comparable with a western manor, a resident linked to an agricultural estate.[32] As well, Grabar has argued that the Large Enclosure of Qaṣr al-Ḥayr al-Sharqī was planned together with an elaborate water system and its concomitant Outer Enclosure for grazing and agriculture, suggesting a rural component to the site.[33]

In the mid-eighth century, towards the end of the Umayyad regime, Jordan-Palestine suffered a major earthquake, known from Christian, Jewish and Muslim sources.[34] This catastrophe has been preserved in earthquake layers in several sites, such as Jerusalem, Khirbat al-Mafjar, Fiḥl (Pella), and Baysān (Bet Shean). Tsafrir and Foerster date the earthquake to January 749 based

---

[26] Walmsley, *Early Islamic Syria*, 111.

[27] Ibid., 110.

[28] Sauvaget, "Chateaux umayyades de Syrie," 45; Grabar, "Umayyad „Palace,‟" 7-8; Kennedy, "Impact of Muslim Rule," 294.

[29] Walmsley, "Production, Exchange and Regional Trade," 315.

[30] Bisheh, "Qasr al-Hallabat," 264-265.

[31] Schlumberger, *Qasr el-Heir el-Gharbi*, 25.

[32] Ibid., 26.

[33] Grabar, Holod, Knustad, and Trousdale, *City in the Desert*, 148.

[34] Tsafrir and Foerster, "Dating of the „Earthquake," 231.

on evidence from excavations carried out at Baysān. There, a hoard of coins was found underneath the debris of the shops at the time of the collapse from the earthquake.[35] The coin latest in date was minted in 131 AH (31 August 748-19 August 749 C.E.). It suggests a *terminus post quem* for the earthquake no earlier than the end of August 748. The coin, which has survived in mint condition, had found its way into the hands of the trader shortly before it was buried underneath the wreckage of the earthquake of January 749.

The early Islamic period witnessed periodic outbreaks of the plague, such as the terrible outbreak of pestilence, the Plague of „Amwās, which devastated Syria from 638-639.[36] It had several important consequences on early Islamic history, as most of the commanders leading the Syrian conquests died in the plague, resulting in the emergence and rise to power of those who survived, namely Mu„āwiya b. Abī Sufyān, the eventual founder of the Umayyad dynasty. These plagues were especially severe between the mid-sixth and the mid-eighth centuries.[37] The region of Jordan-Palestine quickly fell into the hands of the Abbasid revolutionary armies in 750, without any major protracted battles or sieges.

Overview of Islamic Archaeology:

Islamic archaeology emerged as an independent field of inquiry about one hundred years ago, with the past two or three decades witnessing a rapid improvement in archaeological research.[38] Initially, the excavation of Islamic sites was characterized by a desire to recover artifacts, especially to ensure funding and sponsorship for projects.[39] The minor arts of Islam were often treated as objects of beauty or curiosity, rather than invariably tied to the history of the societies

---

[35] Ibid., 234.
[36] Conrad, *Plague in the Early Medieval Near East*, 244-246.
[37] Schick, "Archaeological Sources" 76.
[38] Walmsley, *Early Islamic Syria*, 15.
[39] Vernoit, "Rise of Islamic Archaeology," 1.

which produced them.[40] The collection of medieval Middle Eastern antiquities in the nineteenth

century was later extended to the appreciation of Islamic architecture.[41] Hence, the initial focus

on Islamic art and architecture. Islamic archaeology, as it emerged in the late nineteenth and

early twentieth centuries, was based on two strands of inquiry: (1) an interest in the historical

significance of art; (2) the development of Orientalist studies from the late eighteenth century.

These two strands did not come together until the late nineteenth century.

When scholarly study of the antiquities of Palestine was undertaken in the nineteenth century,

the Dome of the Rock emerged as the first monument from the early Islamic period to garner

attention.[42] While the area of the Ḥaram al-Sharīf in Jerusalem remained inaccessible to non-

Muslims until the middle of the century, Frederick Catherwood was able to produce the first

accurate plans of the Dome of the Rock, the al-Aqṣā mosque, and the Golden Gate in 1833-38.

To this day, the Dome of the Rock remains a source of scholarly interest more than any other

Islamic monument.

The earliest studies in the field of Islamic archaeology in Jordan-Palestine from the first half

of the twentieth century focused almost exclusively on standing architecture, with the ground-

breaking discoveries in the late nineteenth and early twentieth century by explorers, such as

Alois Musil, Rudolf Brünnow and Alfred von Domaszewski, and Antonin Jaussen and Raphaël

Savignac.[43] These expeditions of Jordan-Palestine stood apart from earlier voyages in the

Middle East as they sought to be thoroughly accurate and comprehensive in their work by

describing, mapping and photographing in detail the places. Earlier sources were researched,

and the historical context of the location and buildings was provided.

---

[40] Rogers, *From Antiquarianism*, 26.
[41] Petersen, "What is Islamic Archaeology," 100.
[42] Schick, "Archaeological Sources," 80.
[43] Walmsley, *Early Islamic Syria*, 15-16.

Rudolf Brünnow and Alfred von Domaszewski travelled through southern Syria and Jordan in 1897 and 1898 to document Roman sites; however, they also recorded information regarding a number of early Islamic sites and included complete photographs of the carved frieze at the palace of al-Mshattā.[44] They were instrumental in photographing and planning other early Islamic desert castles and monuments, such as the ˒Ammān citadel, Khān al-Zabīb, Umm al-Walīd, Qasṭal, and al-Muwaqqar. The publications of Alois Musil, who travelled extensively through Jordan in the late 1890s and early 1900s, include exhaustive architectural reports, detailed geographical observations and ethnographic accounts of the nomadic tribes living in the region.[45] His discovery of the eighth century Umayyad bath and audience hall at Quṣayr ˒Amra was the most significant find of this phase of initial exploration.[46] The palace was remarkable in part for its wall paintings, which include naturalistic animal and human figures, some of whom are female and scantily dressed, if clothed at all.[47] These images were incongruent with what was expected of an Islamic building, and provoked considerable interest in the architecture of the first Islamic centuries. Some years later, Antonin Jaussen and Raphaël Savignac, from the École Biblique in Jerusalem, further documented the eighth century desert castles in the eastern desert of Jordan, which Musil had visited, namely Kharāna, Qaṣr al-Ṭūba, and Quṣayr ˒Amra.[48] The large amount of data generated by the works of Musil and others was followed by the more analytical researches of K.A.C Creswell and Jean Sauvaget.

The two seminal works of Creswell, *Early Muslim Architecture* and *The Muslim Architecture of Egypt*, were extraordinarily precise and detailed studies of Islamic monuments. The former was produced as a two-volume work in 1932-40 and the first volume was subsequently revised

---

[44] Schick, "Archaeological Sources," 80.
[45] Walmsley, *Early Islamic Syria*, 16.
[46] Schick, "Archaeological Sources," 81.
[47] Walmsley, *Early Islamic Syria*, 16.
[48] Schick, "Archaeological Sources," 81.

and enlarged into two parts in 1969. An abbreviated version of *Early Muslim Architecture* was published in 1958 under the title *A Short Account of Early Muslim Architecture*. The purpose was to write a history of the origins and development of Muslim architectural tradition, which required the establishment of a precise chronology of the known buildings.[49] With his overriding concern for chronology, Creswell may have ignored the possibility that architectural change may reflect social, economic or religious changes, or that buildings architecturally similar may have been used to house different institutions.[50] However, without a fixed chronology, no further conclusions could be drawn with regards to changes in form and function. Creswell meticulously researched information in all the relevant literature, including medieval texts as well as travelers" and archaeologists" accounts. Ranging widely in his subject matter and analysis, Creswell dealt in detail with the architectural heritage of the Umayyad dynasty in Jordan-Palestine.[51]

The pioneering French scholar Jean Sauvaget was likewise concerned with understanding architecture in context.[52] In particular, Sauvaget"s model on the development of the medieval suq was widely referenced. In "Le Plan de Laodicée-sur-Mur," Sauvaget traces the process of encroachment on an ancient colonnaded avenue by a suq (fig. 2). According to Sauvaget, in the evolution of Syrian towns, medieval suqs developed on the large ancient colonnaded avenues, lined by shops, following a very simple process.[53] The conversion of the broad colonnaded street of classical cities into a suq occurred during a period of political upheaval, beginning in the ninth century. Due to conditions of impoverishment, a lack of political authority, and a lack of greatness in conception, which rendered the old extensive architectural constructions useless,

---

[49] Creswell and Allen, *Short Account*, v.
[50] Rogers, *From Antiquarianism*, 65.
[51] Walmsley, *Early Islamic Syria*, 17.
[52] Ibid., 17.
[53] Sauvaget, "Laodicée," 100-102.

shops gradually encroached onto the side porticos. Partition walls progressively leaned on the columns, thus reducing the public way (lane) to the width of the earliest pavement. When this pattern was accentuated, the shops overflowed onto the pavement itself, narrowing it excessively. Sometimes, the pavement was completely eliminated, and the only walking paths remaining were the old porticoes, now elevated to the rank of "streets."

In essence, Sauvaget contends that this poaching of public space introduced during the Islamic period represents the uncontrolled encroachment of private structure over once wide open streets. Recent archaeological data, however, refutes these claims: namely, the process of private encroachment on public colonnades is evident at Ṣart (Sardis) in Asia Minor as early as the seventh century.[54] Furthermore, in the Umayyad suqs in Tadmur (Palmyra) and Baysān, there is no archaeological evidence for encroachment.[55] This suggests that the early patrons of these Umayyad suqs maintained uniformity of the shops and the integrity of the colonnade avenue, which had not always been the case in Byzantine Asia Minor.

Concurrent with these early architectural and urban studies, the first significant archaeological excavations of Islamic-period sites took place in Jordan-Palestine. With the end of the First World War and the establishment of the British Mandate over Palestine and Emirate of Transjordan, the nature of scholarly study of the Islamic period shifted from the initial exploration and recording of standing architectural monuments to excavation.[56] While archaeologists excavated a number of early Islamic sites, they did so often in pursuit of earlier remains lying beneath them. For instance, Baysān, the site of the first major excavation of an

---

[54] Crawford, *Byzantine Shops*, 7.
[55] Al-As,ad and Stepniowski, "Umayyad Suq," 205-223; Tsafrir and Foerster, "Urbanism at Scythopolis-Bet Shean," 85-146.
[56] Schick, "Archaeological Sources," 81.

early Islamic site in Palestine, was excavated to uncover the site"s ancient, especially Biblical, remains.[57]

The site of Khirbat al-Mafjar, excavated between 1934 and 1948 under the auspices of D. C. Baramki and R. W. Hamilton, unearthed spectacular architectural remains.[58] The work uncovered a walled enclosure (*qaṣr*), a forecourt with a fountain, a mosque, and an imposing reception hall with a huge floor paved with mosaics and adjoining baths.[59] The significance of Khirbat al-Mafjar was the complete publication of an Umayyad complex. In particular, Baramki"s publication of the site"s corpus of Islamic ceramics was one of the earliest in Palestine and one of the largest, leading to Khirbat al-Mafjar becoming a type site for the early Islamic period.[60] The publication has been a reference for all subsequent studies in Islamic archaeology. However, the lack of stratigraphic controls led to Whitcomb"s reassessment of the corpus of ceramics.[61]

Excavations at „*tells*" (archaeological mounds) likewise uncovered Islamic-period remains, though these finds were seldom treated seriously.[62] The excavations conducted at Ḥesbān, a major *tell*-site located south of „Ammān, revealed major Islamic deposits, in spite of the fact that the site was initially selected for its importance as a Biblical center. The seven week season at Tell Ḥesbān conducted in 1971 produced pottery sherds attributable to seven major ceramic horizons, with clear stratigraphic and typological indications.[63] A change in emphasis can be observed at Ḥesbān, where James Sauer presented the sequence of ceramics from the site,

---

[57] Ibid., 81.
[58] Walmsley, *Early Islamic Syria*, 18.
[59] Ibid., 18-19.
[60] Whitcomb, "Khirbet al-Mafjar Reconsidered," 51-52.
[61] Ibid., 51-67.
[62] Walmsley, *Early Islamic Syria*, 19.
[63] Sauer, *Hesbon Pottery*, 8-9.

providing a systematic extension of the earlier model into the late, Islamic period.[64] The chronology and cultural history derived from his archaeological interpretation gained currency in the secondary literature of these periods. The widespread acceptance of this ceramic analysis laid the foundation for serious consideration of archaeological materials as part of regional history of these periods. In short, Sauer emerged as one of the first foreign archaeologists in Jordan to take the material culture of the early Islamic period and seek to differentiate it from preceding Byzantine-period finds.

Other early archaeological work in Jordan-Palestine was focused on large-scale exposure of elite buildings attributable to the Islamic period and the salvaging of the architectural decoration, such as stucco, mosaics and paintings.[65] A consequence of such limited objectives was the lack of attention paid to the wider context of the monuments, or the occupational histories of the buildings. Walmsley cites, for instance, the excavations conducted in the 1930s of the Umayyad Qaṣr al-Ḥayr al-Gharbī as an example where consideration was paid to preserving and publishing the architectural features of the site, while the cultural remains received little attention. The early archaeological expeditions of many early Islamic sites in Jordan-Palestine failed to investigate questions of site settlement histories or the nature of the occupation. However, these early projects laid the foundation for Islamic archaeology as a legitimate field of study.[66] In fact, the immense archaeological finds from Syria-Palestine compelled Creswell to publish a revised and expanded volume one of his *Early Muslim Architecture*. Furthermore, excavations at sites, such as Khirbat al-Mafjar and al-Raqqa, helped to establish a reference corpus of early Islamic ceramics.

---

[64] Whitcomb, "Ḥesban, Amman, and Abbasid Archaeology," 505.
[65] Walmsley, *Early Islamic Syria*, 19-20.
[66] Ibid., 21.

The beginning of the 1980s marked a shift in attitude and practice in the archaeology of Islamic Jordan-Palestine, especially relating to the early Islamic period.[67] The past several decades have witnessed a concentration of research, both conceptual and in the field, unparalleled in previous years or in the experience of other countries of the Levant.[68] In particular, theoretical, methodological and practical approaches were adopted and applied to the examination of social, cultural and economic conditions in Islamic times.[69] The investigation of the Islamic period occupation as an independent research objective was recognized in both regional survey work and site excavation.

In Jordan, for instance, these new objectives were expressed in a series of papers dealing with issues of continuity delivered at the Fourth International Conference on the History and Archaeology of Jordan, held at Lyon in 1989.[70] The Sydney-Wooster excavations at Pella in Jordan, which commenced in 1979, uncovered more than 1,000 sq. m. of dwelling and courtyards on the *tell* dating to the seventh and eighth centuries.[71] The social and economic conditions of Pella during the early Islamic period were examined as a consequence of these excavations. The Jarash international project in the early 1980s proved significant as it revealed occupation up to the tenth century.[72] The Jarash project for excavation and restoration made it possible to reconsider the archaeological history of the site.[73] In particular, an Umayyad residential quarter was found on the north side of the South Decumanus.[74]

---

[67] Ibid., 27.
[68] Whitcomb, "Umayyad and Abbasid Periods," 503.
[69] Walmsley, *Early Islamic Syria*, 27.
[70] Ibid., 27.
[71] McNicoll and Walmsley, "Pella/Fahl in Jordan," 339.
[72] Schick, "Archaeological Sources," 82.
[73] Zayadine, "Jerash Project," 20.
[74] Gawlikowski, "Residential Area,"107-136.

In Israel-Palestine, there was fresh reappraisal of rural settlement patterns from the early Islamic period, especially in the south.[75] Regional survey work undertaken as part of the Israel Antiquities Authority"s „Archaeological Survey of Israel" and small-scale excavations illuminated the widespread and, in some places, expanding occupation in the arid Dārūm and Negev region into the Islamic period. While archaeological surveys were conducted in the central Negev throughout the 1950s and 1960s, the work carried out by the Negev Emergency Survey in the 1980s has provided the impetus for exploration of the Negev Highlands on an unprecedented scale.[76] Gideon Avni, for instance, examined the early mosques in the Negev Highlands to distinguish two types of mosques distributed throughout the Highlands: a more solid structure near the agricultural settlements of the Central Highlands and a less permanent one in the region inhabited by nomads in the Southern Highlands.[77] Mordechai Haiman attributed a wave of agricultural settlement in the Negev desert in the Umayyad period (seventh to eighth century) to two developments: the imperial policy of the Umayyads aimed toward protecting the frontier by encouraging establishment of agricultural settlements; and the gradual transition of semi-nomads from a nomadic life style to permanent settlement sponsored by the state.[78] Avni and Haiman were both receptive to new understandings of ceramic chronologies datable to the Late Antique/early Islamic transition.[79]

Overall, the field of Islamic archaeology has emerged as an independent branch of archaeology from the intellectual melting pot of the 1980s.[80] The last three decades have witnessed advances in the field of Islamic archaeology in Jordan-Palestine, as new information

---

[75] Walmsley, *Early Islamic Syria*, 27.
[76] Avni, "Early Mosques in the Negev Highlands," 83.
[77] Ibid., 92.
[78] Haiman, "Agriculture and Nomad-State Relations," 45.
[79] Walmsley, *Early Islamic Syria*, 27.
[80] Ibid., 29.

relevant to the study of history, architecture and art history emerged from the field. The archaeological material can act as an independent arbitrator of historical events, in the absence of a written record or a biased agenda. Archaeology produces material evidence that, when interpreted adequately, is an unbiased first-hand record of the past.

Chapter 2

Catalogue of Domestic Structures

Introduction:

Private, domestic structures preserve the ways of life lived by everyday people: their domestic arrangements, how they decorated their houses, levels of personal wealth, hygiene and so forth.[81] The house is the home of the family unit, and it forms the primary sphere in Islamic society.[82] As such, the domestic environment can be informative about the larger society.

This chapter will present the archaeological and architectural material of the domestic structures at five sites: ‚Ammān, Jarash, Naḥal Mitnan, Pella, and Umm el-Jimāl. The description of each building will include segments on the geographical and historical setting of the site, the excavation of the domestic structure at the site, the stratigraphy of the domestic structure, and its chronology. The purpose of this chapter is to detail the basic sequence of construction and occupation in the excavated buildings.

‘Ammān

Geographical and Historical Setting of Site:

At ‚Ammān, the Islamic city lies in the bed of the Wādī ‚Ammān, overlooked by the Citadel hill, an L-shaped, steep-sided, limestone projection of the surrounding plateau, with two terraces, 900 m. long (fig. 3).[83] Almost entirely surrounded by slopes, the hill is in an excellent defensive position.[84] The upper terrace consists of two parts: the double enclosure of the palace, about 126 m. x 126 m. at its maximum dimensions, and the hexagon of the main area, approximately 250

---

[81] Walmsley, *Early Islamic Syria*, 127; Idem, "Archaeology and Islamic Studies," 320.
[82] Insoll, *Archaeology of Islam*, 60.
[83] Northedge, "New Urban Settlement," 237.
[84] Idem, *Roman and Islamic ‘Amman*, 20-21.

m. north to south by 150 m. east to west.[85] The double enclosure of the palace is an artificial platform built out from the north end of the hill. To the south, the hexagon is a plateau-like area surrounded by Roman and Umayyad fortification walls.

According to al-Balādhurī, „Ammān was conquered by Yazīd b. Abī Sufyān b. Ḥarb b. Umayya in the wake of the conquest of Damascus.[86] Yazīd marched against „Ammān and achieved an easy conquest, making terms of capitulation similar to those at Boṣrā. The ease of the conquest suggests that „Ammān was indefensible from the south and east, and may not have had a citadel wall at this time.[87] The date for the conquest of Damascus was given by different sources as 634 or 635.

The Umayyads divided Syria into four, and later five, provinces (*jund*, pl. *ajnād*): Qinnasrīn, Ḥimṣ, Dimashq, al-Urdunn, and Filasṭīn (fig. 1).[88] „Ammān was part of the *jund* of Dimashq. Under the Umayyads, al-Balqā' (the steppe-land east and south of „Ammān) and the south were under a united administration, based on „Ammān; this administration formed a sub-governorate of Dimashq.

„Ammān was an Umayyad mint, as some quantity of copper issues has emerged from the city.[89] The coinage with imperial image at „Ammān was very rare: the two known coins have an enthroned imperial figure left and a standing emperor right, with majuscule M on the reverse.[90] Most of the coins bear the name of „Abd al-Malik on the obverse. However, a small number of coins from „Ammān carry the *shahāda* on both sides. „Ammān‟s post-reform issues consist of

---

[85] Ibid., 21.
[86] Al-Balâdhuri, *Origins of the Islamic State*, 193.
[87] Northedge, *Roman and Islamic 'Amman*, 47-48.
[88] Ibid., 48.
[89] Ibid., 49.
[90] Bates, "Coinage of Syria," 218-219.

one type: a fleur-de-lys in a square inscription on the reverse. In general, the coinage parallels that of Damascus.

During the Umayyad period, a citadel was constructed on the „Ammān *tell*, whose elements include: the palace, laid out in the double enclosure at the north end; the rebuild of the fortification circuit; the open cistern; and the buildings of Areas B, C, and the Museum site (figs. 3 and 4).[91] These elements constituted a single monumental construction project as suggested by the regular layout of the Umayyad buildings of Area C and a unified building technique shared by all the construction attributed to this period.

The region of „Ammān was severely affected by an earthquake dated between 746 and 749.[92] As a consequence of the earthquake, the Citadel of „Ammān was damaged, leading to its weakened resistance to the Abbasid armies. The earthquake and the Abbasid revolution, which culminated in 750, virtually coincided.

Excavation of Domestic Structure at Site (Area C):

In 1975, rescue excavations were carried out by the Department of Antiquities of the Hashemite Kingdom of Jordan in the Upper Citadel to prepare for the construction of a new national archaeological museum.[93] The rescue excavations conducted by Mrs. C-M. Bennett lasted from 1975 to 1979 in the three areas of the hexagonal area of the Upper Citadel: Areas B, C, and D (fig. 3). The area of interest for this thesis, Area C, was excavated between 1976 and 1978.[94] It is composed of two parallel lines of 5 m. squares laid out on the west slope of the Qal'a, extending from the Jordan Archaeological Museum to as far as the fortification wall, and

---

[91] Northedge, *Roman and Islamic 'Amman*, 156.
[92] Ibid., 52.
[93] Ibid., 16.
[94] Ibid., 139.

a short distance down the slope outside the wall. Residential Building B is located in Area C inside the fortification wall (fig. 3).

Stratigraphy (Area C):

<u>Byzantine and Early Umayyad Remains: Strata VII and VIII</u>:

The stratigraphic sequence recovered from the excavation of Areas B, C, and D can be summarized as belonging to eleven strata between Middle Bronze and the Ayyubid period.[95] Stratum VIII represents Byzantine urban settlement, while Stratum VII represents early Umayyad level, with provable post-Conquest deposits, predating construction of the Umayyad Citadel (635-735).[96]

Building (c) in Trench C4 and C15 (fig. 5)

A square room, measuring 5.2 x 5.0 m., is found with a threshold facing north (fig. 5).[97] While no interior floor remains, the threshold course and the foundations have survived. It is evidently part of a larger building as a further bonded wall continues to the south. Moreover, there are two areas of a mosaic floor of white tesserae to the north of the structure. They are clearly part of a single mosaic measuring three meters north to south. To the west of the square room is a further room with a well-laid plaster floor. It appears to have been a fairly substantial house.

<u>The Umayyad Citadel: Strata V and VI</u>:

Stratum VI represents an Umayyad level, namely leveling fills for the buildings of Vb, dated by architecture of the Umayyad palace to 735 ± 10 years.[98] Stratum Vb belongs to the Umayyad period, and represents the superstructure of the Umayyad Citadel, dated by the architecture of the

---

[95] Ibid., 139.
[96] Ibid., 12.
[97] Ibid., 141.
[98] Ibid., 12.

Umayyad palace to 735 ± 10 years. Stratum Va belongs to the late Umayyad period, representing post-construction occupation and rebuilding. It was destroyed by the earthquake of 747-8.

Leveling Fill: Stratum VI (fig. 6)

Strata VII and VIII are separated from the next occupation deposits of Stratum V by a considerable volume of fill.[99] These fills are found wherever penetration is made through the floor levels of Stratum V on the inside of the fortification wall. The composition of the fills varies from soil and clays to mixed soil and building rubble, to almost pure building rubble. However, in no place is the material well-compacted.

Stratum VI ranges in depth from 2.2 m., adjacent to the fortification wall (fig. 6), to approximately 0.2 m. in C15.[100] Under Building B, the fill steps up, suggesting the fill levels the site into rough steps. The loose nature of the fill made this area vulnerable to an earthquake.

It seems reasonable to suggest that these fills were deliberately laid.[101] The pottery is a mixture of Byzantine and Umayyad from top to bottom, with concentrations of pottery from one period or another in different places, as is to be expected where various sources of fill material are used. There is no indication of occupational activity or silting.

Building B: Stratum V

Inside the fortification wall, there appear to be two large buildings, A and B, divided by a street, three meters wide, which runs north-south approximately parallel to the fortification wall (figs. 7 and 8).[102] The dimension of Building B is large, with the uncovered western side

---

[99] Ibid., 141.
[100] Ibid., 141-142.
[101] Ibid., 142.
[102] Ibid., 142.

measuring 18 m. (fig. 9).[103] This building is one house (Rooms A, B, C, E, F, G, H), including

one room from another house (Room D) (fig. 7). It is apparent that the building is a residential

block containing more than one house unit. The rooms of the house surround Courtyard J,

although neither the southern wall nor the main door was excavated. Northedge has suggested

that the main door may have opened from the courtyard onto a street to the east which is visible

on the surface.

The courtyard, 8.6 m. wide, has a cistern (figs. 9 and 10) with a shaft 0.42-0.65 m. in

diameter.[104] The cistern appears to have been constructed originally in the Byzantine period as it

has a second ring-shaped stone for a mouth, 2.25 m. below the present mouth. The surround to

the mouth undergoes two phases. In the first phase, the Byzantine cistern is rebuilt with an

extended shaft to suit the new ground level, which is raised by a fill to level the surface for the

Umayyad building. It is built into the east wall of Room A and a channel from the adjacent

plastered basin feeds into it. In the second phase, the channel from the basin is blocked off and a

new surround to the cistern head is built.

Rooms A (4.1 x 5.1 m.), B (4.0 x 5.1 m.), and F (3.6 x 4.2 m. or more) are identified as

residential from their destruction deposits (fig. 11).[105] For instance, Room B contains six pots, a

lamp and a small hearth in the north-eastern corner (fig. 12).[106] Room F provides the best

evidence of a dwelling room: in the south-west corner there is a rectangular stone pan, and on the

west side, the remains of a bread oven. Arranged around the walls of Room F are nine cooking

pots, water jars and cups. Room G (5.8 x 5.1 m.) likely serves as the reception room based on

the analogy of the Museum site.

---

[103] Ibid., 142.
[104] Bennett and Northedge, "Excavations at the Citadel, 1976," 176.
[105] Northedge, *Roman and Islamic 'Amman*, 142.
[106] Bennett and Northedge, "Excavations at the Citadel, 1976," 176.

The adjacent Room E (4.2 x 6.2 m.) has a pair of interconnected basins, one square and open (1.2 x 1.0 m.), and the second deep and round (0.5 m. diameter) (fig. 13).[107] This arrangement is based on the collection of liquid pressed from some material in the upper basin, though it is not certain what is being pressed. Room C (3.5 x 5.7 m.) has three rough store bins, and is used as a storeroom (fig. 14).

There is clear evidence of a violent destruction of Building B at the same period that it was erected.[108] Namely, Rooms A, B, E and F all collapsed on their contents. Furthermore, a skeleton is found on the stone threshold of Room B. The sudden collapse of the building may be attributed to the earthquake of 749, which also left behind extensive destruction levels in the residential area of Pella.[109] Subsequently, the majority of Building B was not re-occupied, which allowed for the preservation of its destruction level.

Building B exhibits a unified constructional technique, seen elsewhere on the *Qal'a*, representing Stratum V construction.[110] Namely, the wall is made of limestone rubble masonry with a standard thickness of 1.0 m., with a range of variation from 0.95 to 1.07 m. However, the two faces of the wall are sometimes not parallel, though they are straight and flat. Small stones are used to wedge the larger masonry firmly, as well as used to smooth the surface for plastering. The wall is mortared with large quantities of a lime mortar containing ash. They are subsequently plastered with the same material. The surface is studded with small pieces of chalk, and stippled with wedge-shaped keying impressions. The foundations are set in a leveling fill to compensate for the slope of the hill.[111]

---

[107] Northedge, *Roman and Islamic 'Amman*, 142.
[108] Ibid., 143.
[109] Ibid., 158.
[110] Ibid., 142.
[111] Bennett and Northedge, "Excavations at the Citadel, 1976," 175.

The material of the floor is a variation of tamped earth.[112] Courtyards and storerooms (Room C) have plain earth surfaces. Rooms B and F have carefully packed surfaces, while Room A has a thin coating of lime. Room D, possibly a reception room, has a laid clay floor.

No evidence has survived of the roofing technique. However, Northedge has speculated that the roof may be barrel-vaulted, similar to Building D in Area B.[113] The rectangular shape of the rooms would have accommodated barrel-vaulting, even at the expense of the regular thickness in the walls. The building is apparently single-storey, as no evidence was recovered of a second storey or of staircases to the roof.

Chronology (Area C):

<u>Byzantine and Early Umayyad Remains: Strata VII and VIII</u>:

The *terminus post quem* of the Byzantine settlement in this area is indicated by the 3rd-4th century date of the building outside the wall in C0-10 (fig. 5).[114] However, it is not possible to establish a foundation date for the building inside the wall. A *follis* is recovered from the last deposit of the passageway in trench C2. It appears to be a copy or a forgery of a type of Constans II (641-668).

Evidence for occupation after the Arab conquest (Stratum VII) is further corroborated by the lack of silting on the floors of Buildings (a) and (b), and in trenches C6 and C8, prior to laying the fills that comprise Stratum VI. Silting may have indicated abandonment, whereas the clean deposition of fills suggests that this settlement continued in occupation until the building operations associated with the construction of the Umayyad citadel began.

<u>The Umayyad Citadel: Strata V and VI</u>:

---

[112] Northedge, *Roman and Islamic 'Amman*, 143.

[113] Ibid., 143.

[114] Ibid., 141.

The latest coins to emerge from Area C are Umayyad post-reform *fulūs*.[115] The Umayyad *fulūs* come from sealed locations in the fill below Room F of Building B and from between two floors of Room A. A coin recovered from Room A may have been minted at al-Ramla, while another coin found in Room F was mined in Damascus.

Stratum V (Umayyad) pottery is recovered from the destruction of Building B.[116] The pottery is found, in smashed and intact conditions, on the floors of Rooms A, B, E and F.[117] With the red-painted ware, the paint, a red iron oxide, contrasts with a pale background, which is of several different kinds: (a) a body fired light red right through (fig. 15:9); (b) a body fired with a pale yellow to pale brown exterior and light red core and interior surface (fig. 15:1-4, 8); (c) a body fired pale yellow to pale brown right through (fig. 15:5); (d) a white to pale yellow wash or paint over a light red body (fig. 15:6).[118] Similar groups of Umayyad pottery have been published from Pella. For instance, Ware 8 from Pella is described as a light orange fabric, sometimes apparently white slipped, with small and sometimes medium white and grey inclusion. It is decorated with bold reddish-brown paint and depicts loops, stars, wavy lines, arcade patterns, and crisscrossed lines.[119]

Excavation of Domestic Structure at Site (Museum Site):

Rescue excavations on the site of the present Jordan Archaeological Museum were conducted by G. L. Harding in 1949.[120] The area is situated on the south side of the western, highest part of the Citadel.[121] The excavations revealed a courtyard and several rooms of a large house dated to the Umayyad period.

---

[115] Ibid., 143.
[116] Idem, *Qal'at 'Amman*, 267.
[117] Ibid., 267-268.
[118] Ibid., 270.
[119] Walmsley, "Tradition, Innovation and Imitation," 661.
[120] Northedge, *Roman and Islamic 'Amman*, 151.
[121] Harding, "Excavations on the Citadel," 7.

Stratigraphy (Museum Site):

The main house, measuring 18.4 x *c.* 20 m., consists of a courtyard (H), with an outside
entrance in the unexcavated area to the west.[122] The courtyard is surrounded by rooms to its
west, north and east (fig. 16).[123] One room on the north side, Room D, has a doorway two
meters wide, and may have functioned as a reception room. Rooms C and E open from Room D
to form a *bayt*.[124] Room P may have served as a latrine.

In the courtyard is a raised stone platform of very rough construction.[125] In addition,
plastered drains in the north-east and north-west corners of the courtyard conduct water from the
roof to the cistern in Room J. This cistern, cut in the rock, is probably earlier than the building
itself. There is an entrance to another cistern against the north wall of F, but it has collapsed.

The door between Rooms D and E has been blocked and used as a cupboard, where a
selection of glass, pottery and lamps are found.[126] A rectangular limestone trough is located in
the south-east corner of Room B, and a circular one in the same corner of Room J. A clay oven
stands against the west wall of F. Iron nails, plain and ornamental, are found in Room F,
probably from the door of the room.[127] No iron hinges were recovered, so presumably the door
revolves in wooden sockets.

The house to the east, of which only one complete room and parts of three others are
preserved, is of finer construction (Rooms K, L and M).[128] A large quantity of plain white
tesserae in Room K suggests that an upper storey had existed here with a mosaic floor. There is
also a large rectangular limestone trough in this room. Further evidence of an upper storey is

---

[122] Northedge, *Roman and Islamic 'Amman*, 151.
[123] Harding, "Excavations on the Citadel," 7.
[124] Northedge, *Roman and Islamic 'Amman*, 151.
[125] Harding, "Excavations on the Citadel," 7.
[126] Ibid., 7, 9.
[127] Ibid., 10.
[128] Ibid., 9.

found in Rooms L and M, where piers for arches to support the roof were excavated.[129] These

piers stand above complete arches carrying a ground floor over a basement (fig. 16). While the

arches of the basement remain intact, those of the ground floor have collapsed and fallen through

into the basement.

The walls are fairly thick and constructed of reused Roman blocks and rough flint rubble held

together by mud plaster.[130] Rooms C, D and F have traces of lime plaster on the walls. Floors

are made of beaten earth. Door sills, with the exception of the stone sill to Room F, are flush

with the floors.

Chronology (Museum Site):

Harding dates these houses to the Umayyad period on the basis of a single Umayyad coin

recovered from the floor of Room J.[131] The remainder of the coins is found in the filling and

consists of two more early Umayyad coins, one Byzantine-Arab transition coin, and one of

Claudius Gothicus.

The main house parallels Stratum V of Building B in Area C.[132] In particular, the

construction is identical to that of Stratum V, while the plan is a mirror image (fig. 17). The

buildings are erected over the equivalent of the Stratum VI fill. Furthermore, the main house

was destroyed suddenly, creating a destruction deposit of Umayyad artifacts in Rooms C, D, E,

F, G, J and N. Therefore, it may be suggested that the building was devastated by the same

earthquake as that of Building B.

Jarash

---

[129] Northedge, *Roman and Islamic 'Amman*, 151.
[130] Harding, "Excavations on the Citadel," 7.
[131] Ibid., 9.
[132] Northedge, *Roman and Islamic 'Amman*, 151.

Geographical and Historical Setting of Site:

Jarash is situated approximately 35 km. north of „Ammān (fig. 18). Its long history is attributable to its strategic location in a fertile valley, close to caravan routes and trade-crossroads that lead south to „Ammān, north to Damascus and Boṣrā, and east to Pella and Baysān.[133]

Jarash was among the cities that capitulated peacefully during the conquest of Bilād al-Shām by Islamic forces.[134] Historians, such as al-Balādhurī and al-Ya„qūbī, record Jarash as one of nine district centers in the *jund* of al-Urdunn, all of which reported to the provincial capital of Ṭabariyya (fig. 18).[135] The *jund* extended to the strategic naval ports of „Akkā and Ṣūr on the Mediterranean Sea. Situated in the farthest south-east corner of the *jund* of al-Urdunn, Jarash was near the important districts of „Ammān/al-Balqā" in the extensive province of the *jund* of Dimashq.

The administrative significance of the town is also reinforced by its production of copper coins in both a Pre-Reform and Post-Reform type (fig. 19).[136] Jarash issued coins in the same style as the more common coppers of Baysān.[137] Baysān and Jarash formed an enclave of autonomous monetary practice which continued into the standing caliph period, exemplified by coins with two standing caliphs in place of one: on the obverse are two enthroned imperial figures and the mint name in Greek, either Scythopolis (Baysān) or Gerasion (Jarash).[138] These coins are clearly derived from a specific Byzantine prototype dating back over a hundred years before their issue. The prototype is an issue of Emperor Justin II and his consort Sophia, who

---

[133] Damgaard and Blanke, "Islamic Jarash Project."
[134] Ibid.
[135] Walmsley, "Friday Mosque," 111-112.
[136] Walmsley and Damgaard, "Umayyad Congregational Mosque," 363.
[137] Walmsley, "Friday Mosque," 114.
[138] Bates, "Coinage of Syria," 215.

reigned from 565 to 578. The Post-Reform issue from Jarash is rather rare.[139] Like all Post-Reform Umayyad coins, this type carries Kufic Arabic on both sides, mostly consisting of the *shahāda*. The mint name is written in Arabic as „Jarash.‟

Jarash became a prosperous manufacturing hub on the Ajlūn highlands.[140] A complex of five Umayyad-period ceramic kilns was established in the North Theater of Jarash during the Umayyad period (fig. 20).[141] Jarash ceramic wares of the early Islamic period were distributed commercially within a wide area, as far north as Tadmur, south into the Mādaba Plain, and west into the Jordan Valley and beyond to the Mediterranean.

Excavation of Domestic Structure at Site:

The Polish mission led by Michael Gawlikowski from the University of Warsaw excavated a sector immediately to the north of the street known as the South Decumanus in 1981-1983.[142] There, lies a residential quarter of 10 rooms, arranged in two wings on both sides of a rectangular courtyard (fig. 20).[143]

Stratigraphy:

<u>Roman Phase:</u>

Evidence for the occupation of the area begins in the first two centuries and consists mostly of several cisterns anterior to the layout of the street (fig. 21).[144] Three of the cisterns, which stand in the path of the South Decumanus, were filled in the process of its construction. A circular well (loc. 15) leads down to a large rock-hewn reservoir 4.25 m. deep (fig. 21). A part of it is cut

---

[139] Walmsley, "Friday Mosque," 114.
[140] Foote, "Commerce," 37.
[141] Ibid., 34.
[142] Gawlikowski, "Residential Area," 107.
[143] Zayadine, "Jerash Project," 19.
[144] Gawlikowski, "Residential Area," 109.

off by the foundation of the stylobate, which elsewhere is laid on the rock surface but here extends all the way down to the bottom of the hollow below.

There are rectangular cisterns once covered with beams located east and west of loc. 15 (fig. 21).[145] One rectangular cistern (loc. 43) has a flight of steps along one of the carefully plastered walls and at least one arch to support the ceiling (figs. 22 and 23). The cistern is cut by a transverse wall, though not directly under the stylobate line, and further north by the much poorer foundation of the shops along the sidewalk of the street. The cistern to the east, loc. 28, is likewise blocked at both ends by the foundations of the stylobate and of the shop façade behind it.[146] The rock is cut to accommodate transverse beams for a cover at surface level.

Another cistern (loc. 29) remained in use longer, as it could be fitted into the line of shops.[147] The cistern has two arches: one supporting a lateral cavity in the rock; the other, at a short distance from the front wall and parallel to it, seems to have carried stone slabs at the entrance.

These cisterns appear to have been part of an elaborate system of public water supply for the area.[148] Behind them are several walls forming an orthogonal system, not in the same orientation as the colonnaded street. The contents of the foundation trenches date the buildings to the first or second centuries, while the higher courses of the wall are attributed to the Umayyad period.

There is evidence of other Roman period remains of the building. The rock face to the north is cut into several sections varying in depth but parallel to the South Decumanus, so as to accommodate housing in front of it (fig. 21).[149] Only one wall is found running south from the rock and under Room 7.[150] A sewage drain leads from the north into the collector under the

---

[145] Ibid., 109.
[146] Ibid., 109.
[147] Ibid., 109.
[148] Ibid., 109.
[149] Ibid., 109.
[150] Ibid., 109-110.

South Decumanus and another cistern (loc. 41) behind the row of shops. The wall standing above it to the west is Roman and some other walls perpendicular to the street may be contemporary, at least in part. Otherwise, the remainder is cleared prior to the erection of the Umayyad House. The clearing is thorough and perhaps repeated following one or several earthquakes.

The later Roman period is better represented on the upper terrace, where there is a cave hollowed from the lower level and dimly lit by two light-wells (loc. 35) (fig. 21).[151] Above it, a square is cut into the rock surface, 3 m. wide and 0.5 m. deep, containing rows of round cavities along three of its edges. This represents the floor of a storage room used contemporaneously with the cave beneath it.

A fissure in the rock along the edge of the terrace may have endangered the further use of the cave, thus resulting in its abandonment.[152] The preserved buildings on the terrace postdate the formation of this fissure. The restoration closely followed a tremor, which occurred about the end of the fourth or in the early fifth century.

After the leveling of debris, a large building is constructed on the eastern end of the rock area.[153] Its ashlar masonry forms a corner, still standing 4 m. high, founded on the rock without a foundation trench. The south wall continues for 16 m. Inside, the late walls form a small compartment in the corner. The original level of occupation is about 0.70 m. above the rock, over an earth and rubble layer having filled and covered the seismic fissure. Outside the building against the western wall, there is a room (loc. 2) with a door opening into the space above the former storage facility. Another door, which is blocked, leads northwards through a wall bonded

---

[151] Ibid., 110.
[152] Ibid., 110.
[153] Ibid., 110.

to the foundations of the north-eastern building. The floor level is about 0.5 m. above the bedrock with a light well into the disused cave beneath.

There is another wall heading south from the lower courses of the north-eastern building.[154] This wall is bonded to the main wall above the brink of the terrace about 3 m. from the corner. An extensive tumble of huge, roughly hewn stones have piled up against it, representing the remains of buildings destroyed by the earthquake and cleared away. The tumble has covered the entrance to the cave and is superimposed by late Byzantine deposits and, partly, by the steps leading down to the Umayyad House.

Further to the west, another house is erected upon the same terrace and includes three rooms (loc. 31, 32, 34) (fig. 24).[155] The walls stand directly on bedrock, with the exception of the south-eastern corner of Room 32, which has a foundation laid around the rock, undercut in this place. The masonry of the walls consists of irregular stones assembled without mortar. While the house is approximately contemporaneous with the north-eastern building, it is possible that at least the upper courses are of later date. The north-western house postdates the tumbling of stones below the terrace, as a door, later blocked, opens above it to the east.

A passageway between this door and an unexcavated space to the west, presumed to be a courtyard, provides the only entrance to Room 32 (fig. 21).[156] Room 34 is directly accessible from the courtyard and opens at its other end into a small room (loc. 31) added later in an angle formed by further rooms to the north. Room 31 is blocked and filled rather early, whereas the other two rooms remain in use until the early seventh century.

Umayyad Phase:

---

[154] Ibid., 110.
[155] Ibid., 110.
[156] Ibid., 111.

After the abandonment of the north-western house, the south foundation of Room 32 was used by the builders of the Umayyad period.[157] This led to a new arrangement of the entire area (fig. 25). A staircase is laid on the stone tumble, leading north, rising 2.4 m. above bedrock (fig. 26). The steps are comprised of two flights of stairs separated by a landing.[158] The steps end at a door opening onto a platform around the corner of the north-eastern building above the Byzantine fill. The stairs are flanked by walls parallel to both sides. The eastern side of the steps is retained by a wall constructed to hold in place a large terrace, which also leans against the north wall of the house. To the west, the upper flight of steps is also bordered by a retaining wall of another terrace above Room 31.

The colonnaded street remains in use since Roman times, as the sidewalk does not seem to have been built over during the early Umayyad period, serving its original purpose along the line of shops.[159] The shops are entirely restored, including the upper foundation courses in the fill of the cistern loc. 43, without any major change in plan (fig. 27).

The Umayyad House extends northwards behind four of these shops for 23 m. (fig. 28).[160] Although incorporating some earlier foundation, it is an entirely new building. The house is laid around a courtyard with the main entrance through a passageway from the street between shops loc. 29 and 13 (fig. 29). There is another door opening on the opposite end into the staircase. An earlier sewage drain runs from the end of the courtyard and beneath the entrance. This serves as the only sanitary facility in the household.

---

[157] Ibid., 111.
[158] Ibid., 111.
[159] Ibid., 111, 113.
[160] Ibid., 113.

The irregular form of the courtyard (loc. 18, 16, 23, 9) is determined by the Roman period foundations under Rooms 17, 24 and 25 (fig. 21).[161] The rooms are arranged in two wings east and west of the courtyard. The western wing consists of a row of rooms demarcated by a rear wall with no openings. While certain parts of this wall may have been retained from older buildings, the northern wall is contemporary with the house.

The depths of the rooms of the west wing vary according to the already existing conditions that the builders encountered in the area.[162] For instance, the northernmost Room 7 (fig. 30), 9.5 m. long and 2.9 m. wide, is longer than the other rooms so as to allow an entrance from the courtyard, in line with the door of the staircase. The room is below ground level on two sides and has a single window opening above the steps, opposite the terrace to the east and its retaining wall. The ceiling could not be lower than about 3.5 m. above the floor, a fact substantiated by the north-western corner of the room, which still stands to a height of 4.2 m. above the floor level. However, an arch springing from two piers set against the long walls for the room is only about 3 m. high and must have carried a partition wall at that level. There is no additional evidence for an upper storey. The floor of the room is covered with a mosaic of which only displaced fragments and a large amount of single cubes remain. At one end, there is a stone bench against the wall.

The main room of the house (loc. 10 and 20) is divided in the middle by an arch spanning an opening 4 m. wide from east to west (figs. 31 and 32).[163] It is south of Room 7 and shorter but much wider (7 m. by 7.6 m.). Rooms 10/20 and 7 apparently serve the whole household for common meals and receptions. Both sections of Room 10/20 are covered separately using this arch, with a minimum height of about 3 m. above the floor, but probably higher. An upper story

---

[161] Ibid., 113.
[162] Ibid., 113.
[163] Ibid., 113.

may have existed, if its entrance is from the higher ground level outside to the west, but no evidence of it has survived. The floor of the room is 0.7 m. below the level of the courtyard. Four steps inside the room lead down from the entrance, which opens against the arched partition into loc. 10. There are windows to the right and left only 0.4 m. wide and 1.2 m. above the courtyard pavement, each one providing light to half of the room. The earthen floor consists of a compact red soil layer 0.5 m. thick.[164]

Further south, Room 17 intrudes into the courtyard space. It is doubled during the Umayyad period by Room 19, in line with the common western wall of the house.[165] The partition between Rooms 19 and 20 extends along the earlier Room 17, built against its northern wall. As a consequence, Rooms 17 and 19 are not aligned on the same axis. Room 17 is cleared in the Umayyad period down to bedrock, removing the earlier foundations. However, there are traces of a pavement some 0.2 m. above the uneven rock. A pit in the bedrock contains a typical Umayyad storage basin.

In Room 17, there are two steps leading down from the courtyard and a window, once secured with iron bars.[166] The window opens 0.8 m. above the floor but is level with the exterior pavement to the south. Room 19 is apparently windowless, with the door connecting to Room 17 being the only opening in its walls preserved up to 3 m. above the floor. Further south, Room 22 with an earthen floor opens from the passage leading to the street.

In contrast, the opposite eastern wing of rooms is not arranged symmetrically. In its northern section, there are four rooms facing the large Room 10/20 across the courtyard (fig. 28).[167] The walls are for a considerable part Roman, cut to the north by the retaining wall of the terrace.

---

[164] Ibid., 113.
[165] Ibid., 114.
[166] Ibid., 114.
[167] Ibid., 114.

Room 25 is entered from the west, while Room 24 is entered from the south through a doorway inherited from the Roman period. Room 25 has a stone bench with a retaining border along its northern wall, used probably for storing household belongings. Both rooms have access to the room immediately behind it (loc. 36 and 37). Room 37 has a completely preserved arch in the middle.

The part of the courtyard (loc. 16) opposite Room 17 extends further east, ending in line with the room of the eastern wing.[168] A small sunken space (loc. 26), reached by steps (fig. 33), leads to a cellar (loc. 27) and an open recess at the same level above the filled cistern loc. 41. From the cistern, steps lead down to an artificial cave dug out in the rock beneath the shop loc. 42. This storage complex is delimited from the courtyard by a stone fence.

The walls of the house, with the exception of fragments from earlier times, are constructed of reused stones varying in size but roughly arranged in courses, with stone chips and mud between them.[169] Usually, there is no core fill between the faces and no bonding stones. The walls are probably mud-plastered, while the roofs are made of wooden beams. The presence of a second storey could not be determined.

<u>Abbasid Phase</u>:

In this structure, there is no evidence of the earthquake of 749 that destroyed the domestic residences at Pella and possibly „Ammān.[170] In fact, the Umayyad House continues in use for some time after this date.

A small room (loc. 21) is built in a corner between Rooms 17 and 10/20 (fig. 34).[171] While the walls of this room lie directly on a Byzantine level forming the floor, this is about 0.5 m.

---

[168] Ibid., 114.
[169] Ibid., 114.
[170] Ibid., 115.
[171] Ibid., 115.

lower than the pavement in the adjacent courtyard and is covered without transition with an eighth century fill. Hence, it appears that the pavement is removed in this place when Room 21 is built. Soon after, the house undergoes further changes. Namely, the house is divided into three separate dwellings. This is achieved by erecting a few partition walls and blocking several doors (fig. 34).[172]

The south wall of Room 24 is rebuilt at this time above the threshold and extends westward to join the corner of Room 21 (fig. 35).[173] Consequently, the new living unit includes the main rooms of the Umayyad House (loc. 10/20 and 7) (fig. 36). The courtyard (loc. 9, 23) is accessible only through the stairs from the north. The floor level remains unchanged, while Room 24 is no longer in use as its two doors are blocked.

A second dwelling is comprised of the courtyard loc. 16, Rooms 17, 19 and 22 (fig. 37).[174] The passage to the street is closed above the sewage drain, thus the courtyard could be accessed from the east, through a doorway in the wall crossing the filled cistern loc. 41. The blocking of the original access to the house results in the formation of a recess (loc. 18) leading to Room 22. It is approached through the former window of Room 17, now level with the floors on both sides. The south-western corner of courtyard loc. 16 acquires a rectangular raised border above a well connected with the sewage drain. This is used for refuse disposal and prevents any direct communication with loc. 18 behind. While the drain remains viable down the South Decumanus, it is blocked uphill from the well.

Another house is developed from the former shops along the street (fig. 38).[175] A wall is constructed through loc. 28/42, thus making the neighboring Room 13 larger. Another room is

---

[172] Ibid., 115.
[173] Ibid., 115.
[174] Ibid., 115.
[175] Ibid., 115.

added above the former cellar (loc. 27) and a part of the passage above the sewer (loc. 14). The resulting room has its floor level with the top of the preserved partition between the two, the cellar having been filled with soil. The same fill is found in Room 13 above the Umayyad level. There is a threshold between Room 13 and the back room (loc. 14/27), which has another entrance through the former passage between the courtyard and the street, now closed at the far end.

This three-room unit opens onto a part of the colonnade, which is enclosed to serve as a courtyard (fig. 34).[176] Only the side walls of the enclosure remain. Any blocking between the columns that might have been preserved is removed during the restoration work in the early seventies.[177] However, a threshold cut in the stylobate is preserved in front of the entrance to Room 13. There is also another threshold in the west wall of this courtyard, suggesting that the area behind it belongs to the same house. The colonnade opens into Room 29 and two other unexcavated rooms further west. Room 29, above the Roman cistern, has evidence of two late levels: the higher level is associated with a pavement in front of it and a door leading west to the next room.

The housing has been at least partially abandoned as a consequence of another earthquake, indicated by the massive stone tumble in several rooms.[178] Most doors are blocked at this occasion and the rooms used, if at all, are at a much higher level. At a later date, the area is installed with pottery kilns.

Chronology:

---

[176] Ibid., 115.
[177] Ibid., 115, 117.
[178] Ibid., 117.

The area north of the South Decumanus has been constantly occupied from the early Roman period to the Abbasid period, interrupted by at least three massive earthquakes.[179] The first earthquake may have occurred before the construction of the north-eastern house and is dated to the late fourth or early fifth century. The next earthquake destroyed the north-western house on the upper terrace, left abandoned, and those beneath that were cleared. This occurred in the mid-seventh century, possibly in 658. Finally, the destruction of the Umayyad House is dated to the late eighth century.

<u>Roman Period</u>:

The cistern (loc. 15) is cut by a transverse wall, though not directly under the stylobate line, and further north by the much poorer foundation of the shops along the sidewalk of the street.[180] Thus, its fill is contemporary with the colonnade and the shops beside it. The fill contains thirteen coins. The latest identifiable coins belong to the reign of Marcus Aurelius, one being dated to 164/165. Consequently, the South Decumanus is dated to approximately 170. The fill of another cistern (loc. 29) contains two late third century coins at the top level of the arches. At the bottom, however, two complete Hellenistic lamps may suggest a fairly early date for the construction of the original building, especially since there are Hellenistic and early Roman deposits behind its north wall (loc. 22).

A wall to the North, running south from the rock and under Room 7, is associated with late fourth century coins.[181] The fill of the cave and of the storage facility above contains late fourth century sherds and coins. In addition, a coin of Justinian is found on bedrock in Room 34.

<u>Umayyad Period</u>:

---

[179] Ibid., 120.
[180] Ibid., 109.
[181] Ibid., 109-110.

The staircase is filled with sterile soil up to the uppermost level of the step. At the bottom

level of fill, a coin of Constans II (641-668) and contemporary pottery are recovered. This coin

dates the filling of the terrace east of the staircase.

Eight coins identified as Arab-Byzantine are discovered in two clusters below the level of

Room 7 and above the Roman wall, buried about 400.[182] These coins are imitations of the *folles*

of Justin II minted in Baysān and, in one instance, in Jarash itself (fig. 39). The Byzantine coin-

type of Justin II was minted for a relatively long period (565/6-578), some 70 years prior to the

Arab conquest of Palestine.[183] This prototype was minted at Baysān and Jarash because the

original type was very popular in Trans-Jordan and adjacent regions. These coins have on the

obverse two enthroned imperial figures and the mint name in Greek, either Scythopolis or

Gerasion.

Though the exact date of their issue is unknown, Gawlikowski argues that they were

gradually replacing Byzantine currency in the first decades of the Islamic government.[184] The

latest genuine Byzantine issues are of poor quality, usually clipped coins of Constans II. The

discovered coins are presumably later than the clipped coins of Constans II, the latest Byzantine

issues commonly found in Syria and Jordan (including the fill associated with this building).[185]

However, these pseudo-imperial issues have been dated to as late as the 680s. The construction

of the house likely followed an earthquake, perhaps the earthquake of 658, which caused

extensive destruction throughout Palestine and Syria. The aftermath of this earthquake was

preserved in the archaeological record of the house at Pella. Therefore, the Umayyad house was

probably built at the beginning of the Umayyad period, approximately 660 or slightly later.

---

[182] Ibid., 111.

[183] Amitai-Preiss, Berman, and Qedar, "Coinage of Scythopolis-Baysan," 136.

[184] Gawlikowski, "Residential Area," 111.

[185] Idem, "Jerash in Early Islamic Times," 471.

Contemporary with the Umayyad house are lamps with handles in the shape of an animal head (fig. 40).[186] This is formed by two pinches on a lamp fresh from the mould. These animal-head lamps do not appear in earlier levels, having evolved around 640. They continue to be used until the middle of the eighth century.[187] In the last quarter of the century of their manufacture, these lamps are sometimes inscribed and dated in Arabic between 105-133/723-750 by Christian and Muslim potters alike.[188]

Abbasid Period:

An Abbasid *dīnār* dated to 770/771 (fig. 39) is recovered from Room 10/20, suggesting that this room is used roughly at its original level as late as 770.[189] The second half of the eighth century is marked by the appearance of bowls with nearly vertical sides, painted in red with festoons and stylized floral motives (fig. 41).[190] The fill of all three late houses yields red-painted pottery, the so-called cut-ware bowls and lamps decorated with a vine scroll, typical of the later half of the eighth century.[191] Furthermore, there is clear evidence of lamps dated to the second half of the eighth century. These lamps mark a definite change of style. The handle is no longer figurative, and the decoration around the channel consists most often of a vine scroll, while there are sometimes engravings of animals, amphorae and even human figures on both the discus and the base (fig. 40).[192]

A comparable unglazed lamp decorated with an undulating vine or rinceau motif is found at al-Fusṭāṭ from ninth-century context (fig. 42), corroborating the date of such lamps at Jarash.[193]

---

[186] Idem, "Residential Area," 118.
[187] Idem, "Jerash in Early Islamic Times," 470.
[188] Ibid., 470.
[189] Idem, "Residential Area," 117.
[190] Ibid., 118.
[191] Ibid., 117.
[192] Ibid., 120.
[193] Scanlon, "Lead Glazed Wares," 67.

The al-Fusṭāṭ lamp is made of buff-brown clay with a simple revered central motif and a prominent decoration of vine leaves and spread grape clusters.

Naḥal Mitnan

Geographical and Historical Setting of Site:

The Negev is an arid desert region in the southern part of Israel. Primarily a transit area, the Negev is unsuitable by climate and topography for settled habitation except under unusual circumstances.[194] The Negev Highlands, between the Mediterranean zone of central Israel and the Saharan zones of the southern Negev and Sinai, constitute an environmental transition area between the sedentary north and the nomadic south.[195] Naḥal Mitnan, located in the western Negev Highlands (fig. 43), is a tributary of Naḥal Ḥorsha. Its 4 km. long wadi channel was intensively cultivated in antiquity by means of agricultural terraces.[196]

Despite the adverse environmental conditions of the Negev, remnants of ancient agriculture, particularly a tremendous network of terraced wadis, are scatted over an area exceeding 3000 sq. km.[197] The agricultural system includes an extensive network of terraced wadis, numerous farmhouses, and various agricultural installations. The archaeological evidence suggests the establishment and occupation of the farms is a process that continued through the sixth, seventh, and eighth centuries.[198] According to Haiman, agricultural settlement in the Negev desert during the Umayyad period was motivated by two reasons: imperial policy aimed toward protecting the frontier by encouraging establishment of agricultural settlements; and state-sponsored

---

[194] Mayerson, "First Muslim Attacks," 168.
[195] Avni, "Early Mosques in the Negev Highlands," 83.
[196] Haiman, "Early Islamic Period Farm," 1.
[197] Idem, "Agriculture and Nomad-State Relations," 29.
[198] Magness, *Early Islamic Settlement*, 137.

sedentarization of semi-nomads.[199] The farms in the Negev Highlands were probably abandoned in the wake of political upheaval, namely the rise of the Abbasid dynasty and the transfer of the capital from Damascus to Baghdad.

Excavation of Domestic Structure at Site:

In 1978, a large-scale emergency survey was initiated on behalf of the Archaeological Survey of Israel and the Department of Antiquities and Museums.[200] Mordechai Haiman led a survey of an area of about 450 sq. km. in the western Negev Highlands from 1979 to 1989, in which approximately 1,500 sites were discovered (fig. 43). Among the sites surveyed was Naḥal Mitnan, where a farmstead, excavated by Haiman, is situated on the southern side of Naḥal Mitnan about 2 km. upstream from its confluence with Naḥal Ḥorsha.[201] The Naḥal Mitnan farm consists of A, the main farmhouse, where excavations were conducted; B, an agricultural installation; C, a semi-sedentary structure; D, a threshing floor; and E, a section of the terraced wadi-channel, enclosed by a stone fence (figs. 44 and 45).

Stratigraphy:

The farmhouse complex measures 15 x 33 m. (figs. 46 and 47).[202] Consistent with structures surveyed in the Negev Highlands, this farmhouse complex is composed of separate dwelling units, each consisting of one to three rooms and a small courtyard.[203] In particular, three units can be identified: one includes Room 102 and Courtyard 101; another includes Rooms 103, 104, 105, and 106, as well as Courtyard 100; and the third, only partly excavated, contains Courtyard 109 and Rooms 108 and 110 (fig. 47).

---

[199] Haiman, "Agriculture and Nomad-State Relations," 45.
[200] Idem, "Western Negev Highlands Emergency Survey," 173.
[201] Bruins, "Ancient Agricultural Terraces," 24.
[202] Haiman, "Early Islamic Period Farm," 1.
[203] Ibid., 3.

On the eastern side is the entrance to the dwelling compound (fig. 47).[204] The narrow wall

bordering the compound on the eastern side apparently demarcates an outer courtyard (L 111)

much larger than the courtyards inside the structure. The outer courtyard may have been utilized

for the activities related to collection of crops before storage or transport, as well as for

sheltering draft or pack animals. Installation 112, adjoining the wall of the outer courtyard, may

have been used as a trough or a stall.[205] Furthermore, Courtyard 113 may have functioned as an

animal pen. North of the farmstead, Structure 114, measuring 3 x 4 m., is constructed of two

rows of rough-hewn stones.

In the northern unit (fig. 48), Courtyard 101 (3.5 x 6.0 m.) has a beaten earth floor containing

fragments of pottery and glass.[206] It leads to Room 102 (4.5 x 3.5 m.) through a doorway

equipped with a stone threshold and lintel (0.8 m. long). The floor consists of beaten earth

mixed with crushed limestone and ash, and it yields potsherds, a stone bowl, a mortar, and two

hammer stones.

The central unit is entered through Courtyard 100 (5.5 x 7.5 m.) with its earthen floor covered

by a thick (0.1 m.) layer of ash.[207] Its finds include pottery, glass, bones, fragments of

grindstones and millstones, and a marble slab. Both Rooms 103 (3.5 x 4.5 m.) and 106 (3.5 x 4.5

m.) contain raised beaten-earth platforms bordered by a row of stones, one course high. These

may have functioned as beds. Finds recovered from Room 103 include a glass weight bearing

the name of ‚Abd al-Malik b. Yazīd, discovered near the southern edge of the platform, pottery,

and a charred beam about 1.5 m. long. Most of the fine ceramics found on the site come from

the platform in Room 106, including an oil lamp, a complete bowl, and fragments of fine bowls.

---

[204] Ibid., 3.
[205] Ibid., 3, 4.
[206] Ibid., 4.
[207] Ibid., 4.

Other finds in the room include potsherds, bones, ostrich egg shells, a fragment of a millstone, and a piece of iron. A pile of ash about 0.5 m. high is found between the edge of the platform and the wall.

Room 105 (3.0 x 3.5 m.), with a slightly sunken floor, has a stone threshold and a step in its entrance (fig. 49).[208] The beaten earth floor, covered by a layer of ash about 0.1 m. thick, yields fragments of grindstones, pieces of iron, bones and fragments of seashells. Room 104 (2.5 x 3.0 m.), which abuts the external walls of Rooms 105 and 103, may be a later addition to the structure (fig. 50). The room has no apparent entrance. While similar rooms found in other Central Negev farmhouses have been interpreted as ritual installations, Haiman argues that Room 104 functions as a granary, with an opening in the upper part of the wall. The practice of storing crops in spaces within the house occurs in traditional rural Arab architecture. In fact, no granaries have been identified in the Negev Highland farms, though there is a prevalence of terraced wadis and threshing floors. The finds in the room are numerous: potsherds, a juglet, a stone bowl, pieces of iron, animal bones, a clay stopper, fragments of glass, four hammerstones, two grinding stones, a marble slab, and a millstone, suggesting that in its final stage, the room serves as a midden.[209]

The southern unit lies at an elevation significantly higher than the rest of the compound: Courtyard 109 is higher than Courtyards 100 and 101.[210] The courtyard is poorly built and badly preserved, and may have been a later addition or an area used for work and storage. Room 108, which is the only room excavated in the southern unit, has no entrance and may have been used for storage.

---

[208] Ibid., 4.

[209] Ibid., 4, 5.

[210] Ibid., 5.

The walls of the farmstead, about 0.7 m. wide and preserved to a height of 1-1.5 m., are built in a distinctive architectonic style. They are constructed of two rows of small, roughly hewn stones, placed on a foundation of large stones (fig. 51).[211] A 5 cm. layer of stony debris covers the floors, which abuts the wall bases. A charred beam recovered from Room 103 indicates that the roof is made of wood. Architectural features include roughly hewn lintels (about 1 m. long), thresholds, and doorjambs. In some rooms (102 and 103), the doorjamb is placed obliquely, narrowing the inner side of the doorway by about 20 cm. in relation to the outside.

Chronology:

A pale glass weight, 2 cm. in diameter and weighing half a *dīnār*, is found in Room 103 (fig. 52).[212] It bears the name of „Abd al-Malik b. Yazīd, the governor of Egypt, and dates to his first term of office, 751-753. Both sides of the weight carry Kufic inscriptions:[213]

Obverse

In the name of Allah.

Ordered „Abd

al-Malik b. Yazīd

a weight

of a half, full weight.

Reverse

[center, mirror image]

Made by

Kail

[margin, retrograde]

[211] Ibid., 1, 3.
[212] Ibid., 8.
[213] Lester, "Glass Weight," 125-126.

…Muḥammad…

The denomination of the weight, which has several parallels, is half a *dīnār*.[214] The three mentioned names and their placement on the weight reflect the administrative hierarchy in Abbasid Egypt. On the obverse is the name, „Abd al-Malik b. Yazīd, the governor and finance director who ruled in the years 133-136/751-753 and 137-141/755-758. The name Muḥammad on the reverse refers to Muḥammad b. Shuraḥbīl, who was in charge of weights and measures during the reign of „Abd al-Malik b. Yazīd. The name Kail most likely refers to the artisan responsible for the minting of the weights. Weights of this type belong to the first period of „Abd al-Malik b. Yazīd"s rule (751-753).

An Umayyad post-reform coin is found in L 114, the isolated structure north of the dwelling compound.[215] It is a bronze *fals* minted in Damascus. In addition, C-14 analysis conducted on the charred beam from L 103 provides two dates: 1455±95 and 1515±55 BP, within range of the 5th-7th centuries. Because these dates are derived from a roof beam, they do not indicate the end of the site"s existence.[216]

Before turning to the ceramics at Naḥal Mitnan, a note of caution should be made about using its material to determine the establishing date of the farmhouse. First, because most of the pottery recovered comes from surveys, diagnostic types of certain periods may not be represented in the sample.[217] Second, this author agrees with Hirschfeld"s assessment that Haiman dates the structure based upon the late finds on the floors representing the period in

---

[214] Ibid., 125-126.
[215] Haiman, "Early Islamic Period Farm," 8.
[216] Carmi and Segal, "Rehovot Radiocarbon Measurements," 126.
[217] Magness, *Archaeology of the Early Islamic Settlement*, 136.

which their use ended and not when it began.[218] Nevertheless, the ceramic corpus is important in establishing the farmhouse‟s use during the early Islamic period.

A lamp, made of light brown coarse clay, white grits, and medium gray slip, is typical of a late eighth century lamp (fig. 53:22).[219] This oil lamp is comparable to the early channel-nozzle oil lamps, dated to the 7th century to early 8th century, presented by Magness in her corpus of ceramic types common at sites in Jerusalem from the second and third centuries to the eighth and ninth centuries (fig. 54).[220] The distinguishing features of this type are the channel connecting the filling hole and wick-hole (which often contains a decorative pattern), and the low knob handle. These features are also evident on the lamp from Naḥal Mitnan.

One type of storage jar recovered from Naḥal Mitnan is made of fine light clay, sometimes with limestone grits.[221] Prevalent colors are light grey or light green (fig. 53:21). This group of jars may be equated with Mahesh Ware of the Abbasid period, which has no antecedent in the Late Byzantine period. The primary characteristics of Mahesh ware at „Aqaba are the prevalence of cream-colored fabric (often bordering on a greenish grey), comb incising, and specific vessel forms.[222] In summary, the coin, the glass weight, the lamp, and the fragments of Mahesh Ware all date the farmhouse to no earlier than the mid-eighth century.[223]

Pella

Geographical and Historical Setting of Site:

---

[218] Hirschfeld, "Farms and Villages," 36.
[219] Haiman, "Early Islamic Period Farm," 8.
[220] Magness, *Jerusalem Ceramic Chronology*, 255-258.
[221] Haiman, "Early Islamic Period Farm," 8.
[222] Whitcomb, "Mahesh Ware," 273.
[223] Haiman, "Early Islamic Period Farm," 9.

Pella is located on the lower eastern scarp of the Jordan valley at the southern end of an extended plateau.[224] It is approximately 30 km. south of Lake Tiberias. From Pella, routes crossed westwards to the Mediterranean Sea via Baysān and the Marj Banī „Āmir, south-eastwards to Jarash and „Ammān, and north-eastwards to Irbid, Adhri,āt and Boṣrā. Throughout its long history, Pella acted as a „gateway community" by providing lodging, food and other facilities for travelers.

In 13/635, one of the earliest battles between Muslims and Byzantine forces occurred nearby in the Battle of Fiḥl (Fiḥl being the ancient Semitic name for Pella that was reinstated in early Islamic times).[225] The Muslims proved victorious over the Byzantine army, leading them to take control of the city immediately after the battle. The inhabitants of Pella took to the fortifications where they were besieged by the Muslims until they sought to surrender, entering into a peace covenant (*ṣulḥ*) with the Arab general Abū „Ubayda „Āmir b. „Abd Allah b. al-Jarrāḥ.[226] Their personal and civic rights and responsibilities were guaranteed upon payment of a land and poll tax.[227] The non-violent submission of the city is confirmed by the archaeological record, as all three churches, the residential quarters and, notably, the military barracks on Tell al-Ḥusn indicate an undetectable transition from Byzantine to Muslim rule. Pella was occupied to sever the link between Damascus and Jerusalem, the two most important centers in southern Bilād al-Shām in the early 7th century.[228]

In early Islamic times, Pella was an administrative district in the military province of Jordan, the *jund* of al-Urdunn (fig. 55).[229] The province, which reached its maximum extent in the early

---

[224] Walmsley, "Households at Pella," 241.

[225] Al-Balâdhuri, *Origins of the Islamic State*, 176.

[226] Ibid., 177.

[227] Walmsley, "Social and Economic Regime at Fihl," 254.

[228] Idem, "Households at Pella," 244.

[229] Idem, "Pella/Fiḥl after the Islamic Conquest," 144.

Umayyad period, stretched from Ṣūr and ,ʿAkkā on the Mediterranean coast to al-Jawlān and Jarash in the east. Pella appears to have joined administratively with Baysān, where there was a large administrative quarter, and Jarash. However, unlike Baysān and Jarash, Pella did not mint coins, or at least no issues have been identified with Pella or Fiḥl as a mint-name to date. This may suggest the absence of any permanent Muslim administration at the site.

There is evidence for two earthquakes at Pella: the first dating to 659/60 and the second, a much larger one, occurring in 749.[230] The former resulted in the houses on the main mound requiring substantial rebuilding and remodeling. The massive earthquake of 749 was even more destructive. The damage from this quake is evident at Pella, as well as neighboring sites, as seen in the complete obliteration of the domestic quarter on the main mound.

Excavation of Domestic Structure at Site:

The excavations at Pella by the University of Sydney from 1979 to 1990 have uncovered more than 1,000 sq. m. of dwellings and courtyards on the eastern end of the main archaeological mound, or *tell*, dating to the seventh and eighth centuries (fig. 56, Area IV).[231] Six courtyard houses, destroyed in the earthquake of 749, have been identified.[232] These units are the result of earlier, mid-7th century modifications to pre-Islamic houses constructed in the time of Justinian the Great (527-65).[233]

Stratigraphy:

The major extant architectural phases can be attributed to the 6th century, and occupation is continuous until the end of the Umayyad period.[234]

Mid-5th century C.E. (Byzantine Phase I):

---

[230] Idem, "Households at Pella," 246.
[231] Idem, "Tradition, Innovation and Imitation," 657.
[232] Idem, *Early Islamic Syria*, 129.
[233] Idem, "Households at Pella," 240.
[234] Watson, "Byzantine Period," 163-164.

Two 10 x 10 plots, in Areas IV and III, provide substantial information on the sequence of domestic occupation at Pella during the Byzantine periods.[235] Five Byzantine phases have been identified. In Phase I, Area IV contains floor levels without any associated architecture (fig. 57).[236] An exception is a rough, uncoursed wall (F76) in the west. An ash pit is nearby, and it runs beneath a 6th century wall (Wall 22) and partly over the remains of a Hellenistic wall (Wall 26). To the east, the remains of a *ṭābūn* (F53) lie partly beneath a 6th century wall (Wall 12), and its associated surface runs over a dismantled Hellenistic wall (Wall 27). This suggests that the Hellenistic walls have been demolished before the next extant architectural phase (II), while Phase II has completely obliterated any structures of the intervening period.

c. 500-525 C.E. (Byzantine Phase II):

This phase is best represented in Area IV where there is a clear sequence of architecture and surfaces (fig. 57).[237] In the southern half of the plot, a building (Rooms D and E) is constructed, directly over the Hellenistic walls, which have been dismantled to floor level at some time prior to Phase I. The condition of the area north of the building is unclear. It is possible that the Hellenistic wall (Wall 20) is still in use. The occupation levels north of Wall 20 are considerably higher than those to the south as indicated by the pottery sherds from the Iron Age. Terracing accounts for the discrepancy in elevations.

A surface associated with Wall 12 lies to the north of the south building.[238] It forms a passageway (P), probably unroofed, between the south building and the retaining wall (Wall 20 or its replacement) for the higher northern building. Two complete rooms of the south building, Rooms D and E, open onto the passageway. Room D also opens westwards to Room C. The

---

[235] Ibid., 163.
[236] Ibid., 164.
[237] Ibid., 164.
[238] Ibid., 164.

floor of Room E is approximately 30 cm. higher than the floor in Room D. The walls, which

have no foundations, reflect terracing: namely, the lowest course of Wall 12 is higher on the east

side of Wall 11 than on the west.[239] An exterior staircase (F41) abuts Wall 12, probably

providing access to an upper storey. Another staircase (F65) is located in the south-west corner

of Room D. Given the lack of foundations of the walls, the upper story may have been fairly

light. When the building is no longer used and the rooms are filled (in Phase IV), the lower

deposits consist of a thick layer of *pisé* and mud-brick remains. This suggests the superstructure

is made of *pisé*. The floors in these rooms are beaten earth flecked with white lime.

c. 525-550 C.E. (Byzantine Phase IIIa):

Phase III has been divided into two sub-phases.[240] Phase IIIa represents the major

architectural changes and initial associated surfaces (figs. 58 and 59). In Area IV, the building

north of Passage P is demolished. A new building is constructed in its place (Rooms F and G),

involving massive trenching and wall foundations. A street running east-west is laid to the north

of this building and its surface is 1.38 m. higher than the surface of the Phase II passageway.

The floor of Room G is paved with mudstone and opens northwards onto the street at

approximately the same elevation. In addition, a door opens southwards into H, but the

associated surface has been removed by later activities. In Room F, the earth floor, lying 80 cm.

below the floor of G, is made of graveled earth. There is no access between this room and the

street, with the exception of a window at street level.

Passage P is raised 35 cm. to the level of Room F, and a north-south section is added to

staircase F41, effectively blocking the passage at this point.[241] It probably communicates with

the southward-opening doorway from Room G. The floor levels in the southern building remain

---

[239] Ibid., 164, 166.
[240] Ibid., 166.
[241] Ibid., 166.

the same as in Phase II. However, the level of the north doorway in Room D is raised by a stone packing and two steps lead up to the new passageway surface. In addition, the doorway in Room E has a similar step upwards to the north.

c. 550-575 C.E. (Byzantine Phase IIIb):

Phase IIIb represents a series of occupational surfaces, largely within the same architectural frame work of Phase IIIa (fig. 58).[242]

c. 575-600 C.E. (Byzantine Phase IV):

The living arrangement in Areas IV and III is substantially altered in Phase IV (figs. 58 and 60).[243] A new room (I) is added to the northern building. The walls of the southern building are dismantled to a uniform level, approximately 1.0 m. above the surface of Room D. Rooms D, E, L, M and the passage areas H and P are then filled to the height of the dismantled walls and the resultant surface is covered with yellow clay. Thus an internal courtyard is created, onto which open Rooms F, G, and I. The walls of Room K are constructed above the courtyard fill and help define the eastern boundary of the enclosure. The western wall is rebuilt to define the western boundary. The massive Phase II/III east-west retaining wall at the south end of Area III remains in use to demarcate the southern edge of the courtyard. A *ṭābūn* and nearby column base are associated with the courtyard. North of the courtyard complex, a second street surface is laid above the original surface.

c. 600-640 C.E. (Byzantine Phase V):

The internal courtyard is also associated with Phase V, namely with the construction of an external staircase abutting the east wall of Rooms I and J, blocking the doorway in Room I (fig.

---

[242] Ibid., 166.
[243] Ibid., 168.

58).[244] The staircase is built directly on the courtyard surface. At the same time, a structure, perhaps a staircase, is added alongside Rooms F and G, though only one course remains. In the north-east corner, another wall is added alongside the inner face of the east wall of Room G. In addition, a rough wall, one course wide and running east-west, is constructed on the courtyard surface in Area III, thus subdividing the southern area of the enclosure. In Room F, a roughly constructed stone bin (F39) runs alongside the length of the east wall and is associated with a soft, fine mustard-brown and grey deposit overlaying the patchy remains of a firm clay surface. The evidence suggests that the room functions as a stable in its final phase.

At the end of Phase V, all the structures associated with this courtyard are destroyed.[245] While the large building complexes to the east and the north are largely renovated and reused, the exposed area is uniformly leveled to create one large courtyard area. This area reveals subsequent major courtyard phases before the final earthquake destruction in 749.

However, one room (Room 32) north of the east-west street is never cleared of debris after the collapse at the end of Phase V (fig. 61).[246] Whereas the courtyard area is cleared and leveled, leaving little trace of the collapse *in situ*, this room preserves the moment in time of the collapse and preceding occupation layers. The room establishes a well-grounded *terminus* for the Byzantine sequence of architectural phases.

There are three phases of occupation established for Room 32.[247] The room is originally constructed in Byzantine Phase IIIa and opens onto the newly established east-west street.[248] While nothing remains of the original floor, there are indications that it is a mudstone pavement. Subsequently, the room appears to have been used to house animals, most likely corresponding

---

[244] Ibid., 168.
[245] Ibid., 168.
[246] Ibid., 168.
[247] McNicoll, et al., "Preliminary Report," 177, 180.
[248] Watson, "Byzantine Period," 170.

to Phases IV/V observed south of the street, and the use of Room F as a stable. The latest occupation evidence is a series of domestic rubbish dumps, consisting of large amounts of small animal bones, carbonized seeds, charcoal and ash, indicating a period of disuse after the stable phase. The room collapsed, filling with a *pisé*-like deposit.[249] The east wall collapsed inwards to the west, retaining the line of the wall face. The evidence suggests an upper storey with *pisé* walls that was occupied at the time of the collapse. It is also evident that people were living in the upper storey rather than on the ground level.

<u>659/60-749 C.E. (Early Islamic Phase)</u>:

The partial collapse of the domestic quarter on the *tell* from the earthquake of 659-60 leads to an urban reorganization.[250] The rebuilding program in Area IV produces large houses with their principal orientation towards a large open space, a development facilitated by the closure of the east-west street and an encroachment on public areas (fig. 62).

Six courtyard houses, each completely destroyed in the 749 earthquake, were excavated in Area IV (fig. 62).[251] All of the houses are probably two-storyed, perhaps three in some instances or at least with roof-top access (possibly House G). The upper floor could be reached through the courtyards by means of stone-built staircases.

Houses A, B, and C, located at the south-eastern corner of the *tell* (fig. 62), generally represent a rebuilding of the terrace houses that faced the southern perimeter of a graveled street prior to 659/60.[252] Following the earthquake, a long wall, running north-south, is built to demarcate the western limit of Houses A and B. Continuing northwards over the now defunct street, this wall eventually turns westwards along the northern limit of the former street, in line

---

[249] McNicoll, et al., "Preliminary Report," 180.
[250] Walmsley, "Social and Economic Regime," 254.
[251] Idem, "Households at Pella," 251.
[252] Ibid., 251.

with the façade of the shops that once lined this part of the street. Thus, a large open courtyard is formed, seemingly approached from the west (unexcavated), with a narrow doorway from the ground floor of House A giving access to it. Small cooking ovens flank the doorway.[253] Rooms along the southern edge of the courtyard may have functioned as storage areas or may have been shops. The absence of a staircase to the upper floor from the courtyard suggests that public access to this court is possible. Additional doorways opening onto the courtyard from House B have not been preserved.

Rooms 3 and 4 of House A are used as stables as both rooms have packed mud floors, over which is a soft mustard yellow layer, interpreted as decayed manure.[254] It is unlikely that these or other ground floor rooms have always functioned as stables since many doorways are blocked before the floors of the final phase are constructed.[255] This suggests that the ground floor rooms are interconnected to an extent unsuitable for the stabling of animals. When the doorways are subsequently blocked, mangers are constructed both in and across them, a development which indicates that the new function and form of these rooms are interrelated.

The internal ground-floor doorways, which once allowed passage between Houses A and B, perhaps before 659/60, have been blocked with a solid wall-like filling with stone feed bins as part of this process.[256] In House A, a subdividing wall, bonded to the blocking between Room 3 of House A and Room 1 of House B, is erected in Room 4. This wall is subsequently destroyed and a support for the upper floor is inserted in the middle of the room in the form of a column.[257] The upper floor of House A is not accessed from the courtyard, but from the eastern side of the building through a passageway, small courtyard and staircase.

---

[253] Ibid., 251, 253.
[254] McNicoll, Smith, and Hennessy. eds., *Pella in Jordan 1*, 132.
[255] Ibid., 135.
[256] Walmsley, "Households at Pella," 253.
[257] Ibid., 253-254.

The disposition of finds in the layered collapse of Houses A and B confirms human occupation of the buildings is primarily reserved for the upper floor rooms.[258] The domestic items recovered include ceramic vessels and lamps, metal objects, such as containers and pins, worked bone, shell and stone, especially small basalt grinders and steatite cooking bowls, and glass vessels and beads. While it is not possible to ascertain the exact layout of the upper floors of Houses A and B, it is likely that it corresponds to the wall plan of the ground level, as the one-meter plus stone-built walls are designed to carry the considerable weight of an upper story and roof.

The re-arrangement of the houses north of the former street after the mid-7th century earthquake is more complicated.[259] East of the blocking wall of Houses A and B, a shop that once opened out onto the former street is converted into a laneway, and the street-side shop is reduced in size by the construction of a thin wall over the paved floor (fig. 62, Room 1, House D). The function of this reduced room is undetermined. The lane opens out into a central courtyard flanked by rooms.[260] The large open courtyard is paved with neatly cut and laid mudstone pavers.[261] Access from the courtyard is possible to all surrounding dwellings. Half-way along the lane is the courtyard gateway, of which only the threshold blocks survive. The gate is double leafed, with doors of unequal size. North of the gateway the courtyard entrance is paved with mudstone and along its west side runs an open drain. An L-shaped staircase on the west side gives access to one or more rooms above the south wing of House G.[262]

---

[258] Ibid., 254.
[259] Ibid., 254.
[260] Ibid., 257.
[261] McNicoll, Smith, and Hennessy. eds., *Pella in Jordan 1*, 136.
[262] Walmsley, "Households at Pella," 257.

Extensive ash deposits and working surfaces made from upturned columns capitals suggest that the central courtyard is used for domestic and or light industrial purposes.[263] For instance, two column bases in the courtyard serve no structural function.[264] They are probably used to prepare dough, which is subsequently cooked in a *ṭābūn* nearby.

The bent staircase in the north end of Room 6 may have given access to the raised area between House D and the courtyard of House H.[265] There is no evidence for animal stabling in House D, although the remains of an earthquake victim in Room 7 of House D indicate occupation. House H has only been partially excavated, and lies very close to the surface, suggesting it is single storeyed. An earthen courtyard on the west side gives access to a single room (1), and to its north are Rooms 2 and 4. Room 2 gives entry to a further Room 3. All of the rooms are roughly paved.

The clearest example of an operating household at the time of the massive 749 earthquake is a large and wealthy unit known as House G (fig. 62), which has a floor area of some 375 sq. m. and living space over two levels of nearly 750 sq. m., and perhaps more, if roof space is also accessed.[266] House G is organized around a paved internal courtyard approximately 8.35 x 9.7 m. (fig. 63). Six supports, comprised of 5 columns and a pier, carry an internal balcony some 3 m. deep on at least three sides (north, west and south).[267] Access to the balcony is by way of a staircase, 1.25 m. wide, against the eastern wall of the internal courtyard.[268] Entry to the rooms of the upper floor, whose arrangement is not known, could be accessed from the balcony.

---

[263] Ibid., 257.

[264] McNicoll, Smith, and Hennessy. eds., *Pella in Jordan 1*, 136.

[265] Walmsley, "Households at Pella," 257.

[266] Idem, "Excavation of an Umayyad Period House," 257.

[267] Idem, "Households at Pella," 259.

[268] Idem, "Excavation of an Umayyad Period House," 517.

House G is approached from an open courtyard on its east side through two doorways.[269] A public outer courtyard leads to a private inner courtyard (fig. 64). Both courtyards are paved to withstand the heavy traffic of people and animals. The inner courtyard has a wide stone staircase ascending to the north along its eastern wall, animal feed benches built against the north and west walls (fig. 63), and an open drain in the south-east corner.[270] The drainage channel indicates that the courtyard is open to the sky.[271] Located between the staircase and the drain is the main doorway of the courtyard, which opens out onto an external courtyard to the east.

Five internal doorways around the courtyard give access to flanking rooms (fig. 64). The inner courtyard opens onto two stand-alone rooms on the south side (1, 2).[272] A single, wide doorway gives access to Room 9. The doorway opening has a threshold and jambs, suggesting it could have been closed. The recovery of many iron nails near doorways indicates they are closed with leaves of nailed wooden planks. A large room (8) could be accessed from Room 9 through double arches by way of a step. Both Rooms 8 and 9 are stone paved and provided with feed benches to accommodate animals, specifically cows. There is an additional doorway in the east wall of Room 9 at its northern end (fig. 62). The doorway leads to another outside court, but is too narrow for large animals and thus may have been used only by humans.

The arrangement of rooms on the west side of the inner courtyard is more complicated than those to the north and south.[273] Three rooms (3, 4 and 5) are originally reached through a single doorway in the south-west corner of the internal courtyard (fig. 64).[274] The stone threshold and jambs indicate that this doorway, like that into Room 9, could be closed by a door, probably

---

[269] Idem, "Households at Pella," 257.
[270] Idem, "Pella/Fiḥl after the Islamic Conquest," 150.
[271] Idem, "Households at Pella," 257, 259.
[272] Ibid., 268.
[273] Ibid., 268.
[274] Idem, "Excavation of an Umayyad Period House," 518.

made of nailed wooden planks. In contrast, the plainer entrance into Room 7 appears to have been left open. There is no entrance from the inner courtyard into Room 6. Room 6, and from it Room 7, is originally accessible from Room 5. In fact, Rooms 5 and 6 once formed one room with a line of feeding mangers in the center (fig. 63). At a later time, two Rooms, 5 and 6, are created by blocking the central opening in the manger, leaving Rooms 6 and 7 devoted to stabling animals.

Access to the southern wing of the building (Rooms 3 and 4) is also closed off by the construction of a long solid blocking wall between two arch piers.[275] Manufacturing activities involving basins and the use of white plaster take place in Room 3 and is subsequently relocated to Room 5. After access to Rooms 3 and 4 is blocked, the activities associated with those rooms are relocated to Room 5, which is provided with a long bench on the south side, used as a worktable intended for making, maintaining or fixing objects. The change in function for Room 5 explains the need to restrict access to it from Room 6, which continues to be used for the stabling of animals until the earthquake of 749.

Domestic items are found fallen from the upper floor, such as unglazed ceramic vessels and lamps, copper objects including kohl sticks and a basin, blown glass vessels with ribbon trailing, bone buttons with incised lines and inlay from wood furniture, and stone items including hand grinders and a two-part basalt quern.[276] Based on the evidence of artifacts in the collapse and the complete entrapped skeletons on the ground floor, it has been suggested that the downstairs area of the house is reserved for the care of domesticated animals and light workshop activities, whereas the primary living quarters are situated upstairs. Just outside the doorway into Room 2,

---

[275] Ibid., 518.
[276] Idem, "Households at Pella," 262.

there is evidence for a small fire on the bench against the west wall of the inner courtyard. This fire is probably used for cooking rather than heating.

Four human victims are recovered from the ground floor: three adults and a child.[277] A single male is found crouched against the west wall of Room 2, with one arm raised above his head as if to protect himself from heavy falling material (fig. 62). An adult male and female with a young child are found in the north-eastern corner of the inner courtyard, huddled together under the staircase. The trapped animals on the ground floor are mainly cows (Rooms 8 and 9, totaling three), small equids (mules or donkeys; inner courtyard, Rooms 6 and 7), sheep, goats, chickens and a cat.[278] With the exception of the chickens and cats, these animals represent wealth, especially the cows and mules.

In the lower floors of all the houses, large, roughly dressed stone blocks are laid to form two faces (fig. 63); both the interior wall cavity and block interstices on the faces are filled with small stones and yellow clay mortar.[279] Well-squared blocks are reserved for wall corners and doorways, where the additional strength is required to carry the weight of the upper floor. In contrast, the walls of the upper storey are made of unbaked bricks made from pebbles and yellow clay, a lighter and more easily managed building material than the heavy stone blocks of the ground floor.

In some cases, upper floors are paved with plain white mosaic over a pebble and mortar base, the walls are plastered and painted (red, yellow, cream and fragments of text in black), and fitted out with fixtures in stone, often reused marble, some of which come from a church (fig. 65).[280] The absence of ceramic roof tiles among the collapsed debris, but the presence of carbonized

---

[277] Ibid., 262.

[278] Ibid., 264.

[279] Idem, "Pella/Fiḥl after the Islamic Conquest," 150.

[280] Idem, *Early Islamic Syria*, 130.

wood beams, suggests the roofs are made of matting over oak beams, sealed with clay. It has been speculated that the upper storey floors are carried on timber joists, as stone slabs for cantilevered roofs of the kind found in Umayyad housing in the Ḥaurān are not evident.[281]

Chronology:

<u>Mid-5th century C.E. (Byzantine Phase I):</u>

The two latest identifiable coins found in Areas III and IV are dated to Julian II, 360-363, and to Honorius, 393-423, respectively.[282] Another recovered coin is more generally identified as 4th-5th century. Stratigraphically, the deposits of Phase I lie between a late Roman context and an early 6th century context (Phase II). Therefore, the evidence suggests a 5th century attribution for Phase I, probably around the middle of that century.

<u>*c*. 500-525 C.E. (Byzantine Phase II):</u>

The few identifiable coins attributed to this phase date to the later 5th century.[283] A bronze „4" from a wall packing can only generally be dated to the second half of the 5th century. More informative are a coin of Marcian (450-457) from the surface of this phase, and a coin of Zeno (474-491). The most notable introduction at this time is late Roman C/Phocaean ware Form 3, particularly Types E and F. This imported ware is assigned to the period from the late 5th century to the middle of the 6th century. Given these dates, it is reasonable to suggest that Phase II is laid down some time in the first quarter of the 6th century.

<u>*c*. 525-550 C.E. (Byzantine Phase IIIa):</u>

The latest coin from these deposits is identified as Justin I, 518-527.[284] However, a date somewhere within the second quarter of the 6th century is suggested for Phase IIIa on the

---

[281] McNicoll, Smith, and Hennessy. eds., *Pella in Jordan 1*, 131.
[282] Watson, "Byzantine Period," 173.
[283] Ibid., 174.
[284] Ibid., 176.

grounds that a sequence of architectural changes in the late Byzantine period at Pella is paralleled by a sequence of progressively later dating coins for each phase, roughly separated by a quarter century.

c. 550-575 C.E. (Byzantine Phase IIIb):

The latest coin to be found from Area III dates to Justinian I, 527-565.[285] The coin evidence suggests a date in the third quarter of the 6th century for Phase IIIb.

c. 575-600 C.E. (Byzantine Phase IV):

No identifiable coins from the Phase IV deposits date later than Justinian I.[286] A coin of Tiberius, 578-582, is found on the surface of the later street in Area IV, which is probably re-laid during the alterations of Phase IV, and in use during Phase V. Whereas in later deposits coins of Heraclius (615-616) are commonly distributed at Pella, they are notably absent in Phase IV deposits. Hence, the coin evidence and the relative position within the phasing sequence suggest a date somewhere within the fourth quarter of the 6th century.

c. 600-640 C.E. (Byzantine Phase V):

The latest identifiable coin found within the collapse is of Heraclius, dated 615-616, from Area IV.[287] It is probable that the destruction at the end of Phase V occurs not long afterwards. The damage represented in Phase V could be attributed to an earthquake. The end of Phase V marks the end of the Byzantine period at Pella.

659/60-749 C.E. (Early Islamic Phase):

Two small hoards of Umayyad gold *dīnārs* are recovered from the debris of House G.[288] The *dīnārs* are all standard issues from the Dimashq mint (fig. 66, **6.001-6.010**).[289] Four of the

---

[285] Ibid., 178.
[286] Ibid., 179.
[287] Ibid., 181.
[288] Walmsley, "Excavation of an Umayyad Period House," 519.

dīnārs, probably contained in a leather purse which had decayed, are recovered in Room 2 in 1981 next to the crushed skeleton of a young adult male. These coins range in chronological date from 96 to 117/714-736 (fig. 66, **6.004-6.006, 6.009**). These early Islamic *dīnārs* carry a mint date: 96/714-15, 97/715-16, 106/724-25 and 117/735-36. In the courtyard near the remains of the couple, six additional *dīnārs* are found at the end of the 1982 season, dating from 91 to 122/709-740 (fig. 66, **6.001-6.003, 6.007-6.008, 6.010**). Specifically, these date to 91/709-10, two to 94/712-13, 110/728-29, 112/730-31 and 122/739-40. However, the best chronological dating can be attributed to a copper *fals* of Damascus minted in 126/743-44, five years before the earthquake of 130/749.[290] It is found in the same room in House G that produced the four *dīnārs*.

According to Walmsley, a clear pattern emerges.[291] The issues of the 90s AH are well represented, with half of the *dīnārs* originating in the seven year period 91-97/709-715, coinciding with the reign of Umayyad Caliph al-Walīd b. ,Abd al-Malik b. Marwān (85-96 AH), who was a prolific builder in the Filasṭīn and al-Urdunn region. The other five specimens are more randomly spread out over the seventeen years between 106 and 122 AH, though they all belong to the long and equally prosperous reign of the Caliph Hishām (105-125 AH). Hence, the economic benefit afforded the local community from the state projects of al-Walīd and Hishām is reflected in the wealth accrued in one household at Pella.

A wide range of domestic objects is found *in situ* in the internal courtyard and Room 2 of House G.[292] In particular, an important corpus of mid-8th century ceramics is recovered, all unglazed, but including oil lamps, cooking vessels and new types of wares, such as a red painted ware and a porous off-white ware for storing water. The 659/60 earthquake destruction level

---

[289] Idem, "Islamic Coins," 59.
[290] Ibid., 61.
[291] Ibid., 59.
[292] Idem, "Excavation of an Umayyad Period House," 519.

provides a firm starting point for the corpus.[293] Shortly after this date, the range of wares and shapes undergoes the first noticeable change in the archaeological record: namely, five wares fade from the corpus (fig. 67, Wares 1-5) while three new ones appear (Wares 6-8).

Ware 6 is a jar with fine ribbing on the upper body and broad ribbing on the lower body.[294] The ware is made of a gritty fabric with many white and mica inclusions, the „sandwich" core with grey-brown center and red-brown faces (fig. 68: 1-2).[295] Appearing after 660, the ware is suddenly absent after about 750.[296]

Ware 7 is a medium-thin walled jar in large and medium sizes, jugs, and water flasks (fig. 68: 3-6, 8).[297] The larger vessels have broad ribbing. The ware is made of a pale cream or greenish to light yellow-brown fabric, aerated, with fine white, orange and/or grey inclusions. Some of the jars and flasks probably originated from Baysān. The large ribbed water jars, which first appear in post-660 deposits, are joined by the smaller jars, flasks, and occasional incised bowls by the mid-eighth century.

Ware 8 is commonly smooth-bodied jars with ring bases, spouted juglets, bowls, and cups (fig. 69).[298] The ware is made of light orange fabric, sometimes apparently white slipped, with small and sometimes medium white and grey inclusions. Decorations are painted in bold reddish-brown, depicting loops, stars, wavy lines, „arcade" patterns and crisscrossed lines. The cups were made at Jarash. The jars appear occasionally around the turn of the eighth century, but are quite common in the layer representing the destruction level of 747/8 (fig. 69:2).

---

[293] Idem, "Tradition, Innovation, and Imitation," 660.
[294] Ibid., 661.
[295] Ibid., 661.
[296] Ibid., 661.
[297] Ibid., 661.
[298] Ibid., 661.

The domestic wares found in Area IV have many features in common with late Umayyad ceramics from sites in the Jordan Valley and the north Jordan range, such as Jarash.[299] In fact, much of Pella‟s pottery comes from the kilns of Jarash, in particular, the cooking pots and casseroles, small jugs and jars, large hand-made mixing craters and some lamps. At Jarash, levels associated with the kiln uncovered in the Portico of the Theater have produced a collection of small vessels and lamps, including wasters, which can be dated to the second quarter of the eighth century on the basis of coin evidence and comparative material.[300] Furthermore, in the collapse of the Roman North Theater at Jarash, the Umayyad period potters exploited still standing architecture to install a complex of kilns.[301]

The corpus of kiln-produced pottery at Jarash is replicated in the 746/7 earthquake destruction levels at Pella.[302] Pella more than any other site provides a firm date for the Jarash kilns and context for the use of these pottery types, in particular, the gray ware basin Type 2, coarse cooking pot ware casseroles and jars, red ware, pitchers, and wide mouth jars and lids. Gray ware and red ware decorative motifs are identical at both sites. It is the utilitarian wares and shapes found in the destruction layers at Pella that correspond to those produced in the Jarash kilns. It suggests that Jarash was a producer and supplier of pottery for a large region, including Pella, as no kilns have been found at Pella.

The discussion of the ceramics corpus at Pella will conclude with a consideration of the pottery recovered from Area XXIX (fig. 56), where there are archaeological remains of Abbasid settlement. The pottery recovered from this area indicates radical alterations in the ceramic

---

[299] Idem, "Fiḥl (Pella) and the Cities of North Jordan," 380.
[300] Ball, et al., "North Decumanus," 355.
[301] Schaefer and Falkner, "Umayyad Potters‟ Complex," 411.
[302] Ibid., 433.

corpus at Pella occurring at the beginning of the 9th century.[303] In particular, limited quantities of three glazed varieties make an appearance: thick turquoise or blue glaze on greenish fabric, polychrome glaze on white slip over orange fabric (fig. 70:2), and "Coptic" glaze on reddish-orange fabric (fig. 70:1). The interior of the "Coptic" glazed ware is divided into zones by painted black lines with bubbly green and yellow glaze.[304] This ware may be a local production based on Egyptian originals. In Syria-Palestine, glazed wares were generally not introduced until the later eighth century at the earliest, thus they represent a small minority in the ceramic assemblage throughout the early Islamic period.[305]

In addition, the widespread adoption of Sāmarrāʿ-style pale cream jars and strainer jugs with thin walls and a knife-trimmed lower body and base emphasizes the stylistic changes in the ceramic corpus at Pella (fig. 70:3-5). This ceramic type, imitating silver vessels, originated in eighth-century Iraq and became a common domestic ware in Sāmarrāʿ.[306] Manufactured at major centers, such as al-Ramla, these wares are characterized by sharp angular profiles inspired by metal moulded patterns (fig. 70:5).

In the span of 50 years, the new international "Islamic" ceramics (glazed and pale cream) replaced the traditional local wares, especially the white-painted jugs and jars produced at Jarash.[307] It is noteworthy that the Jarash kilns, which were producing the less desirable local forms, ceased production during the same half century. Representing a major artistic and technological break with the past, these international wares reflect a developing involvement, by early ninth century communities in the north Jordan Valley, in the cultural traditions of the wider

---

[303] Walmsley, "Social and Economic Regime," 257.
[304] Idem, "Tradition, Innovation, and Imitation," 664.
[305] Idem, *Early Islamic Syria*, 52.
[306] Ibid., 54.
[307] Idem, "Social and Economic Regime," 257.

dār al-Islam.[308] Especially in the context of Pella, the decisive end by earthquake of Late Antique Pella and its institutions may have led to its searching for new, alternative identities, as suggested by the adoption of cream and glazed wares.

Umm el-Jimāl

Geographical and Historical Setting of Site:

Umm el-Jimāl is located 20 km. east of Mafraq in the semi-arid lava region of the southern Ḥaurān (fig. 71).[309] It was part of a grid of towns and cities radiating from Boṣrā and the Jabal al-Durūz through the relatively more fertile parts of the basaltic regions. In this area, sparse agricultural resources were exploited and distributed along the Roman-Byzantine *Limes Arabicus*, and walled civilian settlements were integrated with more military installations to form a secure buffer to prevent nomadic and military incursions into Syria and Palestine.[310] In the sixth century, the military role of Umm el-Jimāl continued to diminish while its growth as a prospering civilian rural community came to a climax.[311]

During the Umayyad period, Umm el-Jimāl continued the occupation of late Byzantine structures rather than initiating the construction of new buildings.[312] Following extensive collapse of structures in the last decade of the Umayyad period, Umm el-Jimāl was not rebuilt as it had been after such disasters in the past. The collapse of many buildings may be associated with the earthquake of 749.[313] This earthquake came on the wake of the final episode of a two-century long pandemic, in which Boṣrā and the Ḥaurān were affected so severely that entire

---

[308] Idem, "Tradition, Innovation, and Imitation," 668.
[309] De Vries, *Umm el-Jimal*, 91.
[310] Idem, "Urbanization in the Basalt Region," 249.
[311] Ibid., 251.
[312] Ibid., 251.
[313] Idem, *Umm el-Jimal*, 231.

villages were ravaged and deserted after the ensuing famine. Furthermore, the shift of political center from Syria to Iraq brought on by the Abbasid revolution led to the Ḥaurān area losing its strategic significance.[314]

Excavation of Domestic Structure at Site (House XVIII):

House XVIII, a large residential complex, is located in the south-east quarter of the town (fig. 72).[315] In 1977, the house was selected as a part of a stratigraphic sampling of domestic architecture because its plan is typical of domestic residences at Umm el-Jimāl and in the Ḥaurān generally (fig. 73). However, it is distinguished by its size and architectural embellishments.

Stratigraphy (House XVIII):

As one of the largest houses at Umm el-Jimāl, the central courtyard measures approximately 24 m. north-south x 19 m. east-west.[316] It represents the most frequently attested domestic plan in the Ḥaurān: rooms are grouped around a rectangular open courtyard, with upper-story apartment units reached by exterior cantilevered stairs (fig. 74). The northern and eastern complexes (fig. 75) each house two sets of apartments, while the western block of rooms (fig. 76) contains a single residence. Smaller rooms flank the entrance on the southern side of the courtyard (fig. 77). There is no evidence for the accommodation of animals in its ground-floor rooms, which lack mangers. The presence of mangers in the courtyard indicates some involvement with animals, but large-scale animal husbandry is largely absent or carried on outside the residence.

The building is constructed out of basalt stone, whose strength lends itself to an unusual style of architecture: corbelling (fig. 78).[317] The method of construction of the wall typically consists

---

[314] Idem, "Umm el-Jimal Project, 1981-1992," 449.
[315] Brown, "Large Residence," 195.
[316] Ibid., 195.
[317] De Vries, "Umm el-Jimal Project, 1972-1977," 53.

of two-face masonry, in which only the outer face of a basalt stone block is dressed.[318] The

efficient method of construction in combination with corbelling is used for the ceilings and

roofs.[319] The base corbel, to be able to support the full weight of the cantilevered roof, is laid

across the entire width of the wall and therefore serves as a header tying the two wall faces

together (fig. 78).

Cantilevering is also applied to the construction of stairways. To conserve space in the

typically narrow rooms, stairways are built onto the exterior facades of the building, usually in

the courtyard, by cantilevering from the walls the treads of stairs (long beams with the portion

inside the wall left rough but dressed to a smooth triangular shape where exposed).[320] In the

courtyard of House XVIII, a single flight of stairs is suspended from the northern facade (fig.

79), while a double stairway is installed in the eastern façade of the courtyard (fig. 80).[321]

In House XVIII, carefully crafted cornices, a double-arched window supported by a central

column (fig. 81), and a finely-worked basalt door (fig. 82) suggest sophisticated attention to

architectural detail.[322] The door is designed with hinge pins, knobs that protrude from the top

and bottom edge so that they could be fitted into socket cups carved into the doorstep and into

the lintel above.[323] The heavy lintel is lowered into place with its socket cup aligned over the top

knob of the door. Once the lintel is in place, the hinge knobs could be locked in place, and the

whole assembly is held together by the weight of the lintel and the masonry loaded upon it.

Lintel relieving is common, as evident in the low-sprung arches used in the courtyard of House

XVIII (fig. 83).[324]

---

[318] Idem, "Restoration at Umm el-Jimal," 45.
[319] Idem, *Umm el-Jimal*, 113.
[320] Ibid., 117.
[321] Ibid., 117.
[322] Brown, "Large Residence," 195.
[323] De Vries, *Umm el-Jimal*, 117.
[324] Ibid., 121.

A cistern C.2 lies in the north-eastern corner of the cellar under the arched central room of the northern of two apartments on the eastern side of the courtyard (fig. 73).[325] Its low arched entrance is in the northern wall near its junction with the eastern wall (fig. 84). Basalt rubble from architectural collapse partially blocks the entrance and covers its silted shaft, whose upper portion is roughly rectangular. The corbelled cistern roof (fig. 85) supports the partition wall dividing the central arched room from the smaller N room.

Chronology (House XVIII):

The lower layer of fill in the cistern has a concentration of late Byzantine pottery, indicating that late Byzantine occupation precedes the Umayyad use of the house.[326] The earliest evidence for occupation is found in the cistern deposit which contains abundant late Byzantine pottery.[327] The Umayyad occupation of the house is not, however, preceded by deposits of the transitional period.[328] Late Byzantine occupation debris, if not even earlier material, is likely to have been removed in preparation for the Umayyad floor. The successive phases can be attributed to continuous Umayyad occupation subsequent to a complete re-flooring in Phase A.

<u>Phase A (Earliest Occupation):</u>

Three early Islamic phases (mid 7th-8th century) are identified from the excavation of square C.1 in the west room.[329] Phase A represents the earliest occupation. A reddish-brown soil layer, resting on basalt bedrock, contains a few undiagnosed sherds and one possible early Byzantine sherd.[330] The layer above it includes bone and glass fragments, tesserae, and early Islamic, early Umayyad, late Byzantine and earlier sherds. Subsequent to it, a cobble and plaster floor covers

---

[325] Brown, "Large Residence," 202.
[326] Ibid., 204.
[327] Ibid., 204.
[328] Ibid., 199.
[329] Ibid., 195.
[330] Ibid., 196.

the square, except where broken along part of the eastern wall (fig. 86). The floor consists of small cobbles cemented together with gray plaster (a plaster coating was partially preserved), in which are Umayyad and earlier sherds.

<u>Phase B (Floor Construction)</u>:

A thin red-brown soil layer lies above the cobble and plaster floor.[331] It contains considerable occupation refuse: bone, tesserae, plaster, glass, fragments of a *ṭābūn*, bronze pins, a marble revetment fragment, a bronze latch, and pottery (Umayyad being the latest). On top lies a badly disturbed floor (though intact along the southern wall) constructed of smooth, flat basalt cobbles resting on a thin, sterile plaster and earth bed.

<u>Phase C (Accumulation of Debris in the Late Umayyad Period)</u>:

Debris, which accumulated on the above-mentioned disturbed floor over the entire trench, consists of ash in the northern portion of the square and red-brown soil in the south with fragments of bone and glass, a *ṭābūn*, and a piece of iron.[332] The dominant pottery type is Umayyad with some late Byzantine of the mid 6th-early 7th century. The remains here represent Abbasid occupation after formal floors were no longer maintained.

Excavation of Domestic Structure at Site (House 119):

House 119 is located at the modern entrance to Umm el-Jimāl, at the east side of the entry drive opposite the Barracks (fig. 72).[333] It was excavated during the 1993 field season at Umm el-Jimāl.

Stratigraphy (House 119):

House 119 is a modest domestic complex *c.* 40 x 40 m. in size (fig. 87).[334] It consists of a large open courtyard, an entry gate, seven small ground floor rooms (including Room C on the

---

[331] Ibid., 196.
[332] Ibid., 196.
[333] De Vries, "Umm el-Jimal Project, 1981-1992," 438.

east of the courtyard) and two larger rooms (Stables A and B) south of the courtyard. The stables, *c.* 7 x 8 m. each, are partitioned lengthwise by walls that contain a doorway and a row of mangers accessible from both sides and are suitable for larger domestic animals, such as cows and horses. Stable A is especially well preserved, with its manger wall intact to the ceiling, and some corbels on it still in place (figs. 88 and 89). However, the rest of the rooms are in relatively poor condition. The arrangement of the stable-mangers on the ground-floor is typical of houses at Umm el-Jimāl.

A wooden door into Stable A is designed with a similar hinge system as that of the stone door of House XVIII.[335] A groove is cut from the socket hole on the edge of the doorstep toward the center of the step (fig. 90). This groove, shallow near the center of the step, becomes gradually deeper as it approaches the socket hole, which is 1 cm., or more, deeper. To be installed, a door is held at an angle, with the top hinge pin inserted into the lintel socket. The bottom pin is then slipped into the groove whose increasing depth allows the door to straighten as the pin is slid toward the socket. When the bottom of the pin reaches the socket hole, it would snap into place, and the door would hang as the stone door does. Though the wooden doors are not preserved, it is reasonable to suggest that almost all doorsteps are originally wooden based on the fact that almost all doorsteps have installation grooves associated with wooden doors.[336]

Chronology (House 119):

A striking feature of the stratigraphy of House 119 is that the dominant construction and occupational loci are Umayyad, preceded by some Byzantine loci, and followed by Abbasid post-collapse squatters" loci.[337]

---

[334] Idem, "Umm al-Jimāl Project, 1993 and 1994," 422.
[335] Idem, *Umm el-Jimal*, 117.
[336] Ibid., 118.
[337] Idem, "Umm al-Jimāl Project, 1993 and 1994," 428.

<u>Early Byzantine Period</u>:

From the excavation of Room C-4, a clear and representative sequence is ascertained for House 119 (fig. 87).[338] In Room C, the first evidence of occupation is a pre-construction un-datable fire pit on bedrock. The south wall of the room (the north wall of Stable B) is also constructed on bedrock, and butted against it, the east and west walls of the room. Laid directly on bedrock is an excellent floor constructed of flagstone set in a very hard plaster-cement (fig. 91), with embedded potsherds dated late Roman and early Byzantine (third-fourth century), which is plastered up against all three walls. Hence, the initial construction and use of the room date to the third-fourth century. With the exception of this cement-flagstone floor and the related walls in Room C, there is no further evidence of occupation for the period.[339] In fact, no floor in a domestic structure at Umm el-Jimāl dated prior to the Umayyad period has been found besides this one.

<u>Late Byzantine Period</u>:

There is no evidence of fifth-sixth century Byzantine occupation.[340] Therefore, there appears to be a gap between the fourth century construction and the Umayyad reuse of the area. However, in sounding Y.9, on the ashy mound south of House 119 (fig. 87), a dump is located containing much Byzantine material. While the two soil layers below the dump prove to be early Byzantine, ten successive layers above them constitute a mass 2 m. deep with a concentration of Byzantine and Umayyad sherds.

<u>Umayyad Period</u>:

Umayyad preparation for reuse of the site may also have involved appropriating badly damaged portions of the Byzantine building, such as the walls of the rooms in Y.1 and 2, which

---

[338] Ibid., 428.
[339] Ibid., 429.
[340] Ibid., 429.

are preserved to one or two courses.[341] In fact, the possible arch straddling the two squares is entirely removed, with the exception of the stubs of the piers where they bonded into the opposing walls. Furthermore, pre-Umayyad wall remnants in the Y.12 courtyard probe only survive at the foundation course level. This suggests that the Umayyad remodeling, though taking advantage of the surviving walls of Room C, may have involved a completely new construction of other parts of the building. The combination of the Umayyad cleanout and the thoroughness of the reconstruction indicate that House 119 may be considered Umayyad rather than an Umayyad reuse of a Byzantine house.

There is little evidence of Umayyad occupation outside of Room C.[342] For instance, in Stable A, there is no accumulation of domestic dung or other living debris on the bedrock in either Y.7 or 8. Furthermore, in Y.8 roof beams are found lying directly on bedrock in association with both Umayyad and Abbasid pottery. This leads to the possibility that Room C is occupied and re-floored while the cleanout and reconstruction are underway, but the completion of the construction work is close to the 747/8 earthquake collapse. Hence, no Umayyad use of the new building actually takes place.

Four ceramic oil lamp fragments are recovered from deposits of the Umayyad House 119.[343] The typological and stylistic characteristics of the four sherds suggest they belong to either the tongue- or zoomorphic handle variants of the Jarash lamps (figs. 92 and 93). However, because each fragment is only a small portion of its complete lamp, it is not possible to determine with certainty to which variant each belongs. The shoulders of all four examples have consecutive radial lines, a common feature of both the tongue- and zoomorphic handle types found in the hippodrome at Jarash (fig. 94). Furthermore, the scallop pattern found on no. 1 occurs on both

---

[341] Ibid., 430.
[342] Ibid., 430.
[343] Lapp, "Byzantine and Early Islamic Oil Lamp Fragments," 437.

forms of the Jarash lamp (fig. 94, no. 24). The tongue- and zoomorphic handle types of the Jarash lamp are contemporary and date to between the second half of the sixth and the second half of the eighth century.[344]

---

[344] Kehrberg, "Selected Lamps and Pottery," 89.

Chapter 3

Analysis of the Archaeological Material

Introduction:

This chapter will examine the residential structures from „Ammān, Jarash, Naḥal Mitnan,

Pella, and Umm el-Jimāl to trace the development of domestic architecture in Jordan-Palestine

during the early Islamic period. The purpose of this chapter is to identify patterns, wherever

possible, in the material record by reducing the domestic buildings to their basic constituent

parts, which include building material, building layout, function of household, and relation of

building to street.

Building Material:

Wall construction material:

The most common building material for the domestic structures at the five sites is stone. The

method of construction of the wall typically involves two-face masonry, suggesting efficiency

and economy. At Umm el-Jimāl, only the outer face of a basalt stone block is dressed.[345] By

using aggregate rubble and clay fill packed between two faces of a lower course as base for the

next course, it is not necessary to dress interior faces of the stones (fig. 95). This reduces the

need to dress five or six faces to only one face and its four edges, which drastically saves skilled

labor cost. In addition, this simple method of wall construction limits the need for carefully

measured and finely dressed blocks to doors, window posts, lintels and arches. In these cases,

careful fitting is required to achieve the proper structural soundness. If fine wall finishes are

needed, the rough texture is smoothed with layers of plaster (fig. 95).[346]

---

[345] De Vries, "Restoration at Umm el-Jimal," 45.
[346] Idem, *Umm el-Jimal*, 113.

Likewise, in the households at Pella, the walls of the lower floors are constructed of large, roughly dressed stone blocks laid to form two faces (fig. 63).[347] The interior wall cavity and block interstices on the faces are filled with small stones and yellow clay mortar. In contrast, the walls of the upper storey are made of unbaked bricks made from pebbles and yellow clay, a lighter and more easily managed building material than the heavy stone blocks of the ground floor.

The use of mortar or aggregate concrete would eventually replace the classical east Mediterranean tradition of setting masonry dry.[348] At „Ammān, the walls of Building B are mortared with large quantities of a lime mortar containing ash.[349] They are subsequently plastered with the same material. At Pella, both the interior wall cavity and block interstices on the faces are filled with small stone and yellow clay mortar.[350] The clay mortar does not have the same strength or hardness as the lime mortar, however. Because the builders of Building B at „Ammān employed a unified constructional technique, seen elsewhere on the *Qal'a* representing Stratum V construction,[351] the use of lime mortar to set the masonry may reflect more available resources not available at Pella.

Floor construction material:

The homogeneity of the wall construction material is also evident in the surfaces found in the domestic structures of the five sites. The most common floor type is earth, and it is found in both rooms and courtyards. However, stone and pavers, when present, are used for the floors of rooms and courtyards where there is heavy traffic of people and animals. Hence, the courtyard

---

[347] Walmsley, "Pella/Fiḥl after the Islamic Conquest," 150.
[348] De Vries, "Restoration at Umm el-Jimal," 45.
[349] Northedge, *Roman and Islamic 'Amman*, 142.
[350] Walmsley, "Pella/Fihl after the Islamic Conquest," 150.
[351] Refer back to Chapter 2, pgs. 19-20, for the dating of Stratum V.

of Household D at Pella is laid with mudstone pavers. In Household G, both courtyards are

stone paved (fig. 63), as are Rooms 8 and 9.[352]

Another type of floor surface includes mosaic floors, which are primarily found on upper

floors, where the living quarters are situated, and the dining/reception room. In the eastern house

over the Museum site at „Ammān, a large quantity of plain white tesserae in Room K suggests

that an upper storey had existed there with a mosaic floor.[353] In addition, the upper floors of the

houses at Pella are paved with plain white mosaic over a pebble and mortar base.[354] The floor of

Room 7 of the Umayyad house at Jarash, which is used for common meals and receptions, is

covered with a mosaic of which only displaced fragments and a large amount of single cubes

remain.[355] Mosaic floors appear to be reserved for rooms where the social function of the

household takes place; hence, the need for decoration.

In House XVIII at Umm el-Jimāl, prior to the construction of the solid Umayyad floors, all

earlier occupation debris is carefully removed down to pre-occupation levels, such that the

Umayyad floors are installed at levels lower than the previous ones.[356] The house is then re-

floored with small cobbles cemented together with gray plaster (fig. 86).[357] Evidence for plaster-

on-cobble floors in all rooms suggests thorough refurbishing.[358]

Such Umayyad refurbishments are an interesting feature. In the case of House 119 at Umm

el-Jimāl, the Byzantine structure is dismantled and all occupation debris removed, so that all that

remains is a single cobble-and-cement Byzantine pavement.[359] This subsequent refuse is stored

in a two-meter thick dump (fig. 87, Y.9). Similar dumps are found throughout the site, attesting

---

[352] Idem, "Households at Pella," 257, 268.
[353] Harding, "Excavations on the Citadel," 9.
[354] Walmsley, *Early Islamic Syria*, 130.
[355] Gawlikowski, "Residential Area," 113.
[356] De Vries, "Continuity and Change," 44.
[357] Brown, "Large Residence," 196.
[358] De Vries, "Continuity and Change," 43.
[359] Ibid., 44.

to such cleaning taking place everywhere. While the radical cleanup may be indicative of a break with past culture, it is more likely motivated by hygienic concerns, in particular, the prevalence of devastating plagues that swept the Levant beginning with the Justinianic plague of 542.[360] The seventh century Umayyad builders may have methodically cleansed the site in order to restore disease-free habitability.

<u>Roof construction material</u>:

The most common roof construction materials are wood and stone. In the absence of walls sufficient to carry the load of stone roofs, wood appears to have been the preferred material. The roof of the Umayyad house at Jarash is made of wooden beams.[361] In the farmhouse at Naḥal Mitnan, a charred beam recovered from Room 103 indicates that the roof is made of wood.[362] At Pella, the lack of ceramic roof tiles among the collapsed debris, but the presence of carbonized wood beams, suggests the roofs are made of matting over oak beams, sealed with clay.[363] The upper storey floors may have been carried on timber joists, as stone slabs for cantilevered roofs of the kind found in Umayyad housing in the Ḥaurān are not evident.[364]

The roof of House XVIII at Umm el-Jimāl, however, is constructed from the same material as the entire building, basalt stone. It is possible to build the rubble-filled walls to surprising heights because their faces are tied together by a tightly laid course of corbels at each new floor level (fig. 78). Because the flat basalt beams for ceilings and roofs laid across these corbels are structurally limited to a length of *c*. 3 m., the rooms have to be narrow.

---

[360] Idem, "Umm al-Jimāl Project, 1993 and 1994," 431.
[361] Gawlikowski, "Residential Area," 114.
[362] Haiman, "Early Islamic Period Farm," 3.
[363] Walmsley, *Early Islamic Syria*, 130.
[364] McNicoll, Smith, and Hennessy. eds., *Pella in Jordan 1*, 131.

While no evidence has survived of the roofing technique of Building B at „Ammān, Northedge has speculated that the roof may be barrel-vaulted, similar to Building D in Area B.[365] The rectangular shape of the rooms would have accommodated barrel-vaulting, even at the expense of regular thickness in the walls.

Building Layout:

The basic layout of the domestic structures at the five sites consists of rooms arranged around, or associated with, an interior courtyard. The courtyard is spatially the focal point of the house: it represents the general space where nearly every movement between the various elements of the house begins, ends, or passes through.[366] Given that the courtyard functions as an element of distribution, the sewage drains, open drains, and the cisterns of the houses are concentrated in the area of the courtyard. At Jarash, for instance, the sewage drain extends from the end of the courtyard to beneath the entrance (fig. 28).[367] This serves as the only sanitary facility in the household. In the main house over the Museum site at „Ammān, plastered drains in the north-east and north-west corners of the courtyard conduct water from the roof to the cistern in Room J (fig. 16).[368]

The centrality of the courtyard space in the internal organization of these houses is corroborated by the layout of the rooms around the courtyard: most of the rooms open directly onto the courtyard. This arrangement is exemplified by Household G at Pella, which is organized around an internal courtyard with five doorways around the courtyard giving access to surrounding rooms (fig. 62). The inner courtyard opens onto two stand-alone rooms on the south

---

[365] Northedge, *Roman and Islamic 'Amman*, 143.
[366] Al-Azzawi, "Oriental Houses," 92.
[367] Gawlikowski, "Residential Area," 113.
[368] Harding, "Excavations on the Citadel," 7.

side (1, 2).[369] A single, wide doorway gives access to Room 9. In the household"s original configuration, it is possible to access Room 5 from the courtyard and loop around through Rooms 6 and 7 back into the courtyard through the doorway in the north-west corner (and vice versa).[370]

The courtyard as the nucleus of the house also dictates that the main entrance leads from the street or outside to the courtyard. In Building B at „Ammān, the main door of the house may have opened from the courtyard onto a street to the east, which is visible on the surface (fig. 9).[371] In Household G at Pella, the main doorway of the courtyard, which opens out onto an external courtyard to the east, is located between the staircase and the drain (fig. 62).[372]

Elementary courtyard process:

Petruccioli has presented a series of typological processes that produces variations in the courtyard house.[373] While the author of this thesis does not adhere to the exact description of each process presented by Petruccioli, she has observed similar processes that have produced variations among the courtyard houses of the five sites. Therefore, it should be noted that while the courtyard houses of this study have been placed into respective categories of processes described by Petruccioli, they do not exactly adhere to the steps that he delineates for each process. In essence, these are models subject to adjustments, as every building culture behaves differently and privileges its own formulation within the universal scheme.

The most elementary typological process involves a courtyard gradually transformed as more and more of its area is covered, so that activities that once took place outdoors have been

---

[369] Walmsley, "Households at Pella," 268.
[370] Idem, "Excavation of an Umayyad Period House," 518.
[371] Northedge, *Roman and Islamic 'Amman*, 142.
[372] Walmsley, "Households at Pella," 257, 259.
[373] Petruccioli, *After Amnesia*, 73-84; Idem, "Courtyard House," 3-20.

incorporated inside.[374] In this first series, the house has a rather low level of specialization. At this stage, the plot size is large enough for division of function on a single level.

At Pella, the transformation of the house into a courtyard house has been preserved in the archaeological record of Households A, B, and C (fig. 62).[375] In the first half of the sixth century, there is a complete redevelopment of living quarters on Pella's main mound.[376] As in other towns of the Levant, the reign of Justinian was accompanied by many instances of urban renewal.[377] Money, from Constantinople and local elites, was invested in urban infrastructure, and this was manifested in Pella with the remodeling and rebuilding of living quarters on the main mound. In the second quarter of the 6th century, the domestic arrangement consists of four-meter wide graveled streets set out on a formal grid, each street flanked by stone and mudbrick terrace-style houses two storeys high, fronted in some cases by shops (fig. 58).[378] Such houses that spread down the *tell* side into the valley on purpose-built terraces are also constructed at Baysān, where the archaeological mound is flattened and terraced in preparation for construction in Late Antiquity.[379]

At Pella, there are structural alterations introduced into the terrace house in the late 6th century (*c*. 575), where rooms have been demolished in the middle of a unit to create a small internal courtyard (fig. 58). The typological process of forming a courtyard house is represented here. A new room (I) is added to the northern building.[380] The walls of the southern building are dismantled to a uniform level, approximately 1.0 m. above the surface of Room D. Rooms D, E, L, M and the passage areas H and P are then filled to the height of the dismantled walls and the

---

[374] Idem, "Courtyard House," 5.
[375] Walmsley, "Households at Pella," 251.
[376] Idem, *Early Islamic Syria*, 129.
[377] Idem, "Households at Pella," 250.
[378] Idem, *Early Islamic Syria*, 129.
[379] Idem, "Households at Pella," 245.
[380] Watson, "Byzantine Period," 168.

resultant surface is covered with yellow clay. Thus, an internal courtyard is created, onto which open Rooms F, G, and I. The walls of Room K are constructed above the courtyard fill and help define the eastern boundary of the enclosure. The western wall is rebuilt to define the western boundary. The massive Phase II/III east-west retaining wall at the south end of Area III remains in use to demarcate the southern edge of the courtyard.

This change in urban planning is part of a greater focalization of activities in the towns of Jordan-Palestine in all spheres: domestic, commercial and religious.[381] However, these changes predate Islam and suggest a society already in transformation.

Taberna process:

Different typological processes generate variations of the elementary courtyard building type, characterized by a single-family house with minimum specialization. One such process, described as the *taberna* process (from the Latin *taberna* meaning shop), occurs when functions other than residential ones are introduced, making a house more complex and specialized.[382] Commercial interests lead to the transformation of the front part of the courtyard house into shops, which is achieved by creating a new and direct access from the outside to the existing cells of the house. This phenomenon is prevalent in the Middle Ages, especially in Arab cities where classical foundations, such as the forum and agora, had been swallowed up, leaving reduced space on the road.[383]

As mentioned previously, in the second quarter of the 6th century, Pella witnesses a major urban renewal.[384] Many buildings of the previous century are replaced by large multi-roomed mansions within a grid of graveled streets, each five meters in width (fig. 58). Lined along the

---

[381] Walmsley, *Early Islamic Syria*, 131.
[382] Petruccioli, *After Amnesia*, 79.
[383] Idem, "Courtyard House," 7.
[384] Walmsley, "Social and Economic Regime," 252.

length of parts of the streets are shops, some of which are provided with a second internal room. Both houses and shops are built as one continuous structure from roughly dressed stone blocks, probably with upper storeys of unbaked yellow clay bricks.

At Jarash, the colonnaded street in front of the Umayyad house remains in use: its sidewalk does not appear to have been built over during the early Umayyad period, serving its original purpose along the lines of shops (fig. 28).[385] The shops are entirely restored, including the upper foundation courses in the fill of the cistern loc. 43, without any major change in plan. In essence, the Umayyad house does not appropriate the shop space for its residential use.

Insula process:

The *insula* process involves progressively filling in a courtyard, coinciding with the transition into multi-family residences of the earlier *domus*.[386] This process includes the vertical extension of units surrounding the courtyard with stairways providing access, representing the development of multi-storey, multi-occupancy courtyard housing.[387] The apartment-block phenomenon is evident at Ostia Antica, where three- and four-storey apartment houses, some with rows of shops on the ground floor, are schematically similar to modern-day condominiums.

Vertical extension of houses is found in the house to the east of the main house over the Museum site at „Ammān (fig. 16). There, an upper story is suggested by the large quantity of plain white tesserae in Room K. Further evidence for an upper storey is found in Rooms L and M, where piers for arches to support the roof were excavated (fig. 16).[388] These piers stand above complete arches carrying a ground floor over a basement. While the arches of the

---

[385] Gawlikowski, "Residential Area," 111, 113.
[386] Petruccioli, *After Amnesia*, 80.
[387] Idem, "Courtyard House," 7.
[388] Northedge, *Roman and Islamic 'Amman*, 151.

basement remain intact, those of the ground floor have collapsed and fallen through into the basement.

However, the domestic structures at Pella and Umm el-Jimāl best represent multi-storey apartment units. In House XVIII at Umm el-Jimāl, upper-story apartment units are reached by exterior cantilevered stairs.[389] The northern and eastern complexes have two sets of apartments, while the western block of rooms contains a single residence (fig. 73). At Pella, all of the houses are probably two-storyed, perhaps three in some instances or at least with roof-top access (possibly Household G).[390] The upper floor could be reached through the courtyards by means of stone-built staircases. The upper floor of Household A is not accessed from the courtyard, but from the eastern side of the building through a passageway, small courtyard and staircase (fig. 62).[391] Hence, the first-floor living quarters of Household A are not connected with the lower storey"s activities, exemplifying „apartment" living in 8th century Pella.

In Household G, six supports, comprised of 5 columns and a pier, carry an internal balcony some 3 m. deep on at least three sides (north, west and south).[392] Access to the balcony is by means of a staircase, 1.25 m. wide, against the eastern wall of the internal courtyard.[393] Entry to the rooms of the upper floor, whose arrangement is not known, could be accessed from the balcony.

In a large number of Syrian villages, especially in the Ḥaurān desert on the border between modern Syria and Jordan, houses preserved to a height of two storeys have been uncovered by Butler and Tchalenko.[394] In one such house, located at Il Medjdel in southern Syria, there is a

---

[389] Brown, "Large Residence," 195.
[390] Walmsley, "Households at Pella," 251.
[391] Ibid., 253-254.
[392] Ibid., 259.
[393] Idem, "Excavation of an Umayyad Period House," 517.
[394] Ellis, *Roman Housing*, 89.

single large square room on the ground floor with possibly a stable in the rear area, and an upper-floor room subdivided into four (fig. 96). Such housing of the Syrian villages is a very specific local form of architecture.[395]

Egypt is another eastern province with a strong indigenous architectural tradition.[396] In Karanis, a village in the Fayum basin, a large number of houses dating from the first to the fifth century has been excavated by the University of Michigan. These houses are usually multi-storey with access to the roof, and a small yard is attached to the house, though it is not integral since it could be sold separately or shared with another house (fig. 97).[397] Papyri documentation provides evidence for the organization of the apartments: at the bottom of the house there is usually a cellar, while upper floors commonly contain dining rooms and bedrooms.[398]

In contrast to the two-story apartment houses at Pella and Umm el-Jimāl, in the aforementioned Syrian and Egyptian houses, the rooms are not organized around courtyards.[399] Rather, where there is sufficient space for a yard, apartment blocks form a frontage to an external court, which consequently has to be surrounded by an enclosure wall to ensure privacy. Hence, one should note that there are other types of housing present alongside the enclosed courtyard house, though the latter becomes more prevalent during the Islamic period.

<u>Subdivision process:</u>

The subdivision process relates to the subdivision of a lot: dividing up older buildings and spaces to create smaller buildings, normally houses.[400] Subdivision represents a style of architecture evident in the urban fabric of Late Antiquity.[401] It was driven by two related social

---

[395] Ibid., 91.
[396] Ibid., 95.
[397] Alston, "Houses and Households," 28.
[398] Ellis, *Roman Housing*, 96.
[399] Ibid., 97.
[400] Petruccioli, *After Amnesia*, 84.
[401] Ellis, *Roman Housing*, 110.

developments: the increasing obsolescence of many early imperial public buildings, and the decline of the peristyle house. Many examples of subdivision date from the fourth century. An example of a subdivided house is the House of the Frescoes at Tipasa, which is divided into four apartments, separated by strategically placed divisions.[402] At Pella, large early sixth-century houses are subdivided into smaller apartments around the start of the next century.[403]

During the Abbasid period, the house at Jarash is divided into three separate dwellings among presumably three owners (fig. 34).[404] This is achieved by erecting a few partition walls and blocking several doors.[405] These three separate dwellings are accessible from different directions. For the first dwelling, the south wall of Room 24 is rebuilt at this time above the threshold and extends westward to join the corner of Room 21.[406] Consequently, the new living unit includes the main rooms of the Umayyad House (loc. 10/20 and 7) (fig. 36). The courtyard (loc. 9, 23) is accessible only through the stairs from the north.

A second dwelling is comprised of the courtyard loc. 16, Rooms 17, 19 and 22 (fig. 37).[407] The passage to the street is closed above the sewage drain, thus the courtyard could be accessed from the east, through a doorway in the wall crossing the filled cistern loc. 41. The blocking of the original access to the house results in the formation of a recess (loc. 18) leading to Room 22. It is approached through the former window of Room 17.

A third house is formed from the former shops along the street (fig. 38).[408] A wall is constructed through loc. 28/42, thus making the neighboring Room 13 larger. Another room is added above the former cellar (loc. 27) and a part of the passage above the sewer (loc. 14).

---

[402] Ibid., 111.
[403] Walmsley, "Byzantine Palestine," 145.
[404] Gawlikowski, "Jerash in Early Islamic Times," 472.
[405] Idem, "Residential Area," 115.
[406] Ibid., 115.
[407] Ibid., 115.
[408] Ibid., 115.

There is a threshold between Room 13 and the back room (loc. 14/27), which has another

entrance through the former passage between the courtyard and the street, now closed at the far

end. This three-room unit opens onto a part of the colonnade, which is enclosed to serve as a

courtyard.[409] The colonnade opens into Room 29 and two other unexcavated rooms further west.

Bayt:

In the Islamic architectural context, a *bayt*, composed of a central hall flanked by a pair of

rooms on either side, is a module frequently repeated in buildings, especially in palaces.[410] It is

an element of eastern influence, although it also appears occasionally in Roman buildings, such

as the palace of the Roman Governor at Boṣrā (fig. 98).[411] On one side of the courtyard are two

bayts, one above the other, with a colonnaded portico, also in two storeys, in front of them.[412]

Based on Butler"s plan and elevation, it is a forerunner of the scheme found at Khirbat al-Minya,

Jabal Says, „Anjar, Qaṣr al-Ḥayr al-Gharbī, and Khirbat al-Mafjar (fig. 99).[413]

Parallels of such a building module are found in the residential structures at „Ammān. In the

main house over the Museum site, Room D may have functioned as a reception room (fig. 16).[414]

Rooms C and E open from it to form a *bayt*. In this *bayt*, the central hall is not flanked by a pair

of rooms on either side, but rather by a single room on either side. While it resembles a Syrian

bayt of the Umayyad *quṣūr*, it is directly paralleled by the proto-*bayts* at Khirbat al-Bayḍā".[415]

Likewise, Building B at „Ammān has a comparable reception Room G, which opens onto Rooms

E and H on either side (fig. 9).

---

[409] Ibid., 115.
[410] Creswell, *Early Muslim Architecture*, 516; Almagro, "Origins and Repercussions," 183.
[411] Almagro, "Origins and Repercussions," 183.
[412] Creswell, *Early Muslim Architecture*, 516.
[413] Ibid., 516.
[414] Harding, "Excavations on the Citadel," 7.
[415] Northedge, *Roman and Islamic 'Amman*, 157.

The absence of *bayts* in the residential structures of this study, with the exception of „Ammān, is notable. It suggests that the *bayt* as a module is reserved primarily for palatial structures. The inclusion of a *bayt* in both households at „Ammān may be explained by the fact that Building B and the house over the Museum site constitute a part of the Umayyad citadel project, which represents a single, planned unit whose elements include the palace, the rebuilding of the fortification circuit, the open cistern, and the Stratum V buildings of Areas B, C, and the Museum site.[416] The project includes the construction of separate courtyard house units of a variety of sizes, ranging from two rooms and a courtyard, to seven rooms, a latrine and a courtyard, up to the residential units of the palace, of which Building 6 has ten rooms, a latrine, a staircase and a courtyard.

Function of Household:

In these domestic structures, there is a deliberate shift towards an all-encompassing house unit suited to multifaceted socio-economic activities of households in the towns of early Islamic Jordan-Palestine.[417] The household is segregated according to social and economic function.[418] In the Umayyad house at Jarash, for instance, rooms are grouped in pairs. There are three sets of two-room suites (loc. 17-19, 25-36 and 24-37), with the room behind apparently windowless (fig. 28).[419] This arrangement reflects the division of living quarters: the front room is reserved for daily activities while the other, darker one, is used for sleeping.

The mixed function of households is evident in houses where living arrangements accommodate animal stabling. In particular, there is significant evidence for troughs and mangers in both urban and rural houses, suggesting the prevalence of animal stabling in the early

---

[416] Ibid., 157.
[417] Walmsley, *Early Islamic Syria*, 132.
[418] Idem, "Households at Pella," 269.
[419] Gawlikowski, "Residential Area," 114.

Islamic period. In the main house over the Museum site at „Ammān, a rectangular limestone trough is found in the south-east corner of Room B, and a circular one in the same corner of Room J (fig. 16).[420] There is also a large rectangular limestone trough in Room K.

In House 119 at Umm el-Jimāl, there are two rooms (Stables A and B) south of the courtyard (fig. 87).[421] The stables are partitioned lengthwise by walls that contain a doorway and a row of mangers accessible from both sides and are suitable for larger domestic animals, such as cows and horses. In general, in the houses at Umm el-Jimāl, much of the ground floor space is devoted to animals while living quarters are situated on the upper floor.[422] However, this arrangement of domestic space is not necessarily motivated by the separation of people from animals, as these building layouts indicate an intimate sharing of space, with people and animals in constant contact with one another.[423]

At Naḥal Mitnan, there is even less of a physical division between the living quarters and the area for agricultural and stabling activities of the household. The outer courtyard (L 111) may have been utilized for activities related to collection of crops before storage or transport, as well as for sheltering draft or pack animals (fig. 47).[424] Installation 112, adjoining the wall of the outer courtyard, is possibly used as a trough or a stall.[425] In addition, Courtyard 113 may have functioned as an animal pen. Room 104 is possibly used as a granary, with an opening in the upper part of the wall.[426] In close proximity to these courtyards and room, both Rooms 103 and

---

[420] Harding, "Excavations on the Citadel," 9.
[421] De Vries, "Umm al-Jimāl Project, 1993 and 1994," 422.
[422] Idem, "Umm el-Jimal Project, 1972-1977," 63.
[423] Idem, *Umm el-Jimal*, 109.
[424] Haiman, "Early Islamic Period Farm," 3.
[425] Ibid., 3, 4.
[426] Ibid., 4.

106 function as the sleeping quarters. They contain raised beaten-earth platforms, used as beds, bordered by a row of stones.[427]

The courtyard houses at Pella resemble the domestic units found at Umm el-Jimāl: the households are segregated according to social and economic function. The ground floor is used for the stabling of animals. For example, in Household A at Pella, Rooms 3 and 4 function as stables (fig. 62), as suggested by the packed mud floors over which lies a soft mustard yellow layer, interpreted as decayed manure.[428] In Household G, Rooms 8 and 9 are stone paved and provided with feed benches to accommodate animals, specifically cows.[429] Rooms 5 and 6 are originally one room with a line of feeding mangers in the center (figs. 63 and 64).[430] At a later period, two rooms, 5 and 6, are formed by blocking the central opening in the manger, leaving Rooms 6 and 7 devoted to stabling animals.

There is little evidence of manufacturing activities taking place in domestic structures of the five sites as compared to other economic activities. This, in spite of the fact that the economics of many towns in early Islamic Jordan-Palestine became increasingly focused on the manufacture of tradable goods, especially in the eighth century.[431] The growing industrialization of towns was manifest, for example, in the glass works at Pella and the ceramic workshops at Jarash and Baysān.[432] The separation of domestic and industrial activities is ensured by the construction of independent manufacturing quarters, which places potentially dangerous and polluting industries outside and upwind of the town.[433] At Pella, however, there are remains of basins and white plaster found in Room 3 of Household G, suggesting manufacturing activities

---

[427] Ibid., 4.
[428] McNicoll, Smith, and Hennessy. eds., *Pella in Jordan 1*, 132.
[429] Walmsley, "Households at Pella," 268.
[430] Idem, "Excavation of an Umayyad Period House," 518.
[431] Idem, "Production, Exchange and Regional Trade," 305.
[432] Ibid., 308.
[433] Ibid., 305.

(fig. 64). After access to Rooms 3 and 4 is blocked, the activities associated with those rooms are relocated to Room 5.[434] The change in function for Room 5 explains the need to restrict access to it from Room 6, which continues to be used for the stabling of animals until the earthquake of 749. The need to prevent stabled livestock from entering the relocated workshop in Room 5 compelled the owners to block the opening between Rooms 5 and 6.

The houses at Pella represent the mixed function of the household: living arrangements accommodate animal stabling, workshop production, storage of foods and some aspects of daily living (cooking and perhaps transit accommodation) at ground floor level, whereas much of the social activities of the household occur in the rooms of the upper floor.[435] The ground floor area of the houses at Pella focuses on the central internal courtyard, where much of the daily life of the household takes place, including cooking, care for domesticated animals, and in one corner (Room 3), light craft activities.

A similar arrangement of houses divided into two storeys and segregated according to social and economic function emerges in early Medieval elite dwellings. Information regarding early Medieval urban housing comes from written sources from the 7th-8th century onwards.[436] Of particular significance is the *Codex traditionum ecclesiae ravennatis*, also known as the *Codice Bavaro*, which consists of a collection of early Medieval leases from the 7th to the 10th century, containing very detailed descriptions of housing belonging to the Episcopal see of Ravenna. According to these documents, the type of house that replaced the old Roman *domus* generally consists of a main building, often with two storeys.[437] The single-storey house is simpler and has less functional division of space, while the two-storey house is slightly more complex. The

---

[434] Idem, "Excavation of an Umayyad Period House," 518.
[435] Idem, *Early Islamic Syria*, 131.
[436] Polci, "Transformation of the Roman *Domus*," 93.
[437] Ibid., 95.

layout of the different rooms is similar with regards to most of the described examples: the ground floor is generally devoted to agricultural activity, shops and stables and to domestic activity, as indicated by the presence of a *canapha*, a sort of warehouse, and of a *coquina*, the kitchen. Ground floor often contains wells, cisterns and in some cases, a room provided with a basic drainage system. Living quarters are confined to the upper floor.

Two houses excavated at the Forum of Nerva by Riccardo Santangeli Valenzani corroborate the textual evidence (fig. 100). Dated to the 9th century, both houses are irregular structures, built in stone.[438] The first house has an upper floor, where the bedrooms of the household and possibly a dining room or some other sort of hall, is situated.[439] An outer wooden staircase leads to the upper floor. It is interesting to note that the areas on either side of the building reveal two unroofed areas within the enclosure wall (fig. 100). This area is probably used for housing domestic animals, indicated by the remains of a hitching point in the wall and part of a drinking trough. There is a slight separation of the animals from the inhabitants, in contrast to the arrangement at Pella and Umm el-Jimāl.

The transfer of living activities to the upper floor has been identified as one of the most characteristic features of the process of transformation of the Roman *domus* into the early Medieval house.[440] These structures are representative of a relatively precise type of residential building, characteristic of the wealthier classes of the Roman population in the ninth and tenth centuries.[441]

Relation of Building to Street:

---

[438] Ibid., 96.
[439] Ibid., 97.
[440] Ibid., 106.
[441] Valenzani, "Residential Building," 106.

Evidence suggests that the construction of gridded domestic quarters and broad paved streets flanked by porticoes, which were previously viewed as Roman urban features, continues well into the sixth century.[442] Byzantine, mostly 6th century Justinianic, re-assertion of orthogonality refutes the notion of post-Roman inability or disinterest in rectilinear urban design.[443] At Pella, for instance, completely new streets are laid out in a grid pattern as part of a major urban re-development of the main *tell*.[444] The *tell* is flattened and terraced, thereby removing nearly all evidence of Roman occupation. Subsequently, two-storeyed houses of stone and clay brick are built around five meter wide graveled streets. Shops face onto the streets for part of their length, but as minor thoroughfares in a domestic context, such streets lack colonnades.

However, streets and sidewalks, where urban activities are concentrated, witness a process which has been termed „encroachment," or the appropriation of public space for private use.[445] The infilling begins in earnest during the later sixth or early seventh century, continuing in the early Islamic period. At Pella, the partial collapse of the domestic quarter from the earthquake of 659-60 results in an urban reorganization.[446] The rebuilding program in Area IV produces large houses with their principal orientation towards a large open space, a development facilitated by the closure of the east-west street and an encroachment onto public areas (fig. 62). Following the earthquake, a long wall, running north-south, is built to demarcate the western limit of Households A and B.[447] Continuing northwards over the now defunct street, this wall eventually turns westwards along the northern limit of the former street, in line with the façade of the shops that once lined this part of the street. East of the blocking wall of Households A and B, a shop

---

[442] Walmsley, "Byzantine Palestine," 143.

[443] Foote, "Commerce," 26.

[444] Walmsley, "Byzantine Palestine," 144.

[445] Ibid., 144.

[446] Walmsley, "Social and Economic Regime," 254.

[447] Idem, "Households at Pella," 251.

that once opened out onto the former street is converted into a laneway, and the street-side shop

is reduced in size by the construction of a thin wall over the paved floor (fig. 62, Room 1, House

D).[448] Hence, Household D unit becomes inwardly oriented to the courtyard, whereas it had

formerly opened onto a public thoroughfare.[449]

The process of encroachment onto public space is also evident at Jarash, where the Roman

model of urbanism is asserted: the city has an orthogonal network of *cardi* and *decumani*, and

monumental public secular and religious buildings (fig. 101).[450] The major north-south *cardo*

divides the city into two east and west parts, connecting the major public spaces in the city, the

Oval Plaza, and the North and South Tetrapylons. In the Byzantine period, however, Jarash

undergoes changes and alterations: streets and public spaces are no longer preserved or

protected, private and public buildings encroach onto the streets, such as the *cardo*, and occupy

considerable areas of the public spaces.[451] Following the early seventh century earthquakes,

several structures are erected in the public area of the Oval Plaza, while extensions of buildings

on both sides of the *cardo* block the porticoes and increasingly narrow the street. Evidently, the

process of encroachment commences prior to the arrival of Islam.

However, in relation to the Umayyad house at Jarash, its layout maintains the integrity of the

orthogonal street pattern and does not trespass onto the shops lined along the South Decumanus.

During the Umayyad period, the colonnaded street in front of the housing remains in use, as its

sidewalk does not appear to have been built over, serving its original purpose along the lines of

shops (fig. 28).[452] The Umayyad house does not appropriate the shop space for its residential

use. On the other hand, during the Abbasid period, a house is developed from the former shops

---

[448] Ibid., 254.
[449] McNicoll, Smith, and Hennessy. eds., *Pella in Jordan 1*, 136.
[450] Zeyadeh, "Urban Transformation," 104.
[451] Ibid., 105.
[452] Gawlikowski, "Residential Area," 111, 113.

along the street.[453] A three-room unit opens onto a part of the colonnade, which is enclosed to serve as a courtyard (fig. 34).[454]

Umayyad adherence to existing street patterns is further articulated by Foote, who argues that at least seven cities in Greater Syria exhibit early Islamic, particularly Umayyad, emphasis on monumental urban expression, and manifest the will and resources to assert formal coherence and orthogonal planning.[455] She cites ‚Anjar and al-Ramla as the first new cities established in Greater Syria since the Roman period to exhibit post-Justinianic, straight, broad street planning. In addition, the linear markets delimiting pedestrian-scale streets at Arsūf, Tadmur, Baysān, Ḥimṣ, and Ṭabariyya demonstrate monumental and rectilinear design. Each of these new shops is built in a unified and coherent manner. Both the orthogonal street pattern of Umayyad established cities, such as ‚Anjar and al-Ramla, and linear markets lining straight avenues suggest an Umayyad concern for urban environments with rectilinear streets.

---

[453] Ibid., 115.
[454] Ibid., 115.
[455] Foote, *Umayyad Markets*, 221-222.

Chapter 4

Conclusion

Urban and Rural Houses in the Early Islamic Period:

<u>Houses within an urban context</u>:

The towns of Syria-Palestine are the centers of cultural, religious and economic life for urban and rural populations in Late Antiquity, and continue as such without significant disruption after the Islamic expansion into the region.[456] Walmsley has identified two trends observable in the urban history of towns in the early Islamic period: the continuation of existing traditions inherited from Late Antiquity, and the introduction of new ideas about the essential elements of a town.[457] „Ammān, Pella, and Jarash are representative of towns, or urban centers, in early Islamic Jordan-Palestine. As such, the residential structures found in these respective sites will be examined within the context of their urban setting.

At „Ammān, the principal area of urban reform of the Citadel undertaken by the Umayyads is concentrated in the large square, with its irregular trapezoidal shape, located at the center of the upper terrace of the Citadel (fig. 102).[458] The layout of the public space is a new urban concept adopted by the Umayyads to accommodate the organization of the newly created architectural elements and the reuse of pre-existing features.

There are three basic elements laid out around this public space: the *dār al-imāra*, the suq, and the mosque, features which are characteristic of an Islamic city (fig. 102).[459] The suq is situated on two sides of the square. Similar markets facing out onto a square is found at al-

---

[456] Walmsley, *Early Islamic Syria*, 72.
[457] Ibid., 77.
[458] Almagro and Arce, "Umayyad Town Planning," 662.
[459] Ibid., 662.

Ruṣāfa, where an L-shaped market flanks a central court.[460] The square as an organizing element is innovative, especially in relation to other known cases of early Islamic town planning.[461] It allows the two most important buildings or complexes, namely the mosque and palace, to be situated on the square, as well as the principal streets, which connect the outer wall gateways, to lead to the square. Thus, the square serves as a general framework for the mosque and palace.[462] The layout of the square is conceived as a multi-functional space, to control all the activities taking place: trade at the suq, religious activities at the mosque, and political functions at the *qaṣr*.[463]

In this new urban layout, the non-palatial domestic quarter is noticeably absent from the central square. Building B, located in Area C, and the main house over the Museum site are situated away from the central nucleus of the city (fig. 3). Building B constitutes a residential block, or *insula*, containing more than one house unit. It is apparent that the residential area is segregated from the public space of the city, adding another dimension to the overall privacy of the domestic quarter. At „Ammān, the domestic area does not intrude on essentially public domains, emphasizing the division of public and private spaces.

The notion of segregating domestic housing from religious and administrative structures is also evident at „Anjar, a new urban Islamic foundation in al-Biqā„ Valley of Lebanon. „Anjar is bisected by a colonnaded *cardo* running north-south and a *decumanus* running east-west, thus forming four quadrants (fig. 103).[464] The south-west quadrant contains the principal area of habitation, while the south-east quadrant contains a mosque and a *dār al-imāra*.[465] In essence,

---

[460] Walmsley, "Economic Developments," 345.
[461] Almagro and Arce, "Umayyad Town Planning," 662.
[462] Ibid., 665.
[463] Ibid., 665.
[464] Hillenbrand, "„Anjar and Early Islamic Urbanism," 62.
[465] Ibid., 62.

concentrated domestic housing is confined to a single one of the four quadrants, while official and religious functions are seemingly concentrated into a single quadrant.[466]

At Pella, in the second quarter of the 6th century, the buildings in Area IV on the *tell* are replaced by large multi-roomed mansions arranged within a grid of streets, each five meters in width.[467] The streets are lined with small shops along part of their length. In addition to commerce, these shops accommodate light manufacturing and food processing industries. The houses and shops are constructed as one continuous structure. However, in the early 7th century, a new central market is established adjacent to the cathedral church in the Byzantine Civic Complex, which constitutes the town center. This process involved a comprehensive remodeling of space and a major change in civic function of the area (Area IX) (fig. 56).[468]

A paved open court on the northern side of the church is transformed into a large enclosed market place with the construction of two-storeyed rooms faced with porches and galleries, similar to the layout of a *khan* (figs. 104 and 105).[469] Standing approximately 8.5 m. high, this structure, for the most part commercial in purpose, is of major importance to the town as it flanks the main entrance into the church.[470] Animals, namely camels, and their keepers stay on the ground floor, while the rooms on the upper storey probably house humans and valuable goods. The existence of a small blacksmith"s shop on the ground floor suggests that light industry takes place on the premises. Pella"s new market center performs both a commercial and an industrial function. As a consequence of the construction of the new market center, the shops in Area IV on the *tell* are closed.[471] One shop is blocked up, another stripped of its paving and used as a

---

[466] Ibid., 65.
[467] Walmsley, "Social and Economic Regime," 252.
[468] Ibid., 253; Idem, "Production, Exchange and Regional Trade," 284.
[469] Ibid., 284-285.
[470] Walmsley, "Households at Pella," 248.
[471] Idem, "Social and Economic Regime," 253.

stable, and a third is converted into a laneway to join the street with an inner courtyard. Coin evidence indicates that these alterations occurred no earlier than 580 and before 659-660.[472] Similar to „Ammān, the domestic structure at Pella is separated from the town center, where commercial, industrial and religious activities are concentrated. It should be noted, however, that this process of eliminating the commercial function of the house by constructing a market in the center precedes the arrival of Islam.

Islamic Jarash had a Muslim community of some size and was accordingly provided with a congregational mosque and possibly a governor"s residence.[473] The principal mosque at Jarash is built in a prominent location, immediately south-west of the plaza that marks the crossroad of the town"s primary street (fig. 106).[474] Based on an aerial photograph of Jarash taken in 1928, an area of ruin is identified to the west of the mosque, facing north onto the South Decumanus (fig. 107).[475] Walmsley has speculated that given its position next to the mosque, it is probably a public building, perhaps the administrative center of Jarash (fig. 108).[476]

West of the *tetrakonia*, the *decumanus* is lined with shops that may have served as the suq of Jarash in the early Islamic period.[477] It would appear that the South Decumanus, rather than the *cardo*, is the main arterial route. Behind some of these shops along the *decumanus* is the Umayyad house. During the excavation by the Yale Joint Mission between 1929 and 1934 of the circular plaza surrounding the South Tetrakonia, housing of the early Islamic period was exposed and removed.[478] In this layout, the residential structure is an integrated part of the urban core of the town, where the congregation mosque, suq, and possibly governor"s residence are situated.

---

[472] Ibid., 254.
[473] Idem, "Friday Mosque," 114.
[474] Idem, *Early Islamic Syria*, 84.
[475] Idem, "Friday Mosque," 116.
[476] Ibid., 116.
[477] Ibid., 117.
[478] Walmsley and Damgaard, "Umayyad Congregational Mosque," 364.

<u>Exchange of urban and rural domestic forms</u>:

The rural house is an expression of an essential, utilitarian architecture that responds to everyday, practical needs, such as shelter, warmth, storage of food, and protection of domesticated animals.[479] As stated by Petruccioli, "it avoids gratuitous innovations, uses the simplest techniques to ensure a certain stability, and efficiently meets the most basic of family needs."[480] The relationship between dwelling and place is first established in a rural setting. Consequently, the first urban building systems are influenced by their rural counterpart. In the early Islamic period, there is evidence for such a process in which urban houses become ruralized.

The apparent convergence of urban house plans with their rural counterparts occurs during a period when the division between villages and towns, structurally and culturally, is becoming obscured. Rural settlement expansion in seventh and eighth century Jordan-Palestine may have created an atmosphere conducive to a process of ruralization of urban space. Regional surveys have documented extensive Islamic occupation in many environmental zones of Syria-Palestine: in general, they indicate an increase in the number of occupied sites in river valleys, and a loss of settlement level in the more rugged mountainous zones.[481] This settlement shift has been explained as a consequence of agricultural changes brought on by a "green revolution" following the establishment of an Islamic state. In particular, Andrew Watson has argued that an agricultural revolution occurred in the early Islamic period, facilitated by a region, unified by religion and political control, receptive to new ideas.[482] According to Watson, during this period,

---

[479] Petruccioli, *After Amnesia*, 68.
[480] Ibid., 68.
[481] Walmsley, "Economic Developments," 350.
[482] Watson, *Agricultural Innovation*, 2.

an entirely new season of agriculture was opened up with the introduction of summer crops.[483] In his view, pre-Islamic agriculture involved widespread fallowing and no agricultural production during the summer, with the exception of a few crops grown on a restricted scale. However, recent archaeobotanical evidence demonstrates that the exploitation of summer as an agricultural season is already well in place by the advent of Islam.[484] So-called "revolutionary" crops, such as rice and hard wheat, appear to predate the arrival of Islam.[485]

Walmsley suggests alternative reasons for the growth of the rural economy: the digging of long irrigation canals and the acquisition and foundation of large farm estates owned by members of the ruling Umayyad family.[486] For example, in north Syria, Maslama b. „Abd al-Malik b. Marwān, the governor from 709 to 719, dug canals originating from the al-Balīkh and Euphrates rivers to irrigate fields, and thus increased both agricultural productivity and land values. In addition, a canal was dug in the middle Euphrates region, beginning at the Khābūr River and extending southward for 50 km. As a result, twenty-six new villages were founded. Rather than the arrival of new crops, agricultural improvements instigated by the Umayyads resulted in the spread of agricultural settlements.

Hence, the vibrancy of rural areas may have contributed to urban space becoming ruralized, with types of buildings already known in a rural context gradually introduced into the city.[487] For instance, the plan of the house units in rural settings, such as Umm el-Jimāl, Subaytah and Msayké, shares many details: the central private courtyard is flanked by rooms used for a variety of functions, with upstairs living quarters reached only by a courtyard staircase.[488]

---

[483] Ibid., 123.
[484] Samuel, "Archaeobotanical Evidence," 422.
[485] Walmsley, "Economic Developments," 350.
[486] Ibid., 350-351.
[487] Polci, "Transformation of the Roman *Domus*," 101.
[488] Walmsley, *Early Islamic Syria*, 132.

In Pella, the adoption of this rural apartment arrangement with stabling on the ground floor and living quarters upstairs provides the most compelling evidence for this ruralization process.[489] The origins of this phenomenon are most likely to be found in practical reasons. As towns and cities become characterized by the presence of agricultural activities and animal stabling, it necessitates the development of a more all-encompassing urban house, suited to multi-faceted socio-economic activities. Hence, the ground floor is used for agricultural and domestic activities and is no longer considered a suitable place for the living quarters of the house.[490]

The influence of rural architecture on traditional urban housing forms can be seen as early as the 5th century in the palace of the Roman Governor at Boṣrā.[491] In this so-called „palace,"the traditional village form is mixed with more classical architectural elements. On the ground floor, the apartments are grouped on the north and south sides of a large open court, reminiscent of the village housing of Syria (fig. 98).[492] However, the peristyle and the colonnaded portico are both classical architectural elements. On the upper floor there is a triconch reception room: a *piano nobile* as at Il Medjdel, but with a fashionable Roman aristocratic form.[493] The *piano nobile* house, in which the reception suites are situated on an upper floor, is associated with houses with a vertical orientation, accommodating stables on the ground floor and living rooms directly above them for the heat, and bedrooms perhaps located on an even higher level.[494] This mixture of urban and rural, rich and poor architecture suggests the movement between urban and rural

---

[489] Polci, "Transformation of the Roman *Domus*," 101.
[490] Ibid., 105.
[491] Ellis, "Late Antique Housing," 6.
[492] Butler and Prentice, *Princeton Archaeological Expeditions*, 256.
[493] Ibid., 259; Ellis, *Roman Housing*, 93.
[494] Ellis, "Late Antique Housing," 14.

styles. Rather than a flight to the countryside or to the city, a more reciprocative exchange is underway, obscuring the distinction between village and town.

Conclusion:

The characteristic form of early Islamic private domestic structures, irrespective of their urban or rural setting, is a house enclosing a courtyard. Each of the houses examined in this thesis has an interior courtyard, which functions as the nucleus and as an element of distribution.[495] All of the rooms to the house have either direct or indirect access to the courtyard. None of these features are considered innovations of the period, as the courtyard house is one of the oldest known architectural forms, particularly prevalent in the Mediterranean area and surrounding regions.[496]

The courtyard type house is a generic domestic form of residence which evolved independently in various places, from the Egyptian and Sumerian civilizations to the Mediterranean, Asia Minor, and to the Indus Valley.[497] Schoenauer has identified the inward-looking urban dwelling with one or more private courtyards in four urban civilizations of antiquity, as well as in classical Greek and Roman civilizations: Ur in Mesopotamia, the Mohenjo-Daro in the Indus, Kahun in Egypt, and Beijing, China.[498]

In particular, Ur, dated to before 2,000 B.C., represents the earliest concept of a house planned around an open space or courtyard in the Middle East: the typical house at Ur in the Larsa Period (nineteenth to the eighteenth century B.C.) consists of a house built around a central courtyard onto which all the rooms open (fig. 109).[499] A staircase leads either to the roof or to the upper floor, where bedrooms and private family rooms are located (fig. 110). A reception

---

[495] Almagro, "Building Patterns," 351.

[496] Ibid., 352.

[497] Petruccioli, *After Amnesia*, 73.

[498] Schoenauer, *Oriental Urban House*, ix.

[499] Ibid., 7, 9; Woolley, *Excavations at Ur*, 180.

room, kitchen, and other household rooms face the courtyard at ground level. This arrangement

of a divided household with living quarters primarily reserved for the upper floor while other

aspects of daily living activities occur around the courtyard on the ground floor is remarkably

similar to that of Pella and Umm el-Jimāl. As well, the similarity of the ancient houses at Ur and

the traditional Baghdad houses in present-day Iraq has been noted by Woolley and

Schoenauer.[500]

The enclosed courtyard house is a product of cultural polygenesis dating to the Bronze Age,

and it has persisted in the Mediterranean area in the form of the classical *atrium* and *pastas*

house to be adopted by Muslims in the *dār al-Islam*.[501] In the context of Greater Syria, the

Umayyads may have inherited the courtyard house from Byzantine models.[502] Petruccioli argues

that the Umayyad adoption of the courtyard type house over other models, such as the earlier

Yemenite model, suggests a Byzantine prototype. The characteristic type of Yemeni house is a

tall, square, tower house with an entertaining room or rooms at the top (fig. 111).[503] It has no

relation to the courtyard houses of antiquity and appears to be a product of Arabia and probably

of South Arabia itself.[504] Rather than continuing the tradition of the Yemenite tower house, a

building technology that could have been transmitted by the Yemenite tribes serving in the army

of the Caliph, the Umayyads opted for the courtyard type.[505]

The house-mosque compound constructed by the Prophet Muḥammad in Medina

symbolically represents the first Islamic house: it became a communal gathering place, a place of

worship, and a center of power.[506] Its essential feature was a large courtyard with two shaded

---

[500] Schoenauer, *Oriental Urban House*, 11; Woolley, *Excavations at Ur*, 182.
[501] Petruccioli, *After Amnesia*, 73.
[502] Idem, "Courtyard House," 13.
[503] Lewcock and Serjeant, "Houses of Ṣanʿāʾ," 436.
[504] Ibid., 496.
[505] Petruccioli, *After Amnesia*, 126.
[506] Hakim, *Arabic-Islamic Cities*, 95; Campo, *Other Side of Paradise*, 53.

areas (fig. 112).[507] "According to traditional accounts, the Prophet"s house-mosque had adobe walls, a large squarish courtyard with porticoes for shade on its north and south sides, and three doorways, one on every side except the qibla side."[508] The Prophet"s residential quarters, or rooms, were situated on the southeast side of the courtyard. Made of adobe, these rooms were covered with roofs fashioned from palm trunks and branches. The number of rooms increased from one to nine; each for the new wife he acquired.[509]

According to Besim Selim Hakim, the courtyard house creates a physical setting suitable for the religious and social requirements of Islam: privacy, interdependence, and *Bāṭin* vs. *Ẓāhir*. The interior courtyard house is an expression of notions of privacy dictated by religious and social norms. Islam recognizes the fundamental right of privacy for the family within its own house. Public and private spaces are demarcated in Islamic society, and even within the house degrees of privacy are expressed architecturally.[510] While an austere face is presented to the outside world, the interior courtyard provides secluded open space for all family activities.

In essence, the courtyard layout ensures privacy from outside or adjacent areas.[511] At Umm el-Jimāl and Pella, the stairs leading to the private, upper living quarters are situated in their respective courtyards. The placement of the stairs in the courtyard emphasizes the courtyard as private rather than public space. Likewise, all of the windows at Jarash face the courtyard, suggesting an inward orientation to maximize privacy. As well, the main entrance at Jarash is through a passageway, which turns at a right angle, obstructing direct view into the courtyard space from the street (fig. 28).

---

[507] Grabar, *Formation of Islamic Art*, 102.
[508] Campo, *Other Side of Paradise*, 51.
[509] Ibid., 52.
[510] Petherbridge, "House and Society," 184.
[511] Hakim, *Arabic-Islamic Cities*, 95.

The courtyard house is accretive by nature, allowing the structure to expand in concert with growing extended families. It could be arranged as multi-unit houses, containing many living units on one or more levels of residence, with the courtyard as a shared space. In such houses, more than one family resides in the building. The grouping of courtyard houses necessitates a level of interdependence between neighbors with regards to the use and rights of shared walls, maintenance of streets, problems related to rain and waste water.[512] This interdependence corresponds with Islamic values as they concern neighborly relations. All of the five houses examined in this study can be identified as a multi-unit residential building in some capacity.

Especially in a rural setting, a multi-unit living arrangement is conducive to interdependence, with families functioning cooperatively in terms of land ownership, division of labor and the sharing of work animals. This is exemplified at Naḥal Mitnan, where the farmhouse is composed of three dwelling units, each consisting of one to three rooms and a small courtyard (fig. 47).[513] However, they constitute one structure as the common entrance to the compound is found on the eastern side. In addition, a shared outer courtyard demarcates the eastern side of the compound. This farmhouse is presumably inhabited by three nuclear families.[514]

An essential value in Islam is the emphasis on the *Bāṭin* (the inner aspect of self or thing), and the subordination of the *Ẓāhir* (the external aspect of self or a thing).[515] The courtyard house and its organizational pattern are suitable for the application of this principle. During the five centuries following the Hellenistic conquest, city plans had been superimposed from the outside, with the focus given to public spaces and obscuring private spaces.[516] At Umm el-Jimāl, however, private residential spaces are of primary focus as comfort and function of the

---

[512] Ibid., 95.
[513] Haiman, "Early Islamic Period Farm," 3.
[514] Ibid., 10.
[515] Hakim, *Arabic-Islamic Cities*, 95-96.
[516] De Vries, *Umm el-Jimal*, 127.

household become overriding concerns. The preoccupation is with the arrangement of space around the courtyard, while the spaces outside the inner sanctum, or public spaces, receive secondary attention.

In concluding, it should be emphasized that the residential architecture of only five sites were examined in this study. This does not provide a sufficient basis for reaching comprehensive conclusions about domestic structures of Jordan-Palestine during the early Islamic period. Further study is required to reconstruct an exhaustive catalogue of housing in both urban and rural sites from this period.

Bibliography

Antonio Almagro, "Origins and Repercussions of the Architecture of the Umayyad Palace in Amman," in *Studies in the History and Archaeology of Jordan*, III, ed. A. Hadidi (Amman, 1987), 181-192.

Idem, "Building Patterns in Umayyad Architecture in Jordan," in *Studies in the History and Archaeology of Jordan* 4, ed. Adnan Hadidi (Amman, 1992), 351-356.

Antonio Almagro and Ignacio Arce, "The Umayyad Town Planning of the Citadel of „Ammān," in *Studies in the History and Archaeology of Jordan*, 7 (Amman, 2001), 659-665.

Richard Alston, "Houses and Households in Roman Egypt," in *Domestic Space in the Roman World: Pompeii and Beyond*, eds. Ray Laurence and Andrew Wallace-Hadrill (Portsmouth, 1997), 25-39.

Nitzan Amitai-Preiss, Ariel Berman, and Shraga Qedar, "The Coinage of Scythopolis-Baysan and Gerasa-Jerash," *Israel Numismatic Journal* 13 (1999), 133-151.

Khaled al-As‚ad and Franciszek M. Stepniowski, "The Umayyad Suq in Palmyra," *Damaszener Mitteilungen* 4 (1989), 205-223.

Gideon Avni, "Early Mosques in the Negev Highlands: New Archaeological Evidence on Islamic Penetration of Southern Palestine," *Bulletin of the American Schools of Oriental Research* 294 (1994), 83-99.

Subhi Hussein Al-Azzawi, "Oriental Houses in Iraq," in *Shelter and Society*, ed. Paul Oliver (New York, 1969).

Aḥmad ibn Jâbir al-Balâdhuri, *The Origins of the Islamic State*, trans. Philip Khûri Ḥitti, vol. 1 (New York, 1916).

W. Ball, J. Bowsher, I. Kehrberg, A. Walmsley, and P. Watson, "The North Decumanus and North Tetrapylon at Jerash: An Archaeological and Architectural Report," in *Jerash Archaeological Project, 1981-1983*, ed. Fawzi Zayadine (Amman, 1986), 351-409.

Michael L. Bates, "The Coinage of Syria under the Umayyads," in *The History of Bilad al-Sham during the Umayyad Period (Fourth International Conference)*, eds. M. A. Bakhit and R. Schick (1989), 195-228.

Crystal M. Bennett and Alastair Northedge, "Excavations at the Citadel, Amman, 1976: Second Preliminary Report," *Annual of the Department of Antiquities of Jordan* 22 (1977-78), 172-179.

Ghazi Bisheh, "Qasr al-Hallabat: An Umayyad Desert Retreat or Farm-Land," in *Studies in the History and Archaeology of Jordan*, II, ed. A. Hadidi (Amman, 1985), 263-265.

Robin M. Brown, "A Large Residence (House XVIII)," in Bert de Vries, *Umm el-Jimal: A Frontier Town and Its Landscape in Northern Jordan vol. 1 Fieldwork 1972-1981* (Portsmouth, 1998), 195-204.

Hendrik J. Bruins, "Ancient Agricultural Terraces at Naḥal Mitnan," *'Atiqot* 10 (1990), 22-28.

Howard Butler and H. Prentice, *Publications of the Princeton Archaeological Expeditions to Syria 1904-5 and 1909*, vol. 2A (Leiden, 1919-1920).

Juan Eduardo Campo, *The Other Sides of Paradise: Explorations into the Religious Meanings of Domestic Space in Paradise* (Columbia, 1991).

Israel Carmi and Dror Segal, "Rehovot Radiocarbon Measurements IV," *Radiocarbon* 34 (1992), 115-132.

Lawrence I. Conrad, *The Plague in the Early Medieval Near East*, Ph.D. dissertation, Princeton University, 1981 (Princeton, 1981).

J. Stephens Crawford, *The Byzantine Shops at Sardis*, Archaeological Exploration of Sardis, Monograph 9 (Cambridge, 1990).

K.A.C. Creswell, *Early Muslim Architecture*, vol. 1 (New York, 1979).

K.A.C. Creswell and James W. Allen, *A Short Account of Early Muslim Architecture* (Aldershot, 1989).

Kristoffer Damgaard and Louise Blanke, "The Islamic Jarash Project: A Preliminary Report on the First Two Seasons of Fieldwork," *Assemblage* 8 (2004), http://www.assemblage.group.shef.ac.uk/issue8/damgaardandblanke.html#fn10.

Fred M. Donner, "The Formation of the Islamic State," *Journal of the American Oriental Society* 106 (1986), 283-296.

Simon P. Ellis, *Roman Housing* (London, 2000).

Idem, "Late Antique Housing and the Uses of Residential Buildings: An Overview," in *Housing in Late Antiquity: from Palaces to Shops*, eds. Luke Lavan, Lale Özgenel and Alexander Sarantis, Late Antique Archaeology, vol. 3.2 (Leiden, 2007), 1-24.

Rebecca Foote, "Commerce, Industrial Expansion, and Orthogonal Planning: Mutually Compatible Terms in Settlements of Bilad al-Sham during the Umayyad Period," *Mediterranean Archaeology* 13 (2000), 25-38.

Idem, *Umayyad Markets and Manufacturing: Evidence for a Commercialized and Industrializing Economy in Early Islamic Bilād al-Shām*, Ph.D. dissertation, Harvard University, 1999 (Ann Arbor, 2006).

Michael Gawlikowski, "A Residential Area by the South Decumanus," in *Jerash Archaeological Project 1981-1983*, vol.1, ed. Fawzi Zayadine (Amman, 1986), 107-136.

Idem, "Jerash in Early Islamic Times," *Oriente Moderno* 23 (2004), 469-476.

Oleg Grabar, "Umayyad „Palace" and the „Abbasid „Revolution,"" *Studia Islamica* 18 (1963), 5-18.

Idem, "Islamic Art and Archaeology," in *The Study of the Middle East: Research and Scholarship in the Humanities and the Social Sciences: A Project of the Research and Training Committee of the Middle East Studies Association*, ed. Leonard Binder (New York, 1976), 229-263.

Idem, *The Formation of Islamic Art* (New Haven, 1987).

Oleg Grabar, Renata Holod, James Knustad, and William Graber Trousdale, *City in the Desert: Qasr al-Hayr East* (Cambridge, 1978).

Mordechai Haiman, "Preliminary Report of the Western Negev Highlands Emergency Survey," *Israel Exploration Journal* 39 (1989), 173-191.

Idem, "Agriculture and Nomad-State Relations in the Negev Desert in the Byzantine and Early Islamic Periods," *Bulletin of the American Schools of Oriental Research* 297 (1995), 29-53.

Idem, "An Early Islamic Period Farm at Nahal Mitnan in the Negev Highlands," *'Atiqot* 26 (1995), 1-13.

Mordechai Haiman and Yuval Goren, "„Negbite" Pottery: New Aspects and Interpretations and the Role of Pastoralism in Designating Ceramic Technology," in *Pastoralism in the Levant*, eds. O. Bar-Yosef and A. Khazanov (Madison, 1992), 143-151.

Besim Selim Hakim, *Arabic-Islamic Cities: Building and Planning Principles* (London, 1986).

Gerald Lankester Harding, "Excavations on the Citadel, Amman," *Annual of the Department of Antiquities of Jordan* 1 (1951), 7-16.

Robert Hillenbrand, "„Anjar and Early Islamic Urbanism" in *The Idea and Ideal of the Town between Late Antiquity and the Early Middle Ages*, eds. Gian P. Brogiolo and Bryan Ward-Perkins (Leiden, 1999), 59-98.

Yizhar Hirschfeld, "Farms and Villages in Byzantine Palestine," *Dumbarton Oaks Paper* 51 (1997), 33-71.

Timothy Insoll, *The Archaeology of Islam* (Malden, 1999).

Ina Kehrberg, "Selected Lamps and Pottery from the Hippodrome at Jerash," Syria 66 (1989), 85-97.

Hugh Kennedy, "The Impact of Muslim Rule on the Pattern of Rural Settlement in Syria," in *La Syrie de Byzance à l'Islam, VIIe-VIIIe siècles. Actes du Colloque international; Lyon-Maison de l'Orient Méditerranéen, Paris-Institut du Monde Arabe, 1990* (Damascus, 1992), 291-297.

Eric C. Lapp, "Byzantine and Early Islamic Oil Lamp Fragments from House 119 at Umm al-Jimal," *Annual of the Department of Antiquities of Jordan* 39 (1995), 437-445.

Ayala Lester, "A Glass Weight from the Times of ,Abd al-Malik B. Yazid," *'Atiqot* 10 (1990), 125-126.

Ronald Lewcock and R. B. Serjeant, "The Houses of Ṣan,ā'," in *Ṣan'ā' an Arabian Islamic City*, eds. R. B. Serjeant and Ronald Lewcock (London, 1983), 436-500.

Jodi Magness, *Jerusalem Ceramic Chronology circa 200-800 CE* (Sheffield, 1993).

Idem, *The Archaeology of the Early Islamic Settlement in Palestine* (Winona Lake, 2003).

Philip Mayerson, "The First Muslim Attacks on Southern Palestine (A.D. 633-634)," *Transactions and Proceedings of the American Philological Association* 95 (1964), 163-199.

A. W. McNicoll, P. C. Edwards, J. Hosking, P. G. Macumber, A. G. Walmsley, and P. M. Watson, "Preliminary Report on the University of Sydney"s Seventh Season of Excavations at Pella (Ṭabaqat Faḥl) in 1985," *Annual of the Department of Antiquities of Jordan* 30 (1986), 155-198.

A. W. McNicoll, R. H. Smith, and J. B. Hennessy, eds., *Pella in Jordan 1: First Interim Report* (Canberra, 1982).

Anthony McNicoll and Alan Walmsley, "Pella/Fahl in Jordan during the Early Islamic Period," *Studies in the History and Archaeology of Jordan* 1 (1982), 339-345.

Alastair Northedge, *Qal'at 'Amman in the Early Islamic Period*, Ph.D. dissertation, School of Oriental and African Studies (London, 1984).

Idem, *Studies on Roman and Islamic 'Amman Volume 1: History, Site and Architecture*, British Academy Monographs in Archaeology, No. 3 (Oxford, 1992).

Idem, "Archaeology and New Urban Settlement in Early Islamic Syria and Iraq," in *Studies in Late Antiquity and Early Islam II, Settlement Patterns in the Byzantine and Early Islamic Near East*, eds. G.R.D. King and A. Cameron (Princeton, 1994), 231-265.

Idem, "Archaeology and Islam," in *Companion Encyclopedia of Archaeology*, ed. Graeme Barker (London, 1999), 1077-1106.

Andrew Petersen, "What is Islamic Archaeology," *Antiquity* 79 (2005), 100-106.

Guy T. Petherbridge, "Vernacular Architecture: The House and Society," in *Architecture of the Islamic World*, ed. George Michell (London, 1978), 176-208.

Attilio Petruccioli, "The Courtyard House: Typological Variations Over Space and Time," in *Courtyard Housing: Past, Present and Future*, eds. Brian Edwards, Magda Sibley, Mohammad Hakmi and Peter Land (New York, 2006), 3-20.

Idem, *After Amnesia: Learning from the Islamic Mediterranean Urban Fabric* (Bari, 2007).

Michele Piccirillo, *The Mosaics of Jordan*, eds. Patricia M. Bikai and Thomas A. Dailey (Amman, 1992).

Barbara Polci, "Some Aspects of the Transformation of the Roman *Domus* Between Late Antiquity and the Early Middle Ages," in *Theory and Practice in the Late Antique Archaeology*, eds. L. Lavan and W. Bowden, Late Antique Archaeology 1 (Leiden, 2003), 79-109.

J. M. Rogers, *From Antiquarianism to Islamic Archaeology* (Cairo, 1974).

Delwen Samuel, "Archaeobotanical Evidence and Analysis," in *Peuplement rural et aménagements hydroagricoles dans la moyenne vallée de l'Euphrate, fin VIIe-XIXe siècle: Région de Deir ez Zōr-Abū Kemāl, Syrie: Mission Mésopotamie syrienne, archéologie islamique, 1986-1989*, ed. S. Berthier (Damascus, 2001), 347-481.

James A. Sauer, *Hesbon Pottery, 1971: A Preliminary Report on the Pottery from the 1971 Excavations at Tell Hesban* (Barren Springs, 1973).

Jean Sauvaget, "Le plan de Laodicée-sur-Mer," *Bulletin d'Études Orientales* 4 (1934), 81-114.

Idem, "Chateaux umayyades de Syrie: Contribution à l'étude de la colonization Arabe aux Ier et 11e siècles de l'hégire," *Revue des etudes islamiques* 35 (1967), 1-49.

George T. Scanlon, "Moulded Early Lead Glazed Wares from Fustat: Imported or Indigenous?" in *In Quest of an Islamic Humanism: Arabic and Islamic Studies in Memory of Mohamed al-Nowaihi*, ed. A. H. Green (Cairo, 1984), 65-96.

Jerome Schaefer and R. K. Falkner, "An Umayyad Potters" Complex in the North Theatre, Jerash," in *Jerash Archaeological Project, 1981-1983*, ed. Fawzi Zayadine (Amman, 1986), 411-459.

Robert Schick, "Archaeological Sources for the History of Palestine: Palestine in the Early Islamic Period: Luxuriant Legacy," *Near Eastern Archaeology* 61 (1998), 74-108.

Daniel Schlumberger, *Qasr el-Heir el-Gharbi: Textes et planches* (Paris, 1986).

Norbert Schoenauer, *Oriental Urban House*, 6000 Years of Housing, vol. 2 (New York, 1981).

Irfan Shahid, "The Jund System in Bilād al-Shām: Its Origin," in *Proceedings of the Fourth International Conference on the History of Bilad al-Sham. Bilad al-Sham during the Byzantine Period*, eds. M. A. Bakhit and M. Asfour, vol. 2 (Amman, 1986), 45-52.

Yoram Tsafrir and Gideon Foerster, "The Dating of the „Earthquake of the Sabbatical Year" of 749 C.E. in Palestine," *Bulletin of the School of Oriental and African Studies* 55 (1992), 231-235.

Idem, "Urbanism at Scythopolis-Bet Shean in the Fourth to Seventh Centuries," *Dumbarton Oaks Paper* 41 (1997), 85-146.

Riccardo Santangeli Valenzani, "Residential Building in Early Medieval Rome," in *Early Medieval Rome and the Christian West*, ed. J. Smith (Leiden, 2000), 101-112.

Stephen Vernoit, "The Rise of Islamic Archaeology," *Muqarnas* 14 (1997), 1-10.

Bert de Vries, "The Umm el-Jimal Project 1972-1977," *Bulletin of the American Schools of Oriental Research* 244 (1981), 53-72.

Idem, "Urbanization in the Basalt Region of North Jordan in Late Antiquity: The Case of Umm el-Jimal," in *Studies in the History and Archaeology of Jordan II*, ed. A. Hadidi (Amman, 1985), 249-256.

Idem, "The Umm el-Jimal Project, 1981-1992," *Annual of the Department of Antiquities of Jordan* 37 (1993), 433-460.

Idem, "Restoration at Umm el-Jimal," in *Siti e Monumenti della Giordiania*, ed. Luigi Marine (Florence, 1994), 45-52.

Idem, "The Umm el-Jimāl Project, 1993 and 1994 Field Seasons," *Annual of the Department of Antiquities of Jordan* 39 (1995), 421-435.

Idem, *Umm el-Jimal: A Frontier Town and its Landscape in Northern Jordan, Fieldwork 1972-1981*, vol. 1 (Portsmouth, 1998), 91-127.

Idem, "Continuity and Change in the Urban Character of the Southern Hauran from the 5th to the 9th Century: The Archaeological Evidence at Umm al-Jimal," *Mediterranean Archaeology* 13 (2000), 39-45.

Alan Walmsley, "Pella/Fiḥl after the Islamic Conquest: A Convergence of Literary and Archaeological Evidence," *Mediterranean Archaeology* 1 (1988), 142-159.

Idem, "Fiḥl (Pella) and the Cities of North Jordan during the Umayyad and Abbasid Periods," in *Studies in the History and Archaeology of Jordan*, eds. S. Tell, G. Bisheh, F. Zayadine, K. ʾAmr, and M. Zaghloul (Amman, 1992), 377-384.

Idem, "The Social and Economic Regime at Fihl (Pella) between the 7th and 9th Centuries," in *La Syrie de Byzance à l'Islam VIIe-VIIIe siècles. Actes du colloque international, Lyon - Maison de l'Orient Méditerranéen, Paris - Institut du Monde Arabe (11-15 septembre 1990)*, eds. P. Canivet and Jean-Paul Rey-Coquais (Damascus, 1992), 249-261.

Idem, "Tradition, Innovation, and Imitation in the Material Culture of Islamic Jordan: The First Four Centuries," in *Studies in the History and Archaeology of Jordan* 5 (Amman, 1995), 657-668.

Idem, "Byzantine Palestine and Arabia: Urban Prosperity in Late Antiquity," in *Towns in Transition: Urban Evolution in Late Antiquity and the Early Middle Ages*, eds. N. Christie and S. T. Loseby (Aldershot, 1996), 126-158.

Idem, "Production, Exchange and Regional Trade in the Islamic East Mediterranean: Old Structures, New Systems?" in *The Long Eighth Century*, ed. Inge L. Hansen and Chris Wickham (Leiden, 2000), 265-343.

Idem, "Islamic Coins," in *Pella in Jordan 1979-1990: The Coins*, eds. Kenneth Sheedy, Robert Carson, and Alan Walmsley (Sydney, 2001), 57-66.

Idem, "The Friday Mosque of Early Islamic Jarash in Jordan: The 2002 Field Season of the Danish-Jordanian Jarash Project," *The Journal of the David Collection* 1 (2003), 111-131.

Idem, "Archaeology and Islamic Studies: The Development of a Relationship," in *From Handaxe to Khan: Essays Presented to Peder Mortensen on the Occasion of His 70th Birthday*, eds. Kjeld von Folsach, Henrik Thrane, and Ingolf Thuesen (Arhus, 2004), 317-329.

Idem, *Early Islamic Syria: An Archaeological Assessment* (London, 2007).

Idem, "Economic Developments and the Nature of Settlement in the Towns and Countryside of Syria-Palestine, ca. 565-800," *Dumbarton Oaks Papers* 61 (2007), 319-352.

Idem, "The Excavation of an Umayyad Period House at Pella in Jordan," in *Housing in Late Antiquity: From Palaces to Shops*, eds. Luke Lavan, Lale Özgenel and Alexander Sarantis, Late Antique Archaeology, vol. 3.2 (Leiden, 2007), 515-521.

Idem, "Households at Pella, Jordan: The Domestic Destruction Deposits of the Mid-Eighth Century," in *Objects in Context, Objects in Use: Material Spatiality in Late Antiquity*, eds. Luke Lavan, Ellen Swift and Toon Putzeys, Late Antique Archaeology 5 (Leiden, 2008), 239-272.

Alan Walmsley and Kristoffer Damgaard, "The Umayyad Congregational Mosque of Jarash in Jordan and Its Relationship to Early Mosques," *Antiquity* 79 (2005), 362-378.

Andrew M. Watson, *Agricultural Innovation in the Early Islamic World: The Diffusion of Crops and Farming Techniques, 700-1100* (Cambridge, 1983).

P. M. Watson, "The Byzantine Period: Byzantine Domestic Occupation in Areas III and IV," in *Pella in Jordan 2. The Second Interim Report of the Joint University of Sydney and College of Wooster Excavations at Pella 1982-1985*, eds. Anthony McNicoll, J. Hanbury-Tenison, J.B. Hennessy, T.F. Potts, Robert Smith, Alan Walmsley and P. Watson (Sydney, 1992), 163-181.

Donald Whitcomb, "Khirbet al-Mafjar Reconsidered: The Ceramic Evidence," *Bulletin of the American Schools of Oriental Research* 271 (1988), 51-67.

Idem, "Mahesh Ware: Evidence of Early Abbasid Occupation form Southern Jordan," *Annual of the Department of Antiquities of Jordan* 33 (1989), 269-285.

Idem, "Hesban, Amman, and Abbasid Archaeology in Jordan," in *The Archaeology of Jordan and Beyond: Essays in Honor of James A. Sauer*, eds. James A. Sauer, Lawrence E. Stager, Joseph A. Greene, and Michael D. Coogan (Winona Lake, 2000), 505-515.

Idem, "Umayyad and Abbasid Periods," in *The Archaeology of Jordan*, eds. Burton MacDonald, Russell Adams, Piotr Bienkowski (Sheffield, 2001), 503-513.

Idem, "The Spread of Islam and Islamic Archaeology," in *Changing Social Identity with the Spread of Islam: Archaeological Perspectives*, ed. Donald Whitcomb (Chicago, 2004), 1-7.

Leonard Woolley, *Excavations at Ur: A Record of Twelve Years Work* (London, 1955).

Fawzi Zayadine, "The Jerash Project for Excavation and Restoration," in *Jerash Archaeological Project 1981-1983 I*, ed. Fawzi Zayadine (Amman, 1986), 7-28.

Ali Zeyadeh, "Urban Transformation in the Decapolis Cities of Jordan," *ARAM* 4 (1992), 101-115.

Figures

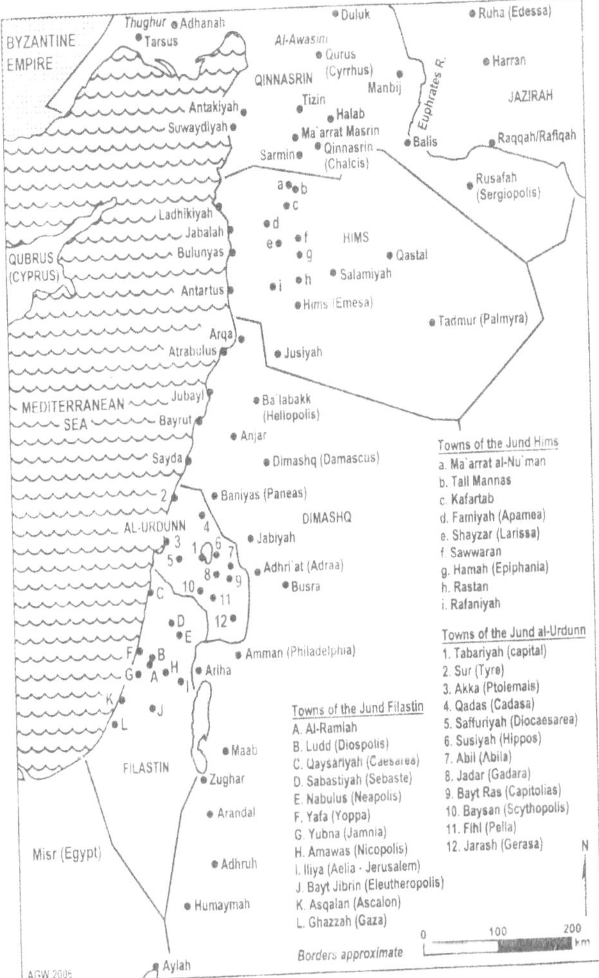

Figure 1. The five provinces (*ajnād*) of early Islamic Syria-Palestine, after *c.* 685 (from Walmsley, *Early Islamic Syria*, fig. 7).

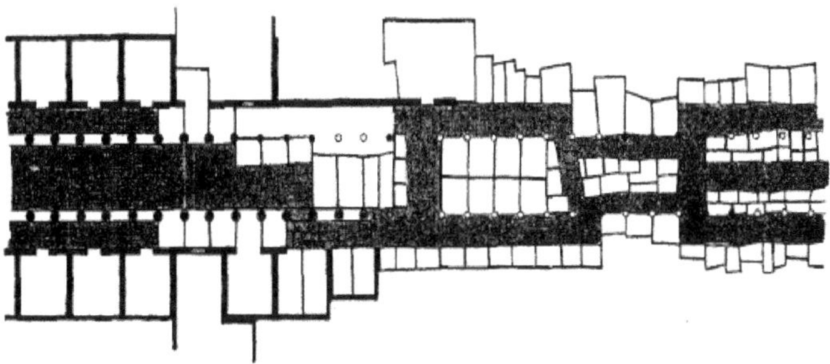

Figure 2. The transformation of the colonnaded avenue into the linear bazaar of Damascus (from Sauvaget, "Laodicée," fig. 8).

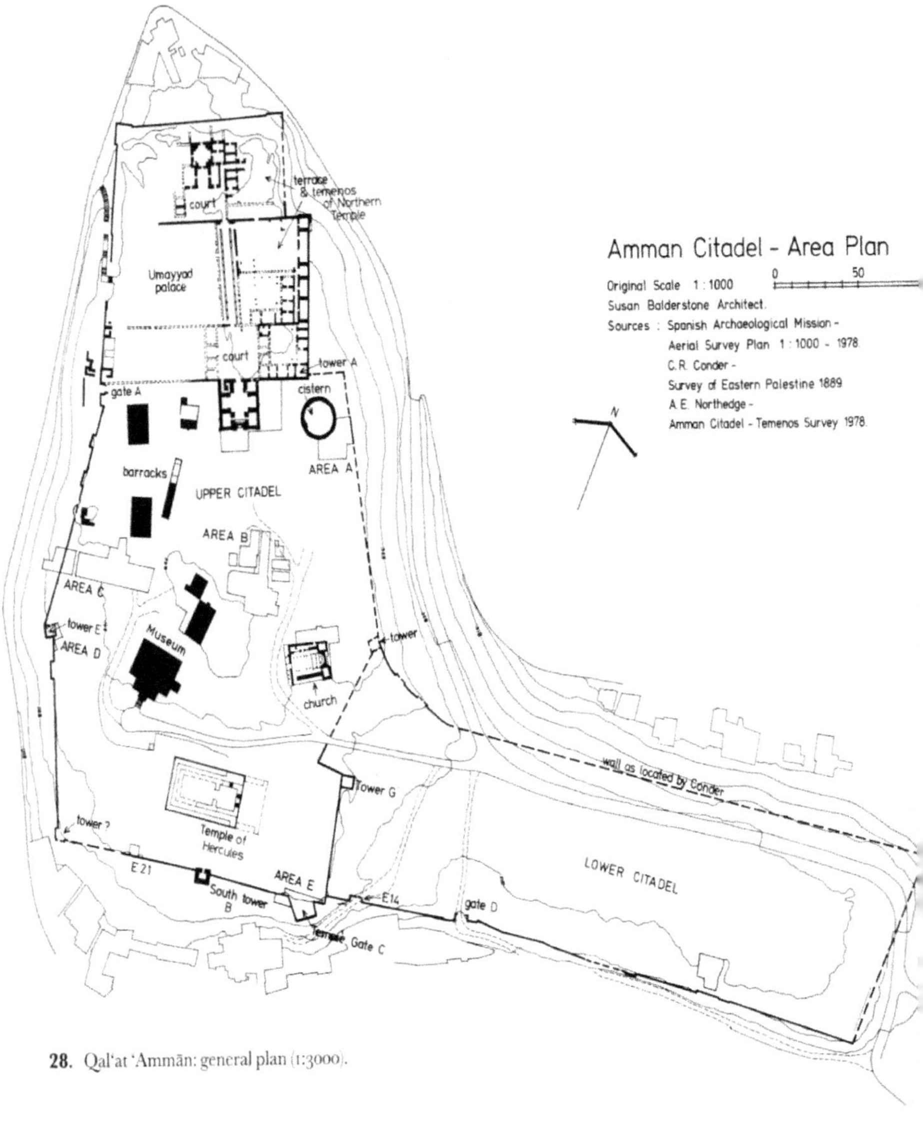

28. Qal'at 'Ammān: general plan (1:3000).

Figure 3. „Ammān Citadel: General plan (from Northedge, *Roman and Islamic 'Amman*, fig. 28).

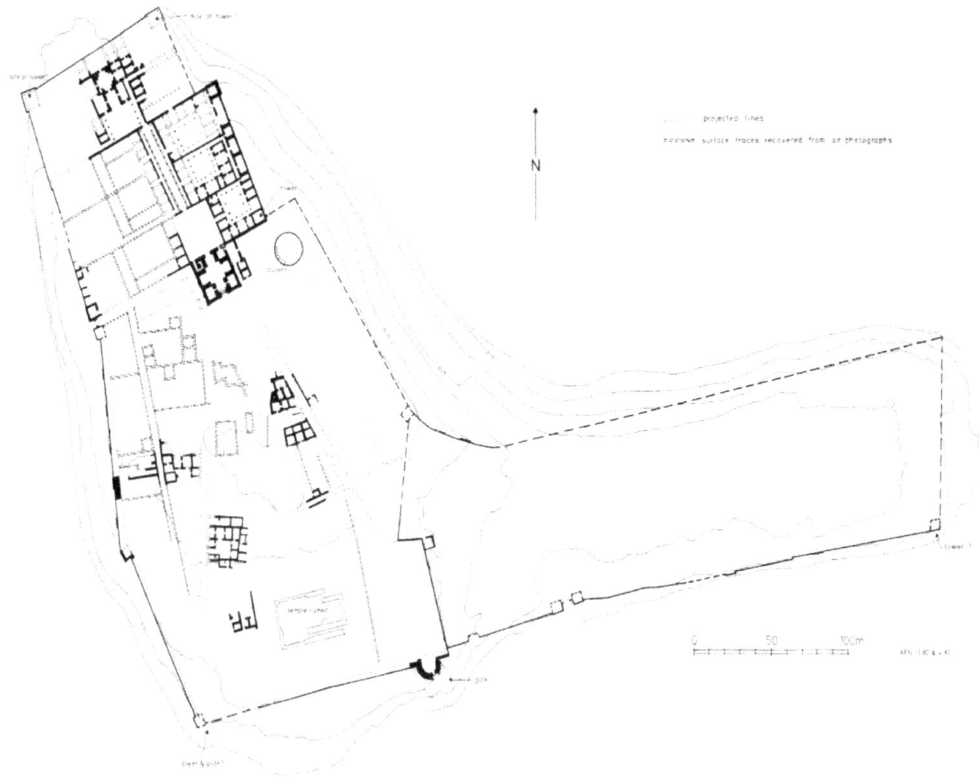

Figure 4. The Umayyad Citadel (from Northedge, *Roman and Islamic 'Amman*, fig. 165).

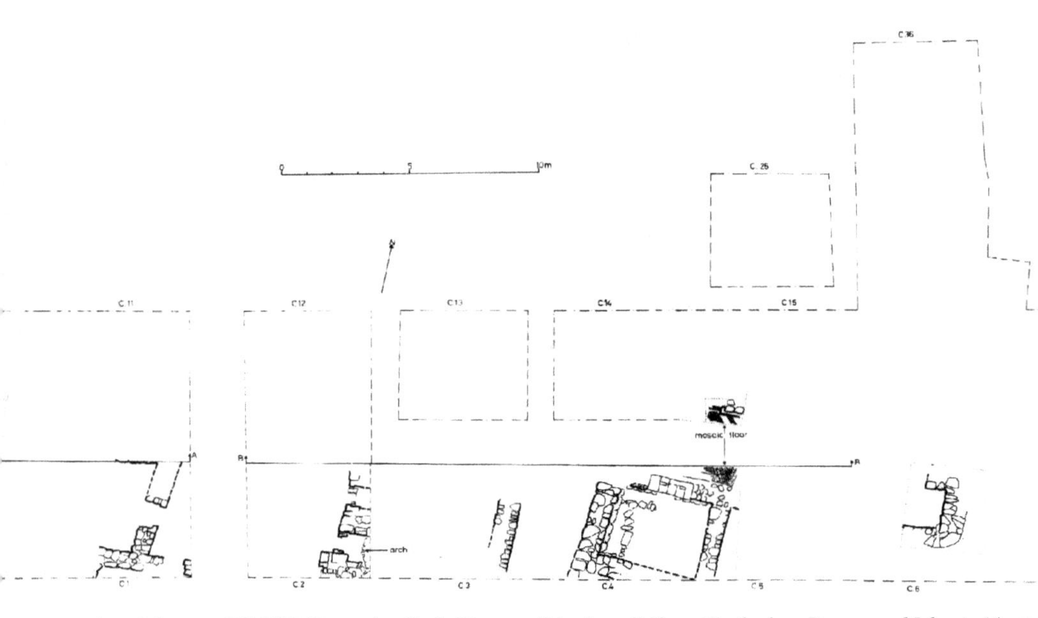

re 5. Remains of Stratum VII-VIII (Byzantine-Early Umayyad) in Area C (from Northedge, *Roman and Islamic 'Amma*

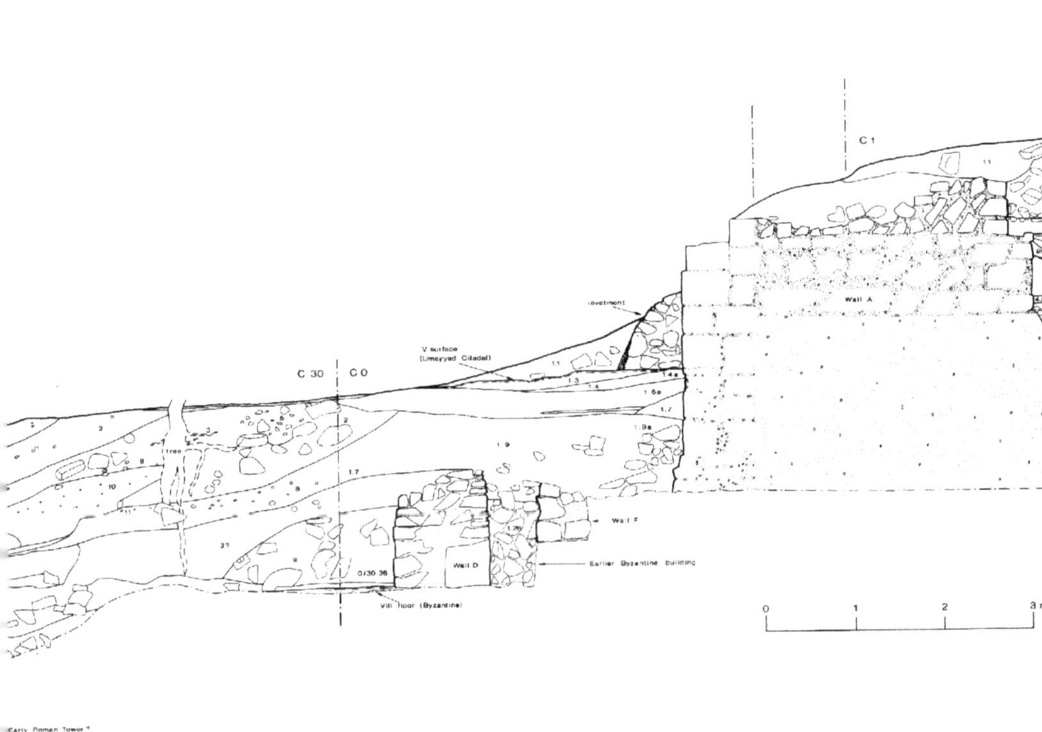

...ctor 8 for fortification wall in Area C, and the area outside the wall, looking north (from Northedge, *Roman and Islamic*

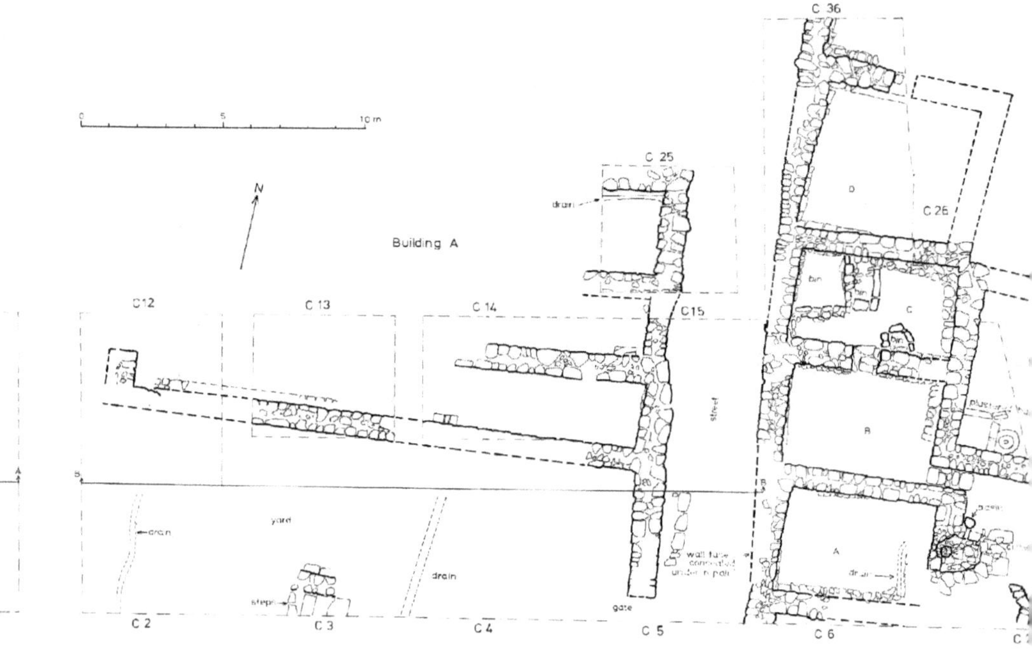

Umayyad Citadel) in Area C (from Northedge, *Roman and Islamic 'Amman*, fig. 126). This author has added the letter '

Figure 8. Area C street, showing later Stratum III surface and buttressing of Umayyad Building B (from Northedge, *Roman and Islamic 'Amman*, pl. 68a).

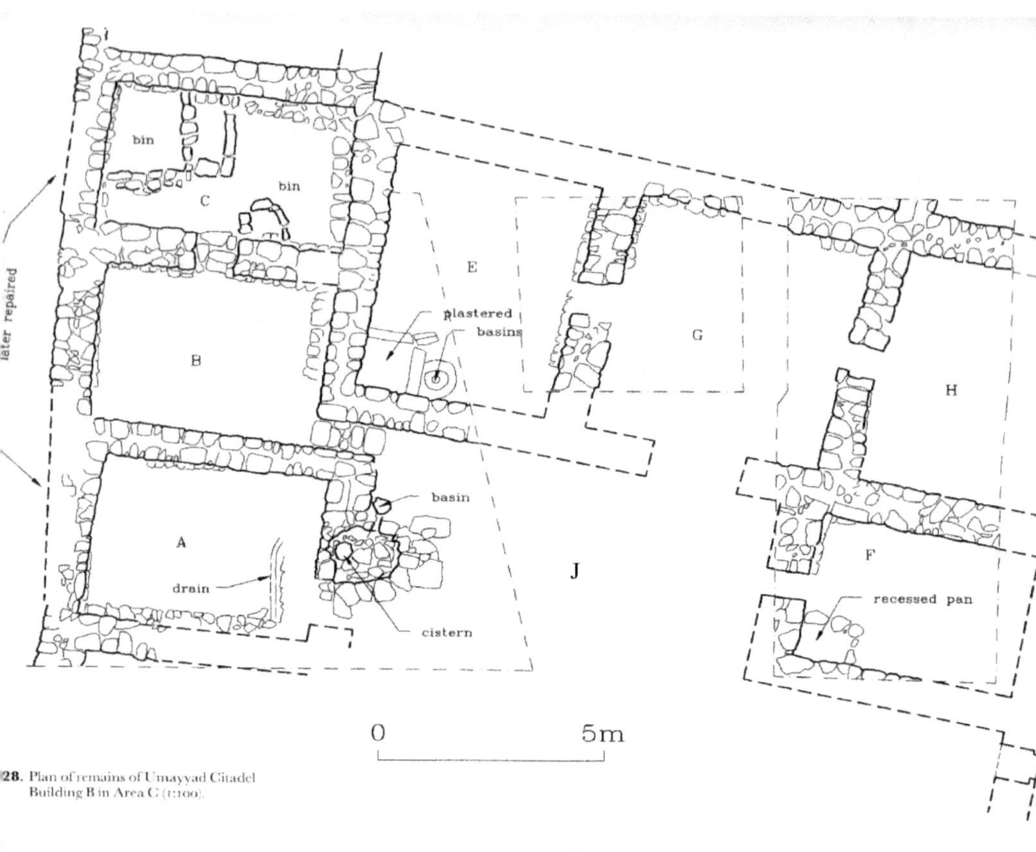

28. Plan of remains of Umayyad Citadel Building B in Area C (1:100).

...f Umayyad Citadel Building B in Area C (from Northedge, *Roman and Islamic 'Amman*, fig. 128). This author has add... identify the courtyard.

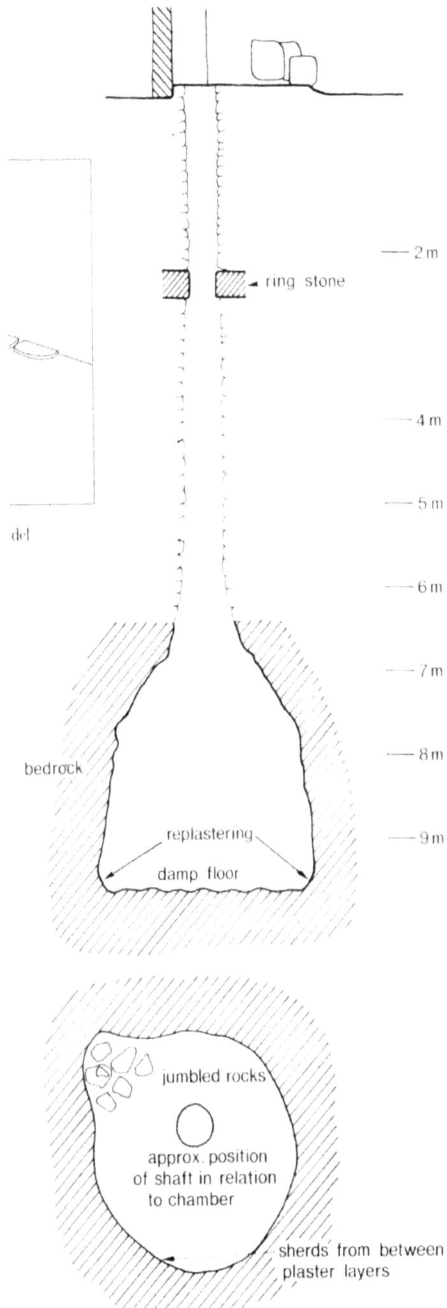

Figure 10. Cross-section of cistern in Umayyad Citadel Building B (from Northedge, *Roman and Islamic 'Amman*, fig. 130).

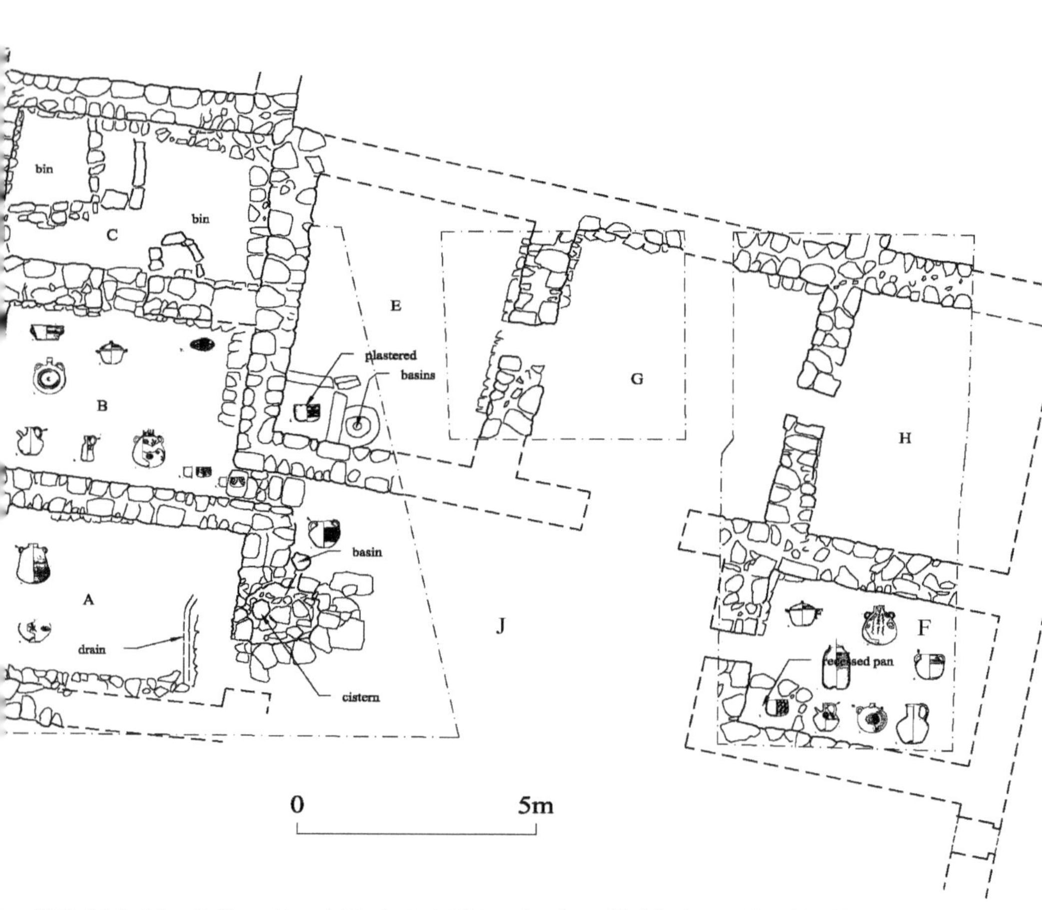

...yad Citadel Building B (from Alastair Northedge). This author has added the letter "J" to identify the courtyard and the

Figure 12. Room B, Stratum V Umayyad Building in Area C, looking northwest (from Northedge, *Roman and Islamic 'Amman*, pl. 68b).

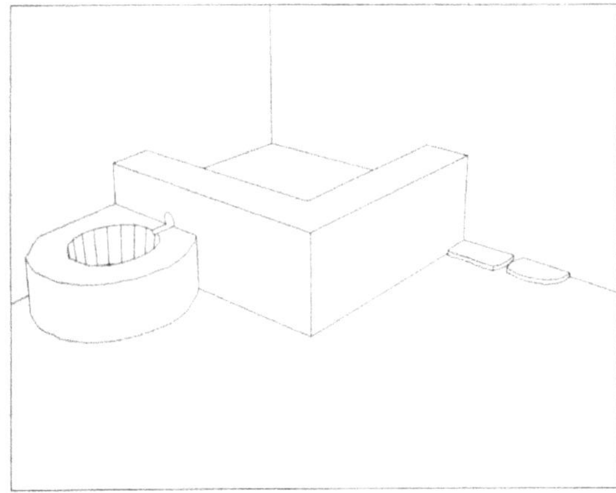

Figure 13. Perspective reconstruction of basins in Umayyad Citadel Building B (from Northedge, *Roman and Islamic 'Amman*, fig. 129).

Figure 14. Storeroom C, Stratum V Umayyad Building B in Area C, looking west (from Northedge, *Roman and Islamic 'Amman*, pl. 69a).

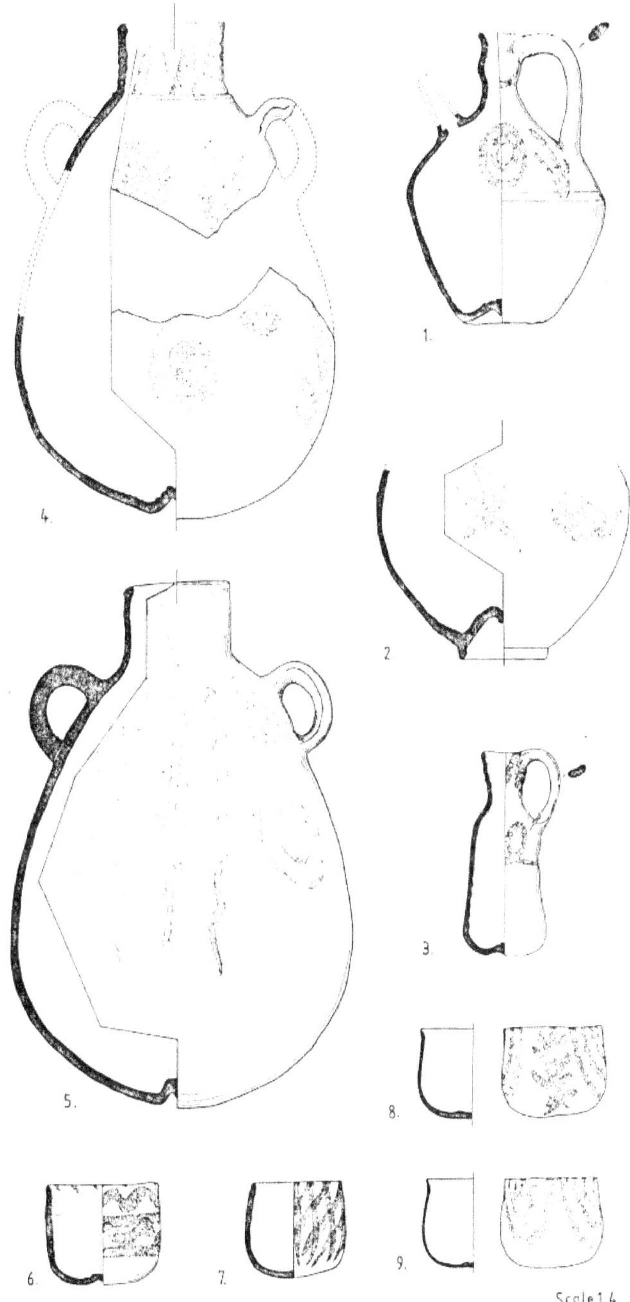

Figure 15. Pottery from the Umayyad earthquake destruction (from Northedge, *Qal'at 'Amman*, fig. 71).

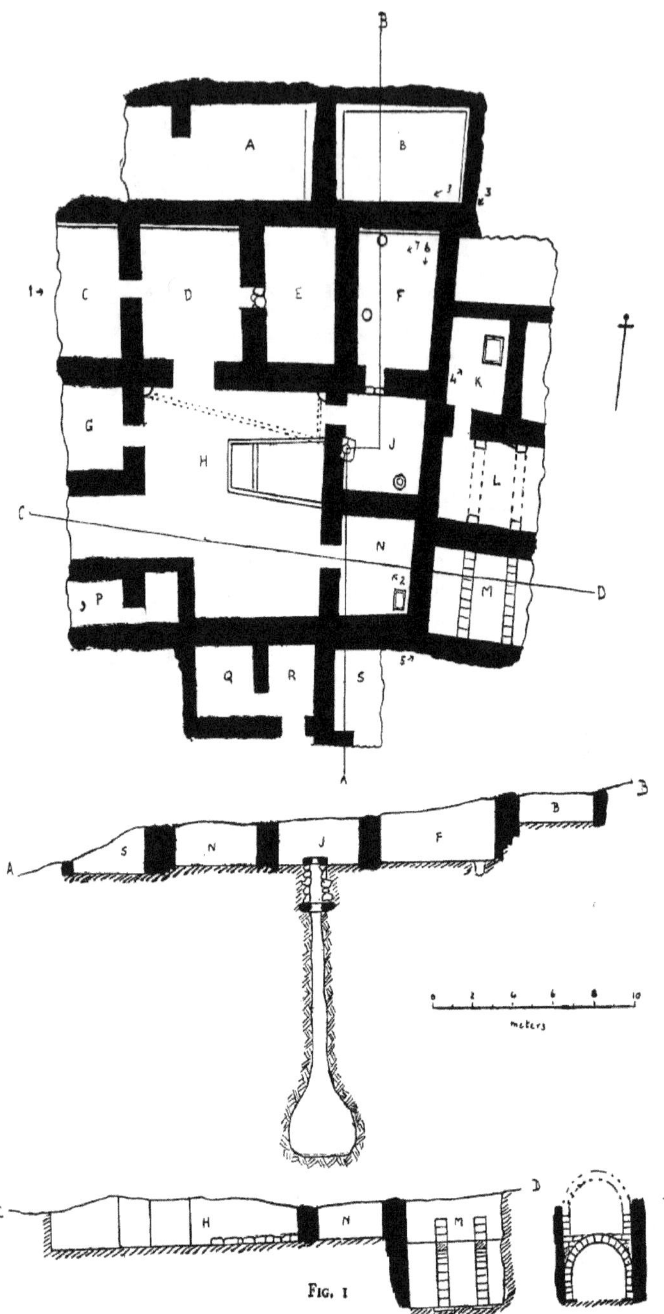

Figure 16. House under the Archaeological Museum, „Ammān Citadel (from Harding, "Excavations on the Citadel," fig. 1).

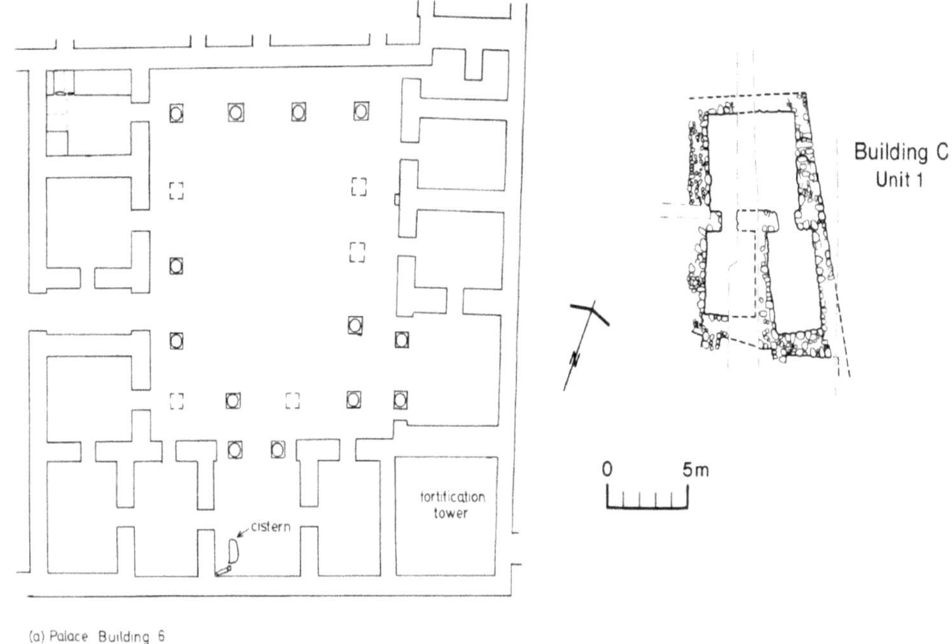

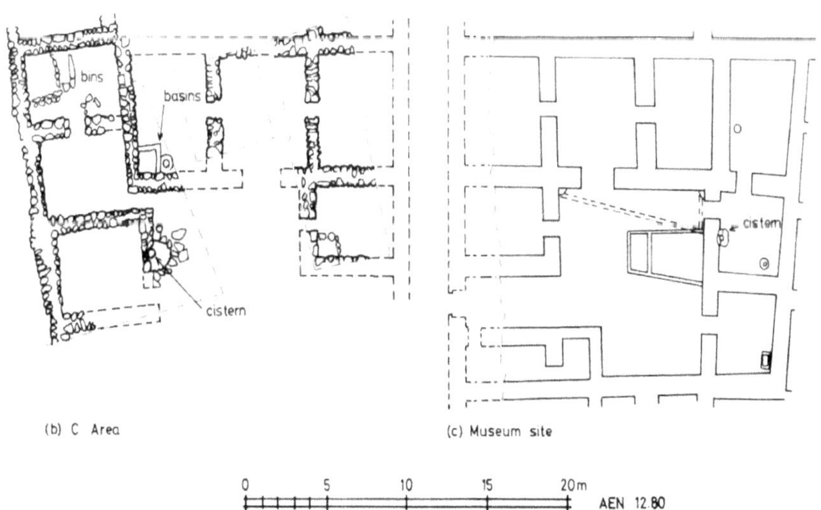

Figure 17. Umayyad Citadel comparative house plans (from Northedge, *Roman and Islamic 'Amman*, fig. 166).

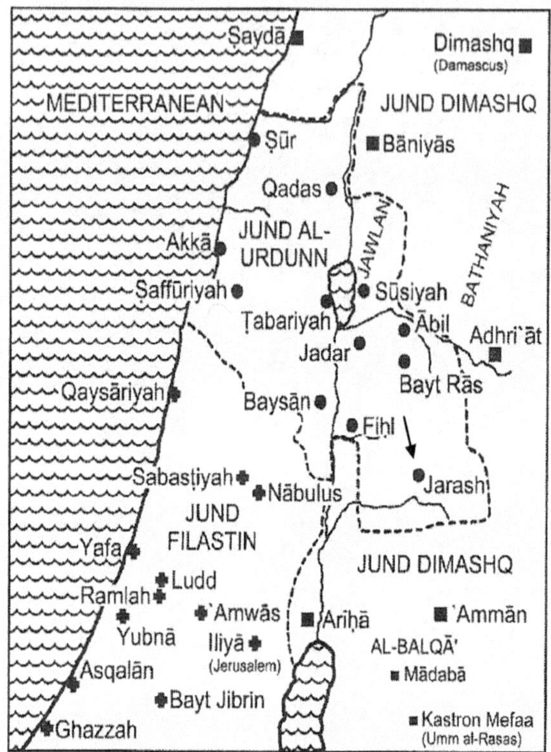

Figure 18. Geographical extent and major towns of the *jund* of al-Urdunn in the early Islamic period (from Walmsley, "Friday Mosque," fig. 2). This author has added an arrow to indicate Jarash.

Figure 19. Typical Pre-Reform (Arab-Byzantine) issue from Jarash (from Walmsley, "Friday Mosque," fig. 3).

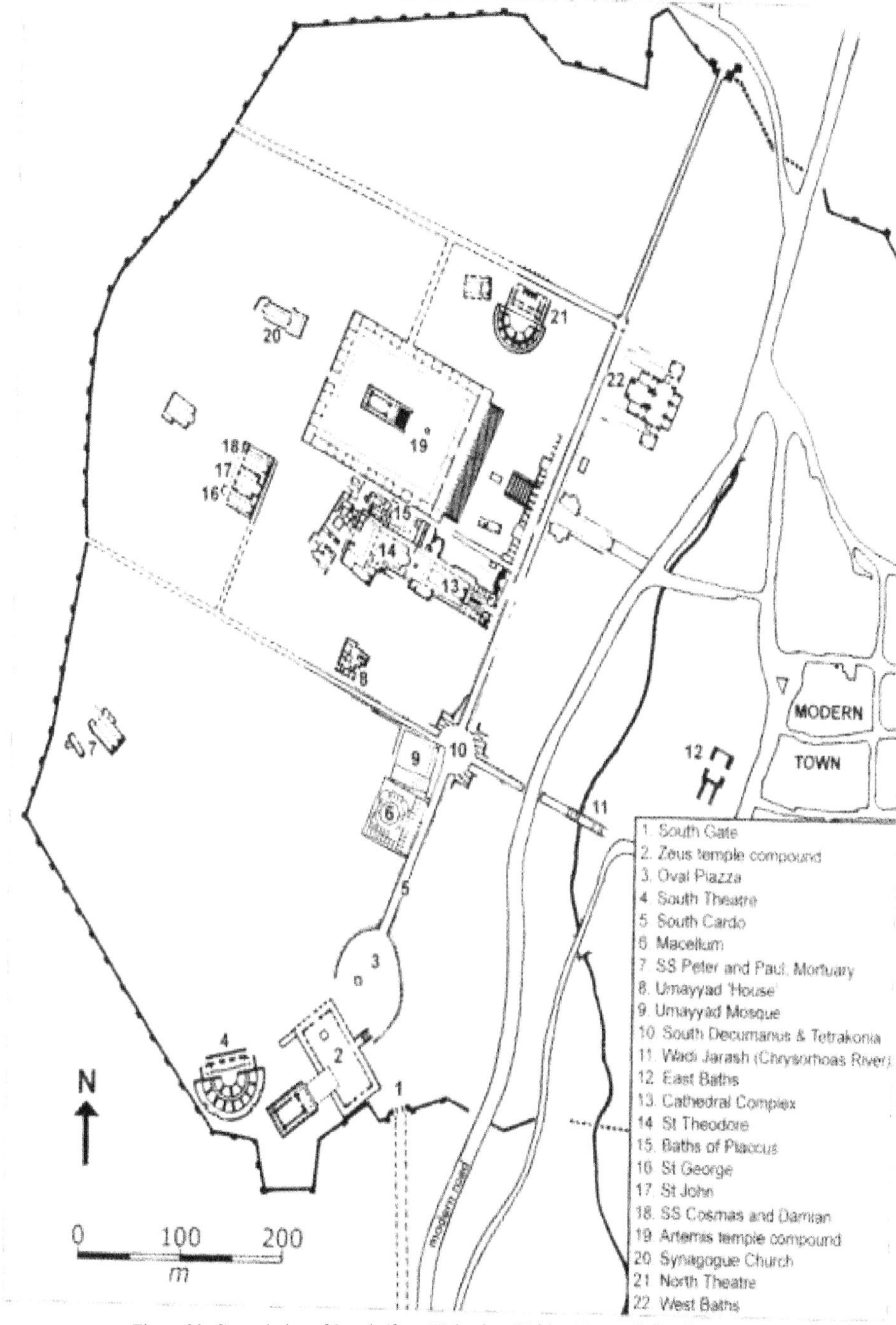

Figure 20. General plan of Jarash (from Walmsley, "Friday Mosque," fig. 1).

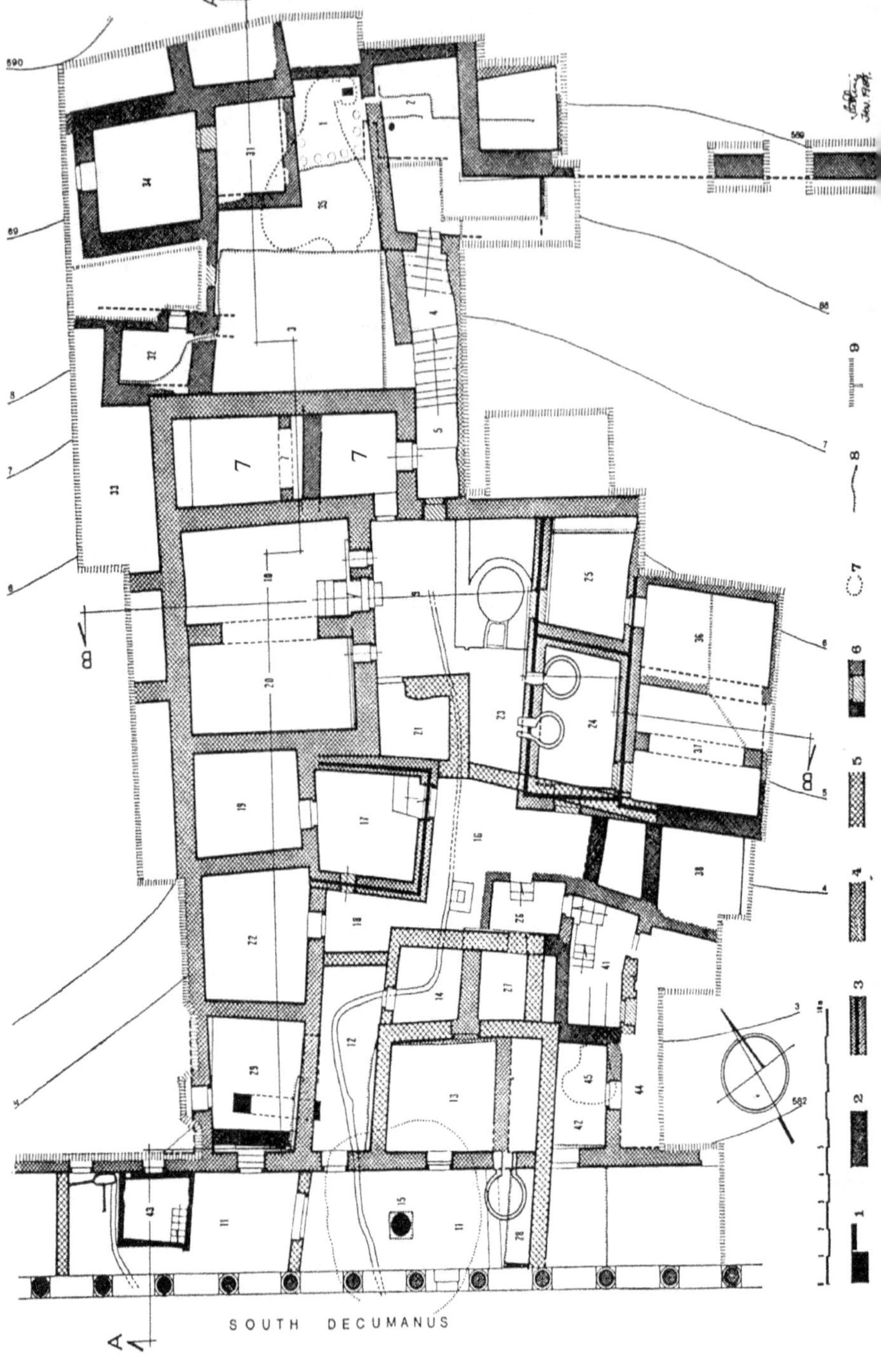

Figure 21. South Decumanus area, general plan (from Gawlikowski, "Residential Area," fig. 1). This author has added the number 7 as it is not clear in the figure.

Figure 22. The cistern loc. 43, SE corner; to the right, the stylobate foundation (from Gawlikowski, "Residential Area," pl. IIA).

Figure 23. The cistern loc. 43, seen from the east (from Gawlikowski, "Residential Area," pl. IIB).

Figure 24. The north-west house, with the Umayyad House in the foreground (from Gawlikowski, "Residential Area," pl. IVB).

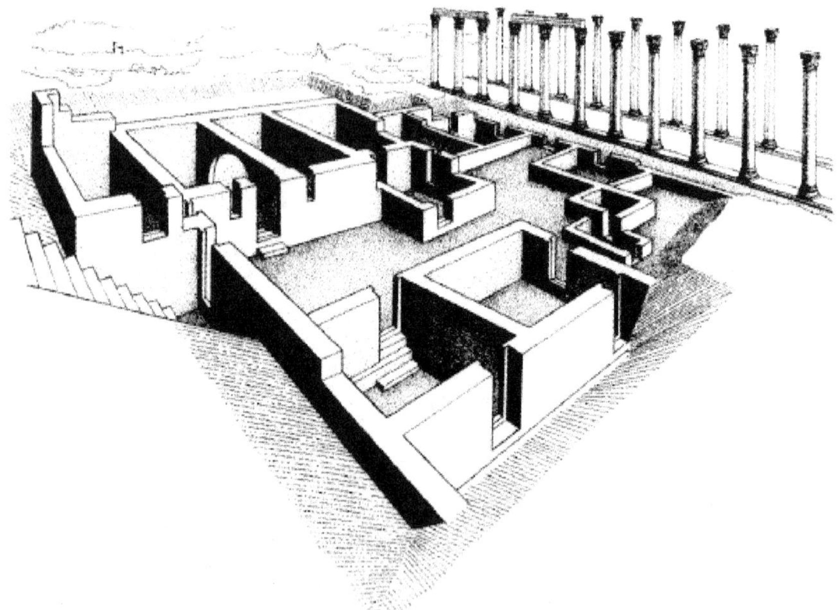

Figure 25. Umayyad House, view of existing restoration by A. Ostrasz (from Gawlikowski, "Jerash in Early Islamic Times," fig. 2).

Figure 26. The staircase of the Umayyad House (from Gawlikowski, "Residential Area," pl. VA).

Figure 27. Entrance to a shop above cistern loc. 43, on Umayyad foundations (from Gawlikowski, "Residential Area," pl. VB).

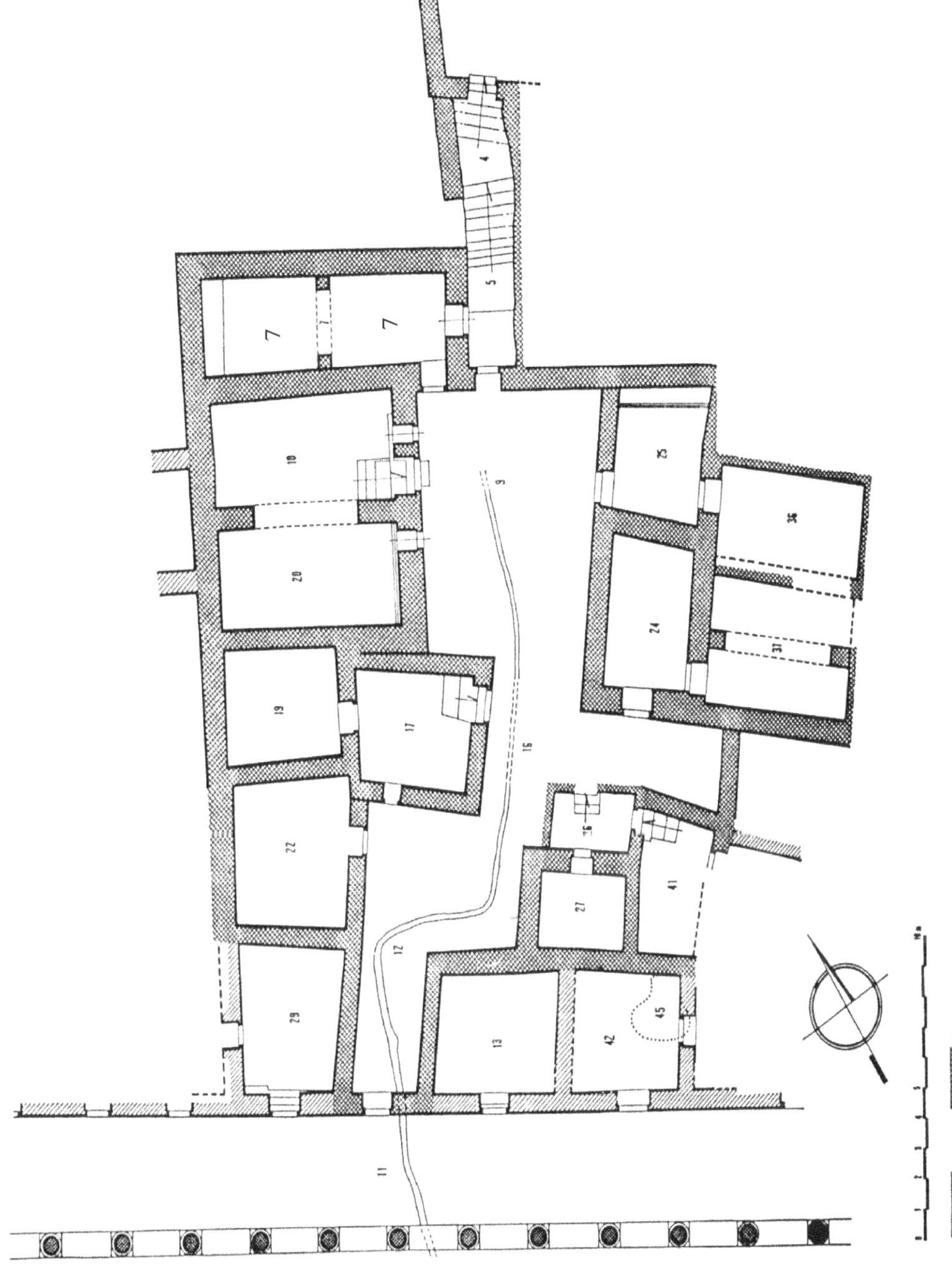

Figure 28. The Umayyad Period House (from Gawlikowski, "Residential Area," fig. 2). This author has added the number 7 as it is not clear in the figure.

Figure 29. Entrance to the Umayyad House, above the sewer (loc. 12) (from Gawlikowski, "Residential Area," pl. VIA).

Figure 30. Room 7 as seen from its window-sill (from Gawlikowski, "Residential Area," pl. VIIB).

Figure 31. Room 10/20 looking from inside the door (from Gawlikowski, "Residential Area," pl. VIIIA).

Figure 32. Loc. 20 from the west; to the left, the late wall between the arch piers (from Gawlikowski, "Residential Area," pl. VIIIB).

Figure 33. The underground Room 26 seen from the east (from Gawlikowski, "Residential Area," pl. VIB).

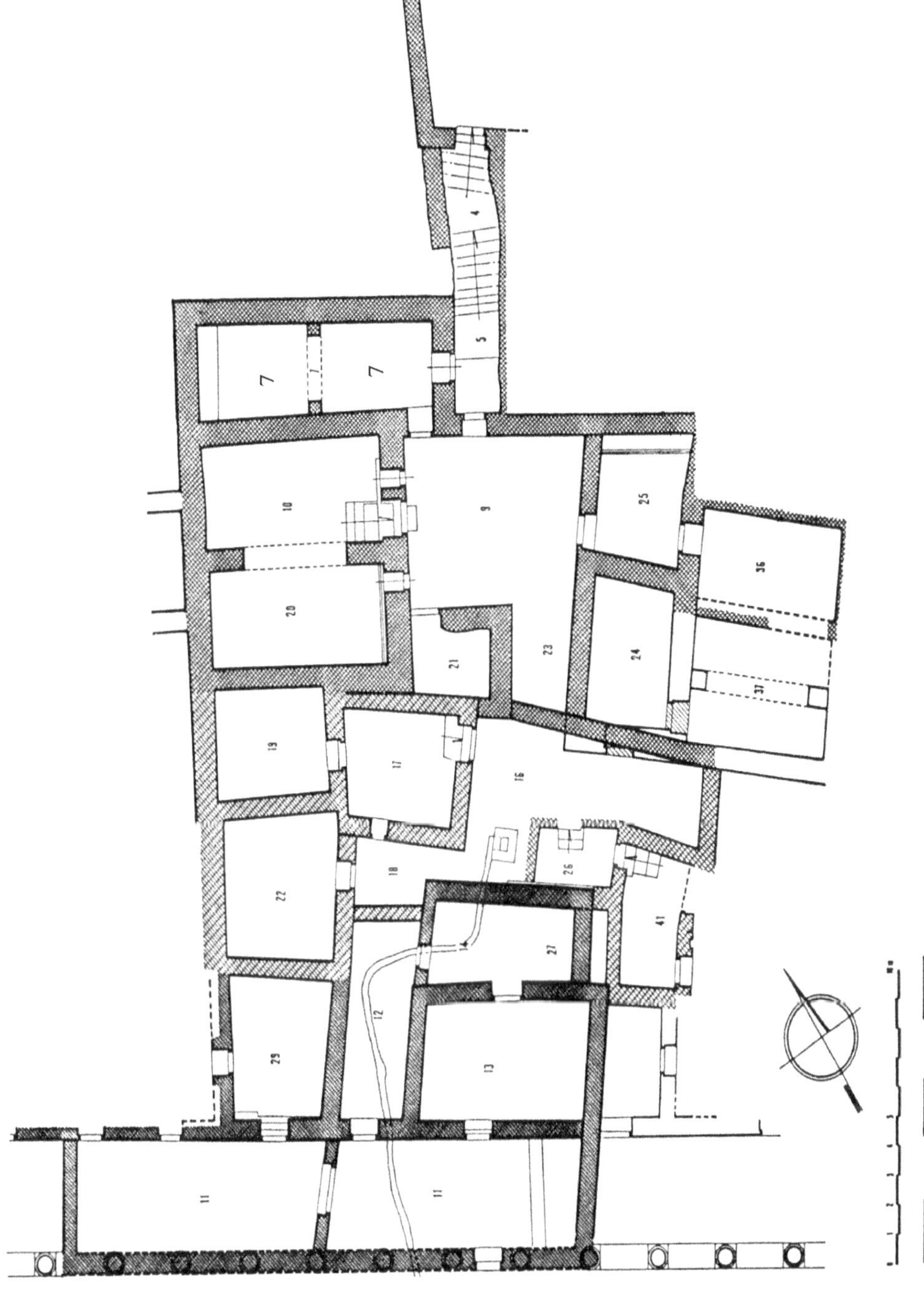

Figure 34. The early Abbasid period (from Gawlikowski, "Residential Area," fig. 3). This author has added the number 7 as it is not clear in the figure.

Figure 35. Northern part of the Umayyad House; behind the wall, loci 21, 23 and 25 (from Gawlikowski, "Residential Area," pl. IIIA).

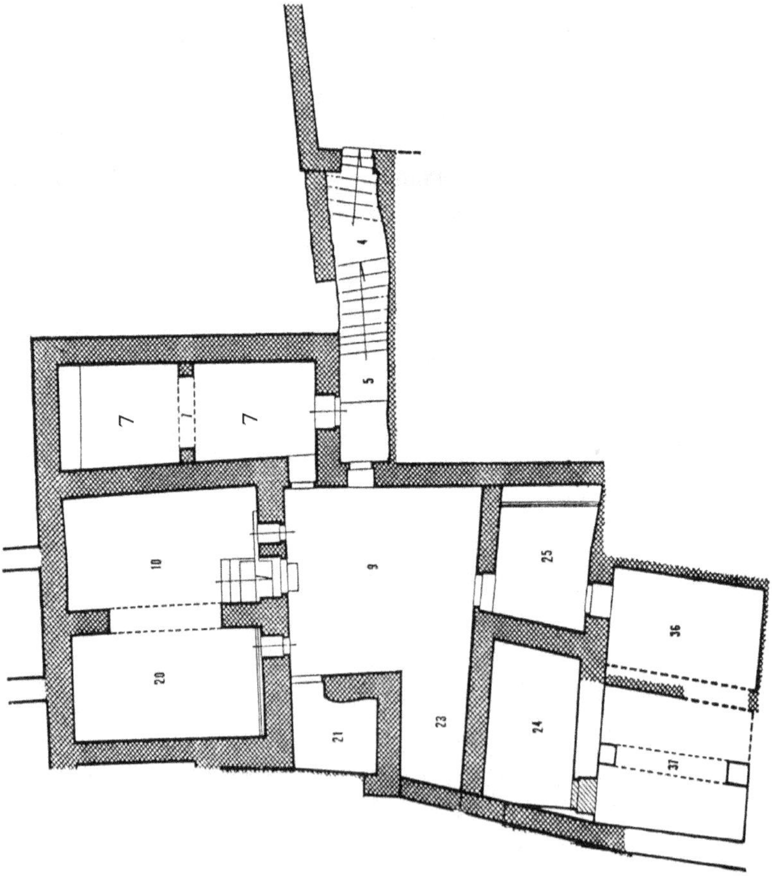

Figure 36. Early Abbasid period house, first dwelling (from Gawlikowski, "Residential Area," fig. 3). This author divided the image into each subdivided dwellings.

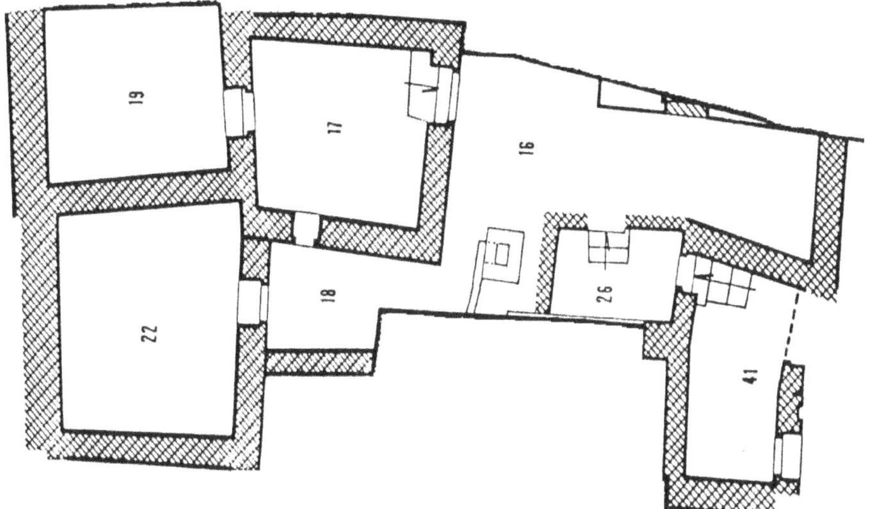

Figure 37. Early Abbasid period house, second dwelling (from Gawlikowski, "Residential Area," fig. 3). This author divided the image into each subdivided dwellings.

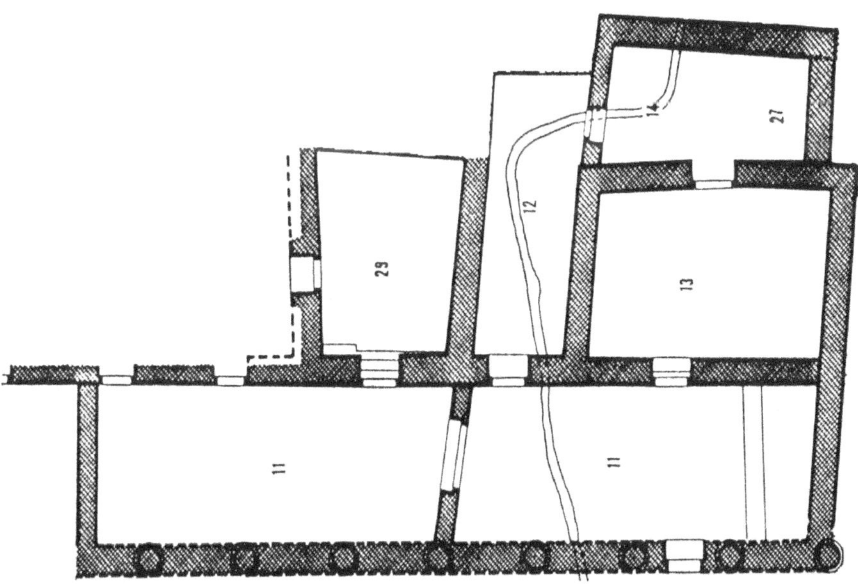

Figure 38. Early Abbasid period house, third dwelling (from Gawlikowski, "Residential Area," fig. 3). This author divided the image into each subdivided dwellings.

Figure 39. Coins recovered from house (from Gawlikowski, "Residential Area," pl. XV).

A. Umayyad lamps (Group III).

B. Abbassid lamps (Group VI).

Figure 40. Lamps recovered from house (from Gawlikowski, "Residential Area," pl. XIV).

Figure 41. Red-painted pottery from Jarash: bowls, 8th century (from Gawlikowski, "Jerash in Early Islamic Times," fig. 4).

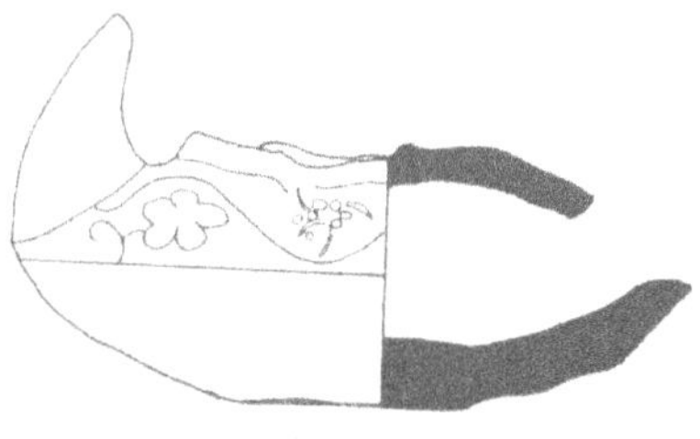

Figure 42. Unglazed lamp from al-Fusṭāṭ (from Scanlon, "Lead Glazed Wares," fig. 11).

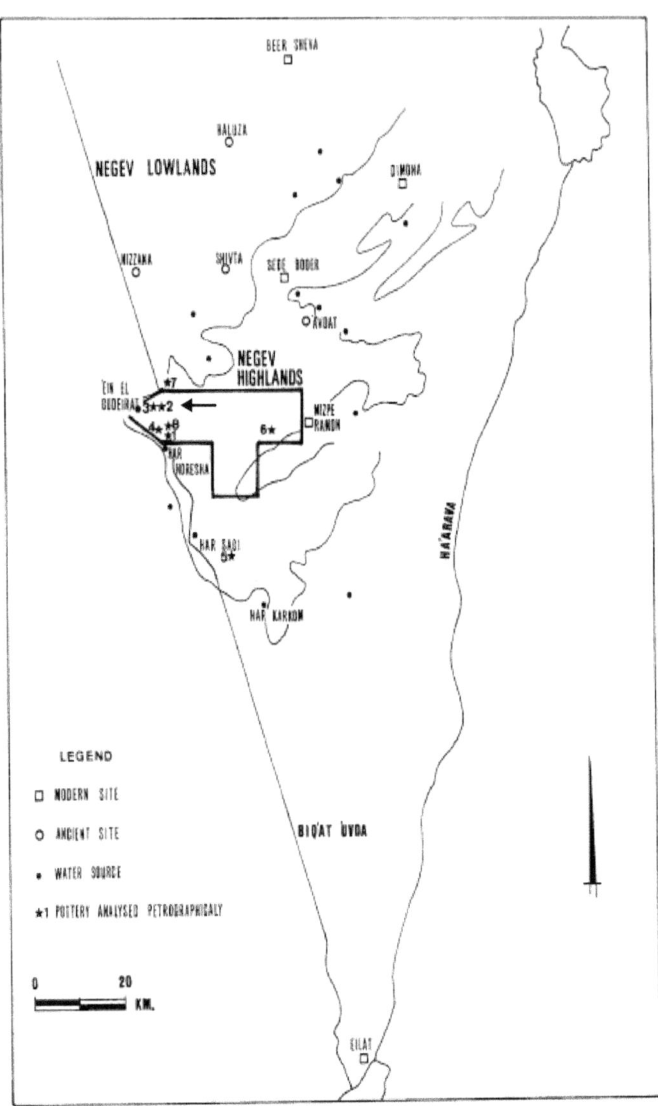

Figure 43. Map of the Negev. The bold frame marks the western Negev highlands survey zone. 2-3. Naḥal Mitnan (from Haiman and Goren, "New Aspects," fig. 1). This author has added an arrow to indicate Naḥal Mitnan.

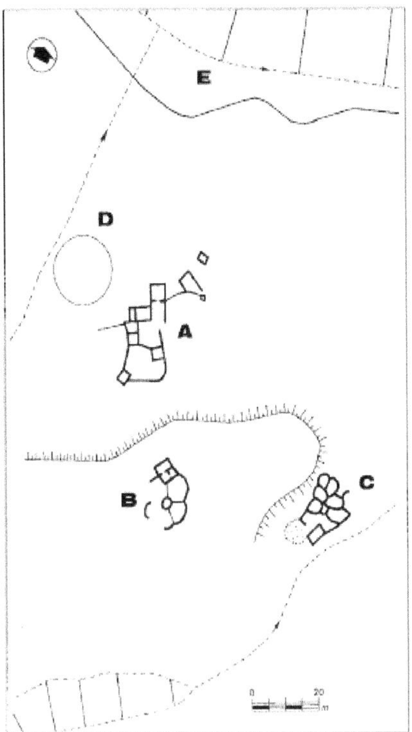

Figure 44. The elements of the Naḥal Mitnan farm (from Haiman, "Early Islamic Period Farm," plan 2).

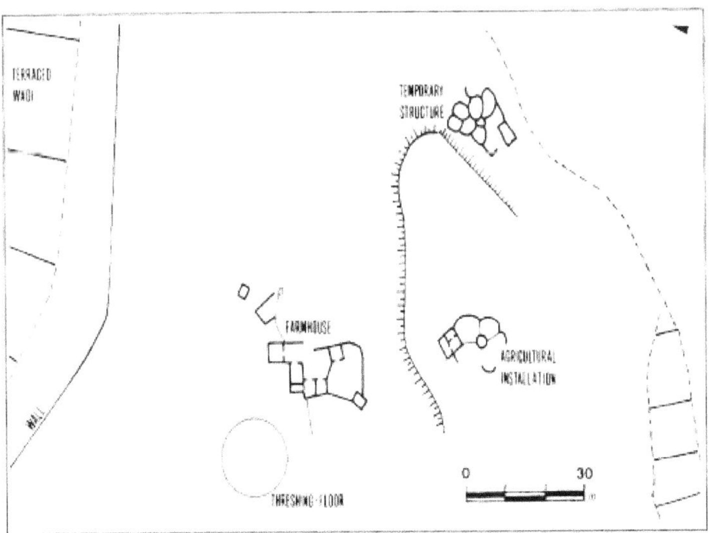

Figure 45. Early Islamic period farm at Naḥal Mitnan (from Haiman, "Agriculture and Nomad-State Relations," fig. 11).

Figure 46. The excavated farmhouse of Naḥal Mitnan, looking east toward Courtyard 111 and the east bank of Naḥal Mitnan (from Haiman, "Early Islamic Period Farm," fig. 2).

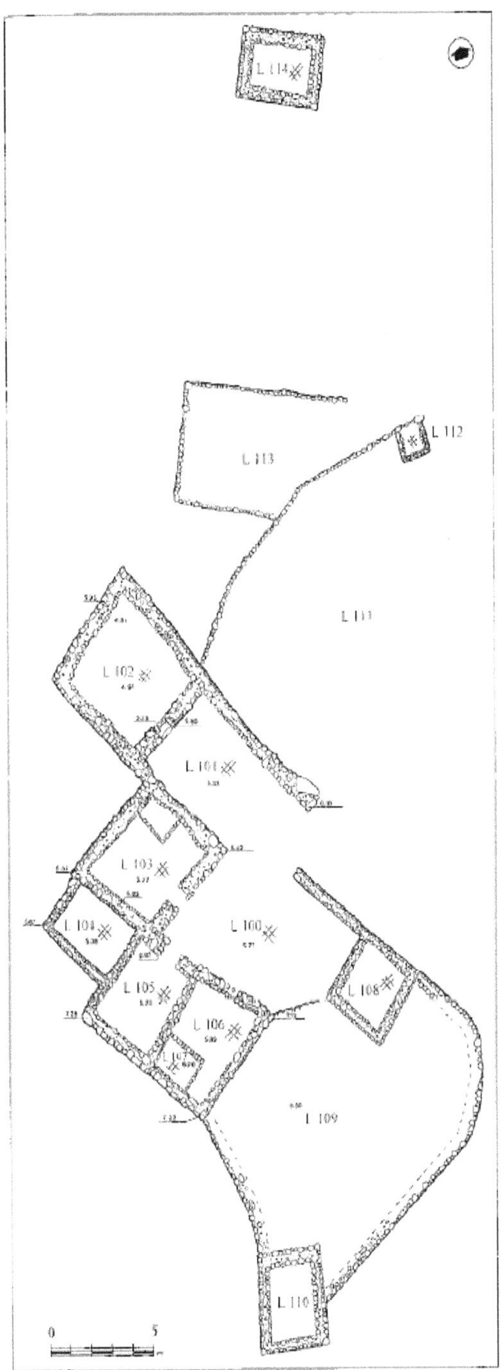

Figure 47. The excavated farmhouse (from Haiman, "Early Islamic Period Farm," plan 3).

Figure 48. Courtyard 101 and Room 102 at the rear (from Haiman, "Early Islamic Period Farm," fig. 5).

Figure 49. Room 105, looking west (from Haiman, "Early Islamic Period Farm," fig. 6).

Figure 50. Room 104, looking east (from Haiman, "Early Islamic Period Farm," fig. 7).

Figure 51. Wall detail (from Haiman, "Early Islamic Period Farm," fig. 3).

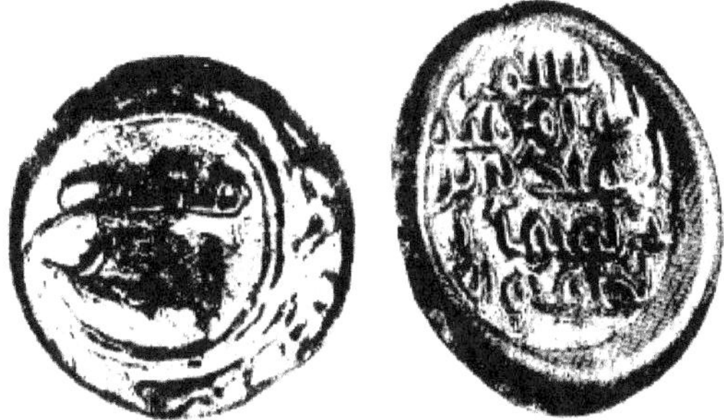

Figure 52. Glass weight from the time of „Abd al-Malik b. Yazīd (from Lester, "Glass Weight," fig. 1).

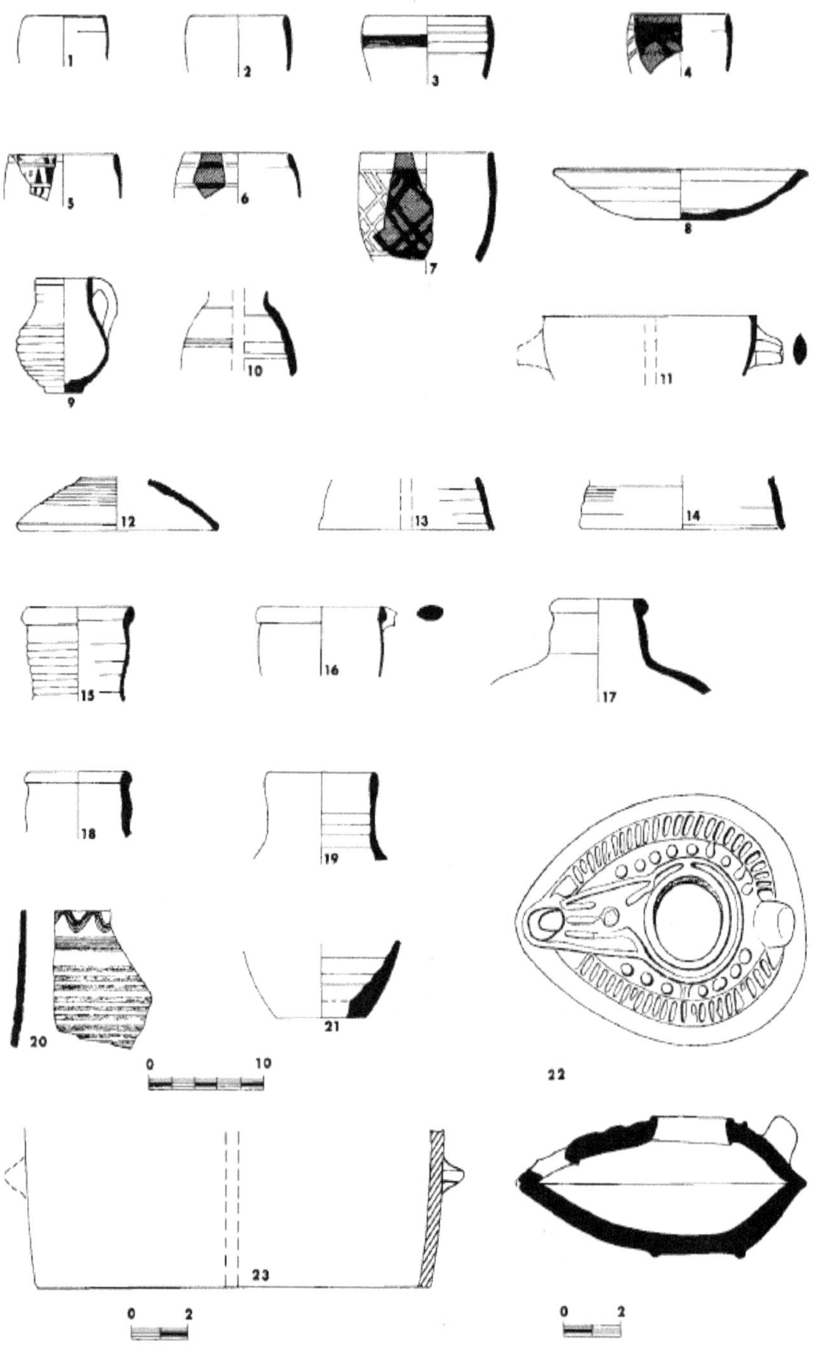

Figure 53. Pottery from Naḥal Mitnan (from Haiman, "Early Islamic Period Farm," fig. 8).

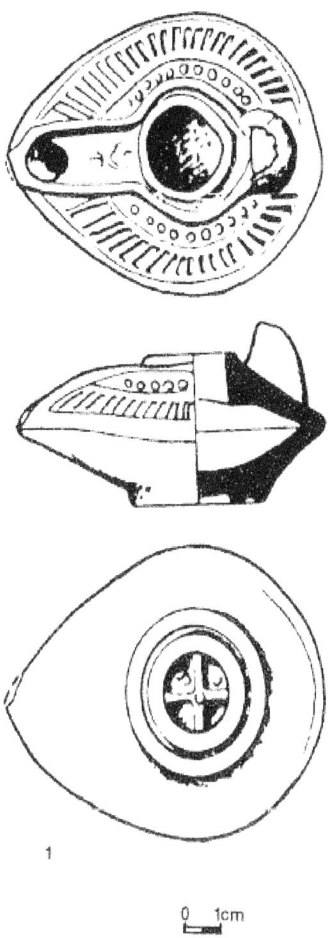

Figure 54. Early channel-nozzle oil lamp (from Magness, *Jerusalem Ceramic Chronology*, 257).

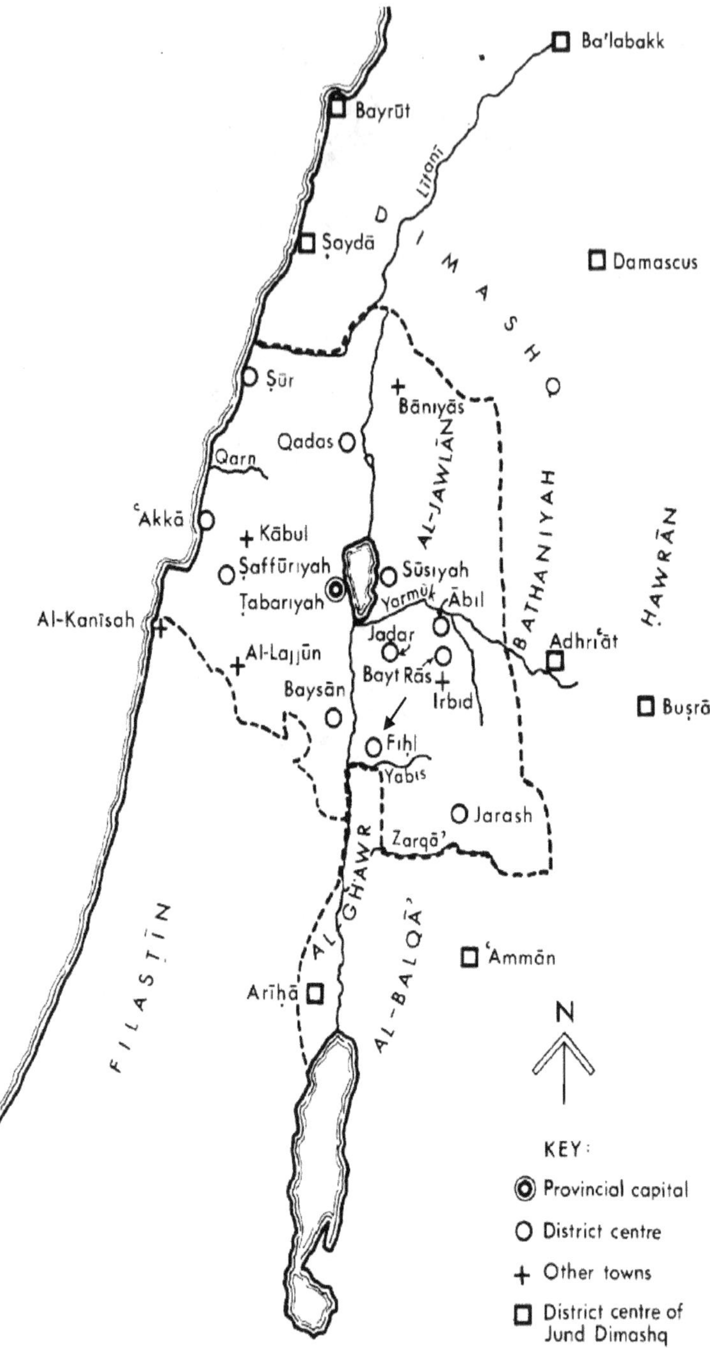

Figure 55. The borders and administrative centers of Umayyad *jund* of al-Urdunn (from Walmsley, "Pella/Fiḥl after the Islamic Conquest," ill. 1). This author has added an arrow to indicate Fiḥl (Pella).

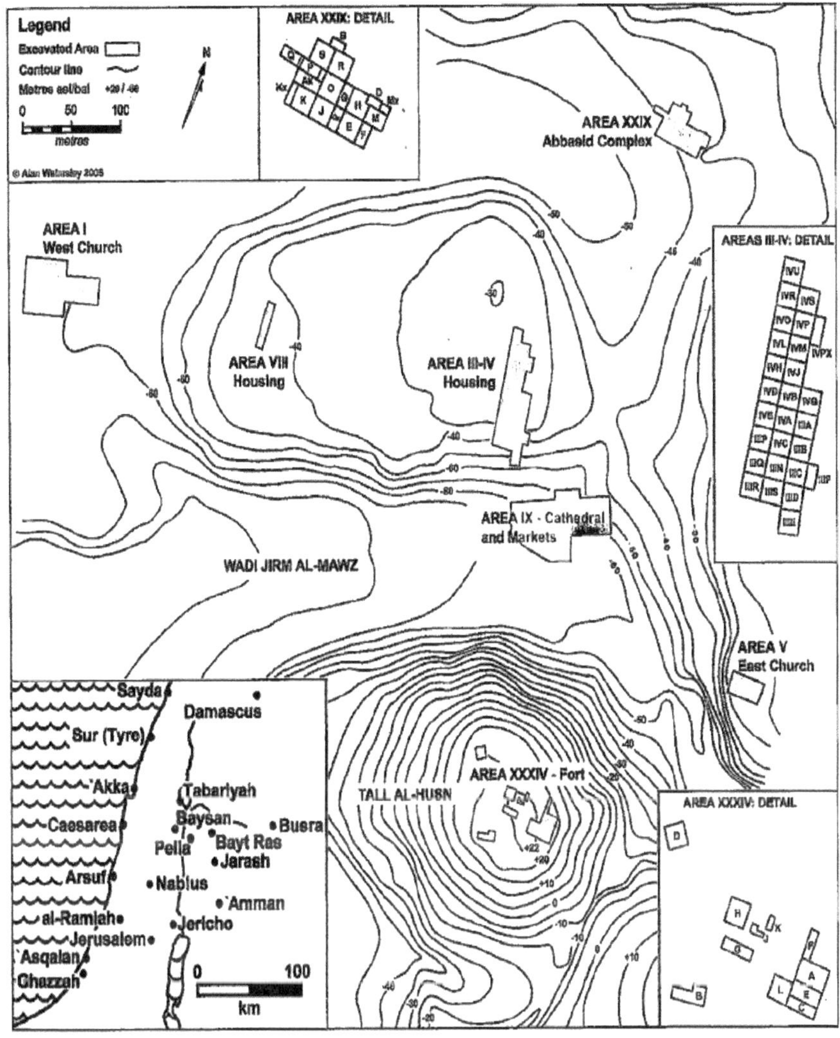

Figure 56. Map of archaeological areas at Pella (from Walmsley, "Households at Pella," fig. 1).

Figure 57. Area IV. Schematic plan of Byzantine Phases I-II (from Watson, "Byzantine Period," fig. 26).

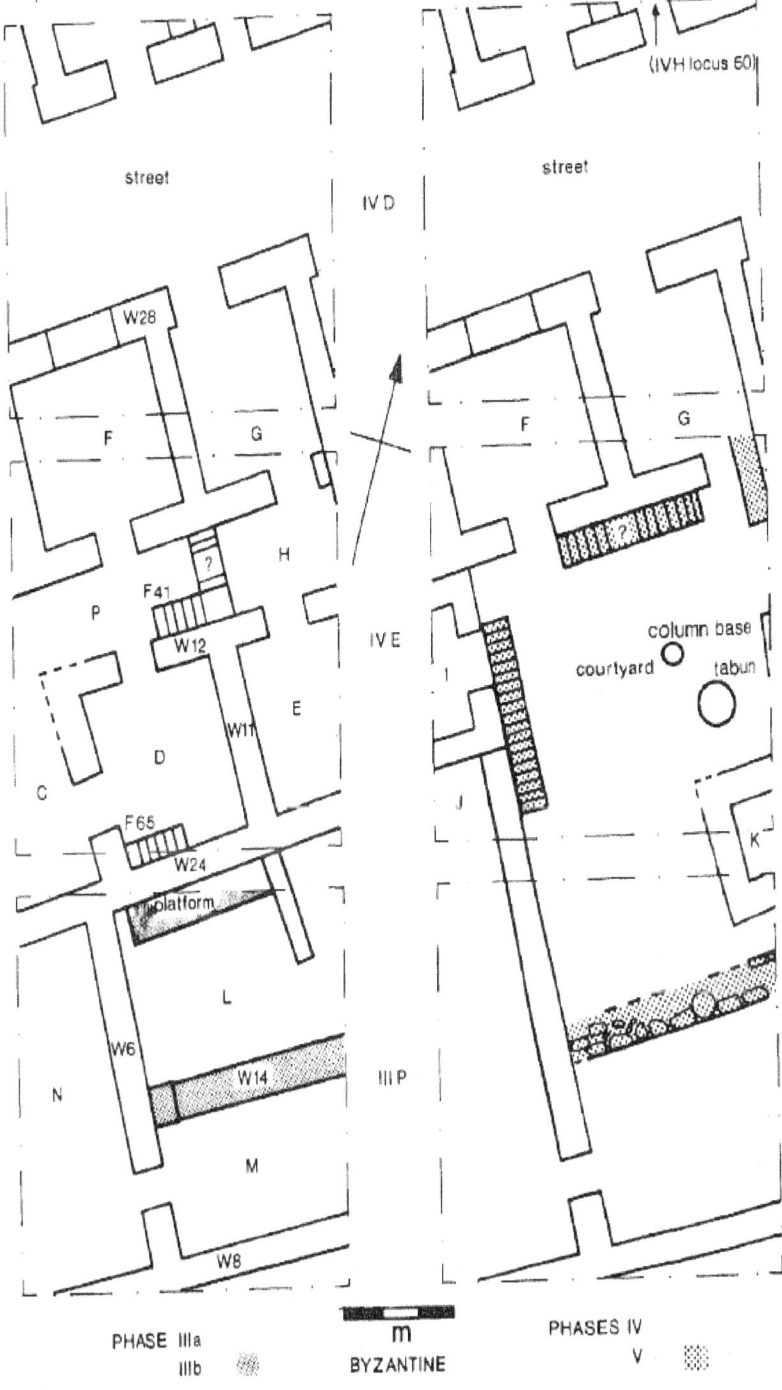

Figure 58. Area IV. Schematic plan of Byzantine Phases III-V (from Watson, "Byzantine Period," fig. 27).

Figure 59. View east showing walls of Byzantine Phases III-IV (from Watson, "Byzantine Period," Pl. 118a).

Figure 60. View east showing walls of Byzantine Phases IV-V and intrusive graves (from Watson, "Byzantine Period," Pl. 118b).

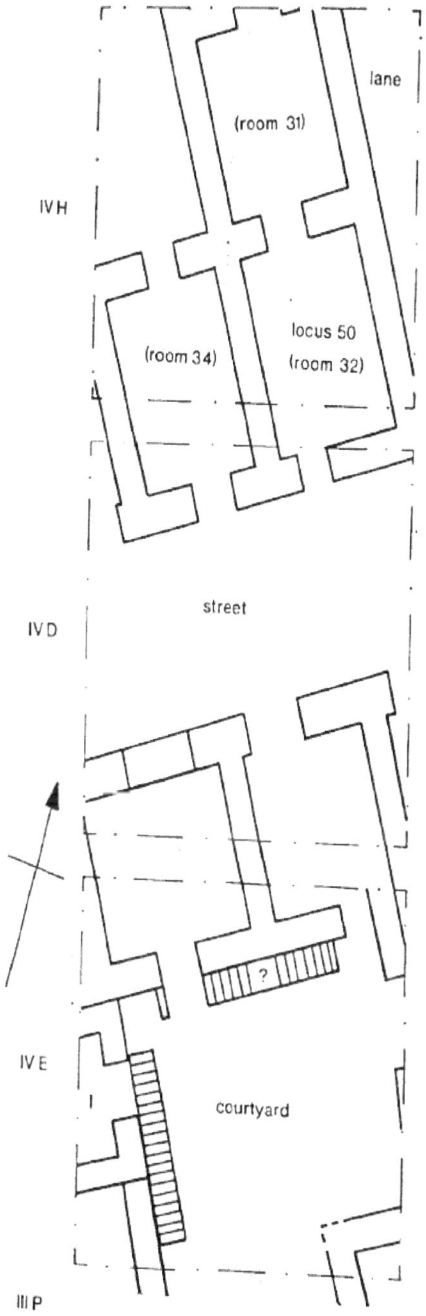

Figure 61. Schematic plan of Area IV in the Byzantine period (from McNicoll, et al., "Preliminary Report," fig. 3).

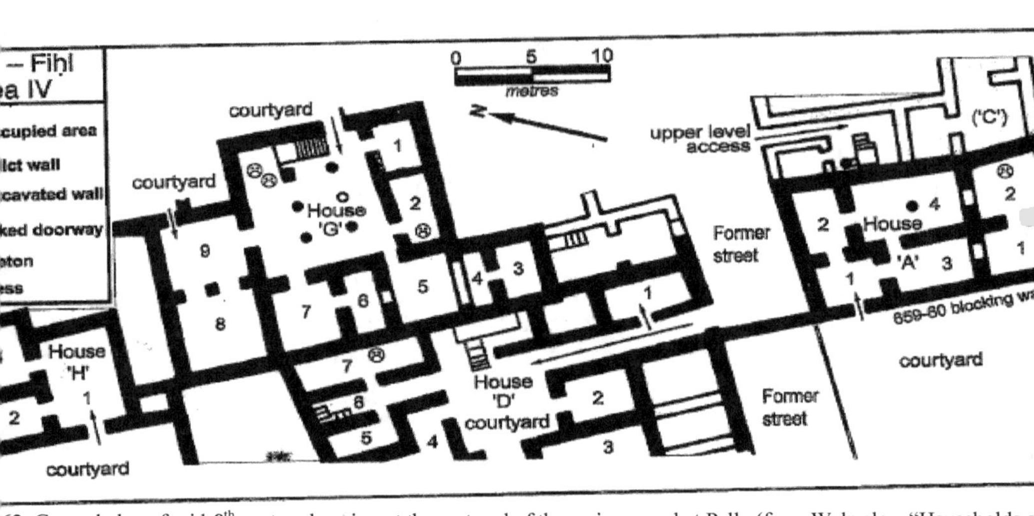

62. General plan of mid-8th century housing at the east end of the main mound at Pella (from Walmsley, "Households a

Figure 63. The central internal courtyard and western flanking rooms in House G (from Walmsley, "Economic Developments," fig. 10.

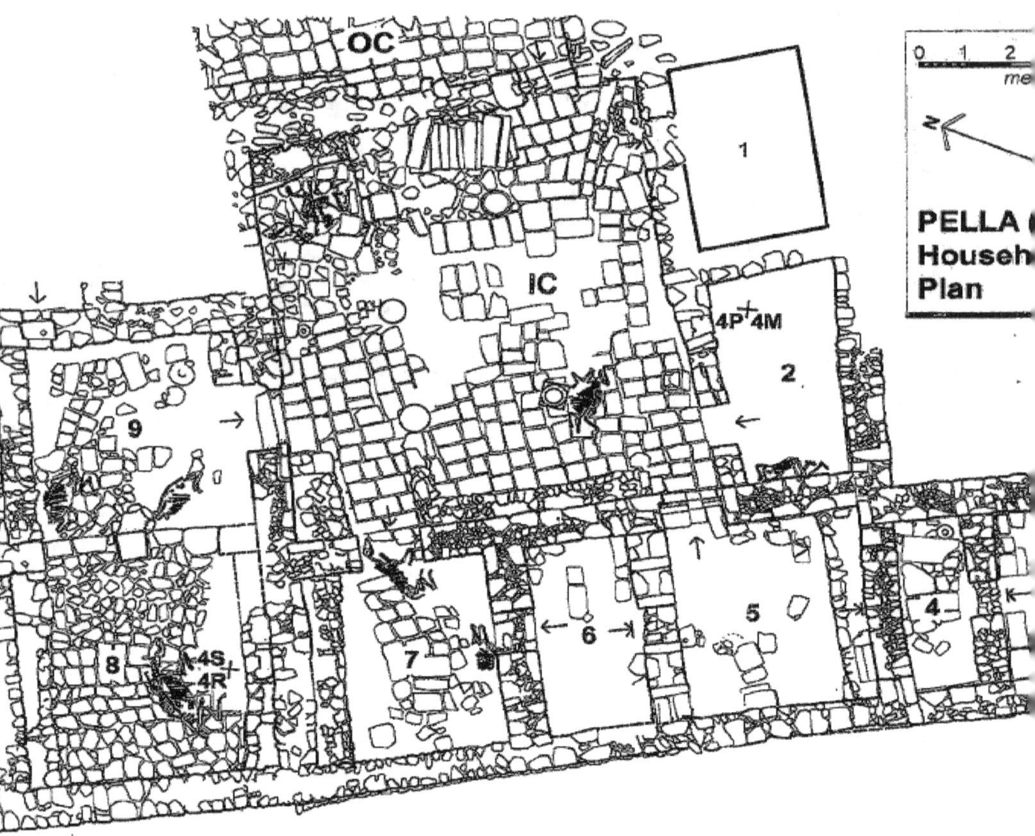

Figure 64. Detailed plan of House G (from Walmsley, "Households at Pella," fig. 12). The arrows indicate entry wa

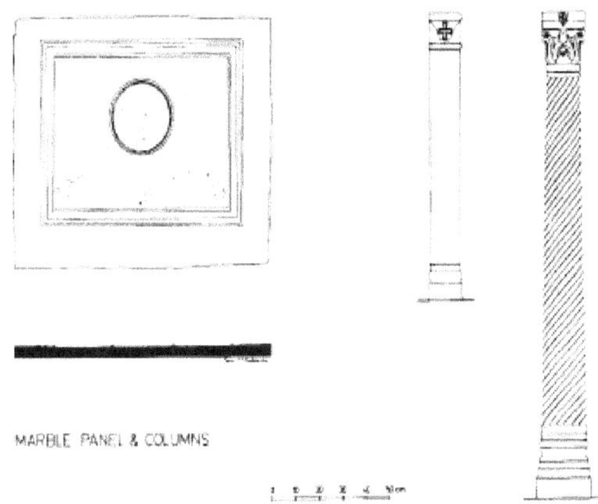

Figure 65. Marble panel and columns recovered from House G (from Walmsley, "Pella/Fiḥl after the Islamic Conquest," ill. 4).

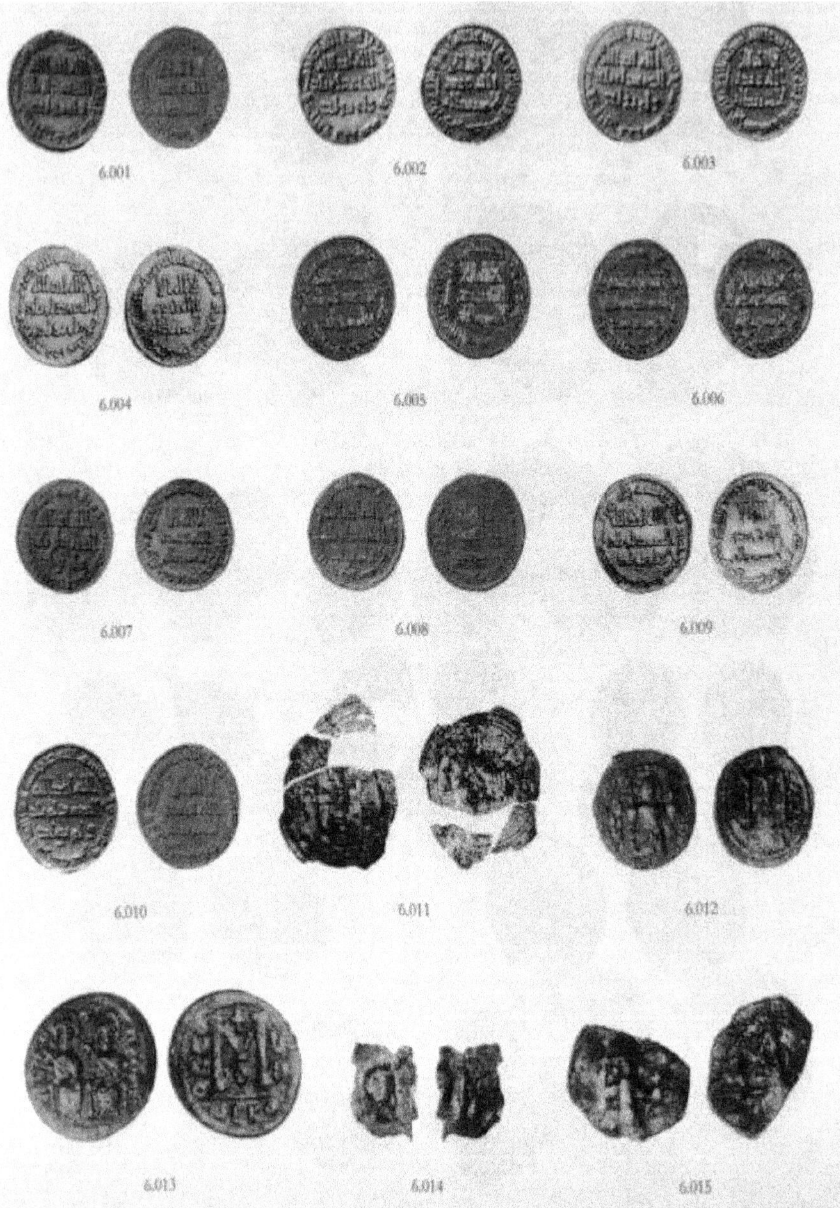

Figure 66. Coins recovered from Pella (from Walmsley, "Islamic Coins," pl. 14).

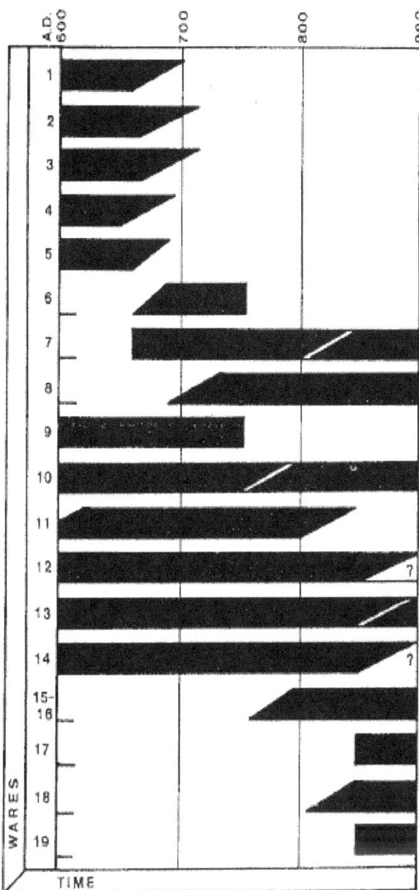

Figure 67. Occurrence of pottery wares at Pella, *c*. 600-900 C.E. (from Walmsley, "Tradition, Innovation, and Imitation," fig. 4).

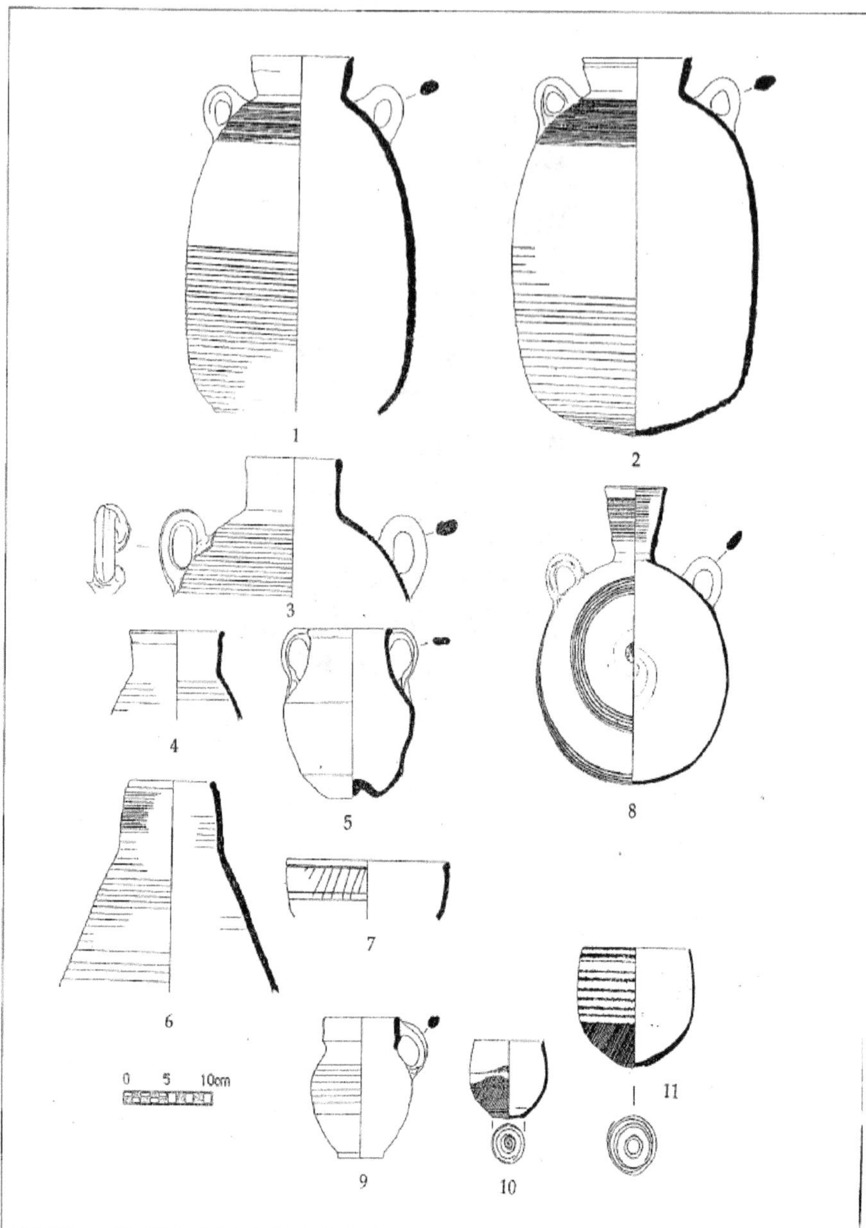

5. 1. CN10299, Ware 6, mid-8th c.; 2. CN154, W.6, mid-8th c.; 3. CN10061, W.7, early 8th c.; 4. CN10040, W.7, mid-8th c.; 5. CN10252, W.7, late 8th c.; 6. CN10237, W.7, early/mid-9th c.; 7. CN246, W.7, mid-8th c.; 8. CN16030, W.7, mid/late 9th c.; 9. CN2021, W.9, mid-8th c.; 10. CN16002, W.10, early 9th c.; 11. CN10246, W.10, late 8th c.

Figure 68. Pella pottery wares 6-7, 9 (from Walmsley, "Tradition, Innovation, and Imitation," fig. 5).

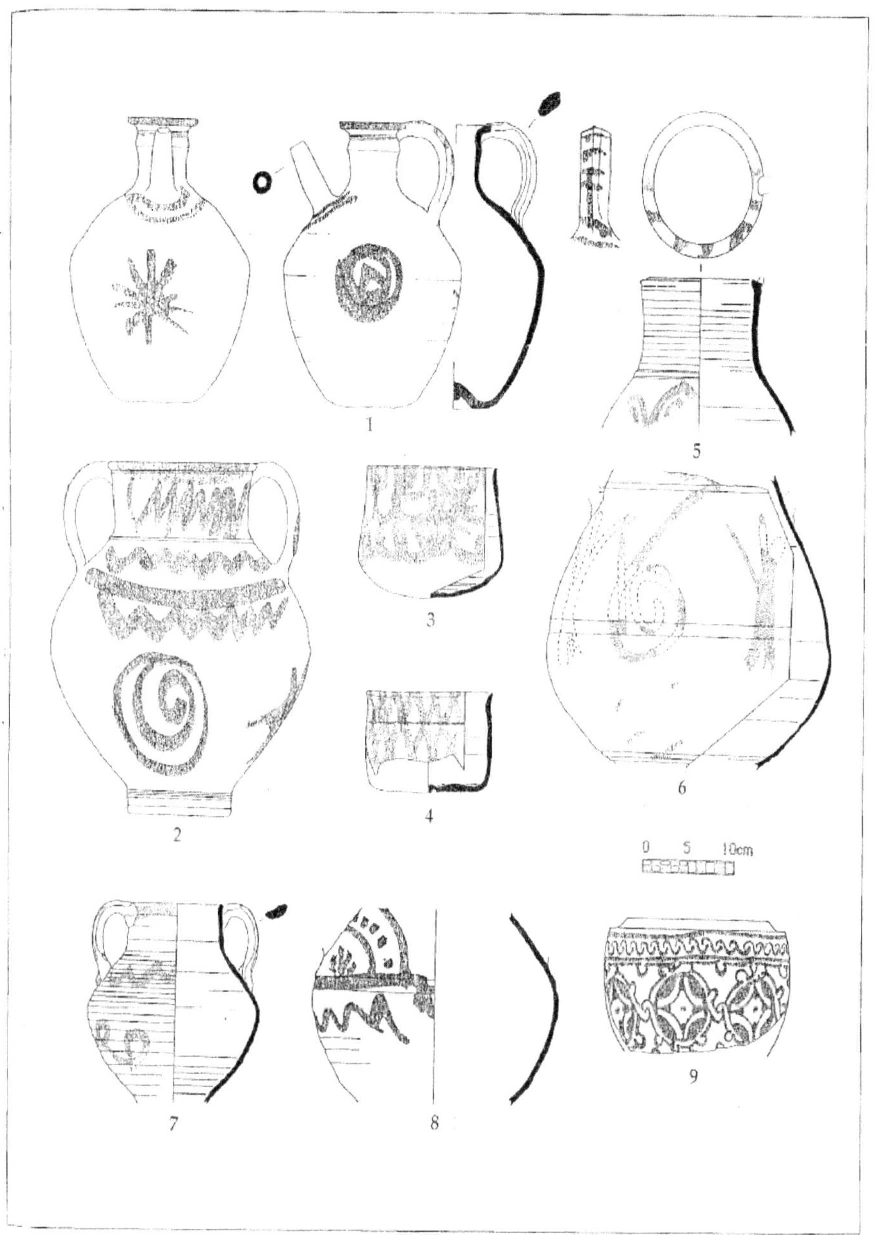

1. CN1869, W.8, mid-8th c.; 2. CN2030, W.8, mid-8th c.; 3. CN16053, W.8, early 9th c.; 4. CN16055, W.8, early 9th c.; 5. CN16051, W.8, early 9th c.; 6. CN16060, W.8, early 9th c.; 7. CN16049, W.8, early 9th c.; 8. CN10245, W.8, late 8th c.; 9. CN16001, W.8, early 9th c.

Figure 69. Pella pottery ware 8 (from Walmsley, "Tradition, Innovation, and Imitation," fig. 6).

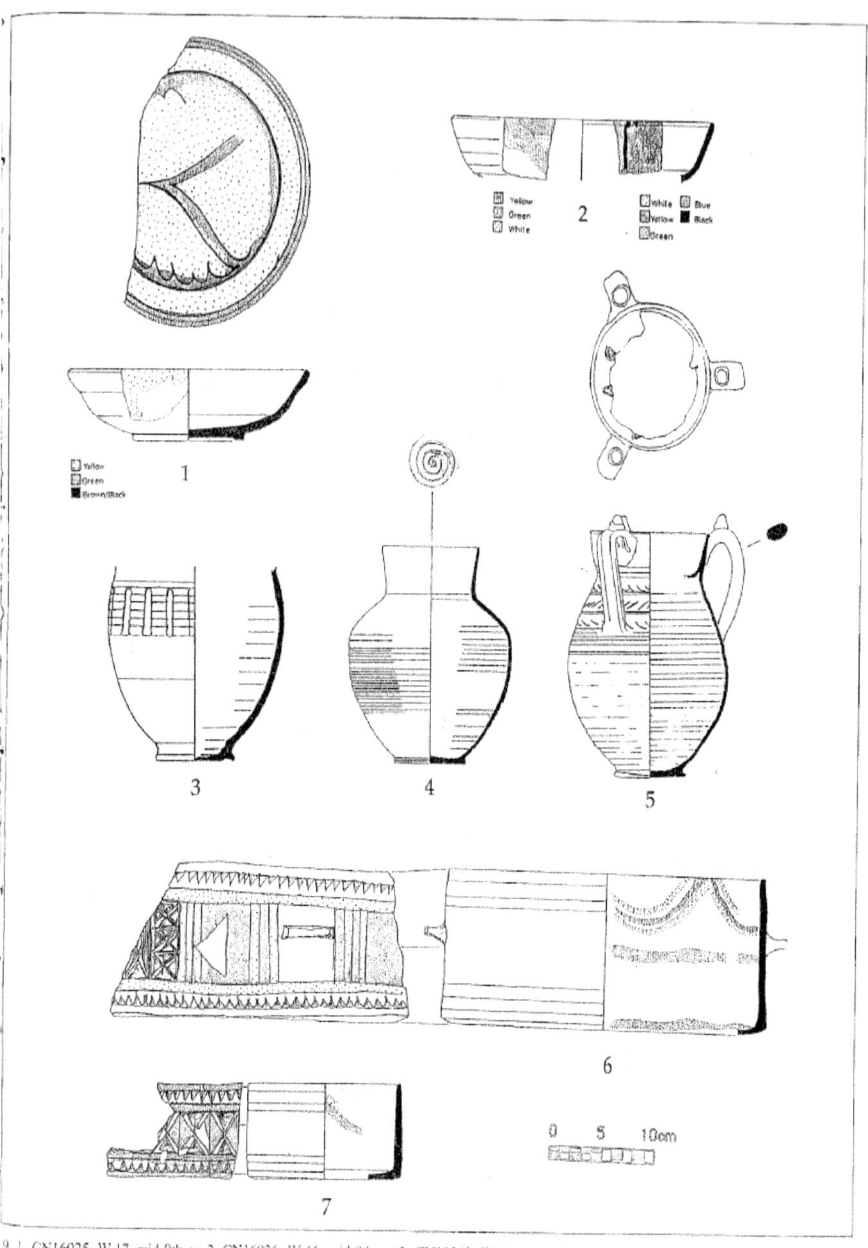

9. 1. CN16025, W.17, mid-9th c.; 2. CN16036, W.16, mid-9th c.; 3. CN10242, W.18, early/mid-9th c.; 4 CN16022, W.18, mid/late 9th c.; 5. CN16027, W.18, mid/late 9th c.; 6. CN16031, W.19, mid/late 9th c.; 7. CN16032, W.18, mid/late 9th c.

Figure 70. Pella pottery wares 16, 17, 18, and 19 (from Walmsley, "Tradition, Innovation, and Imitation," fig. 9).

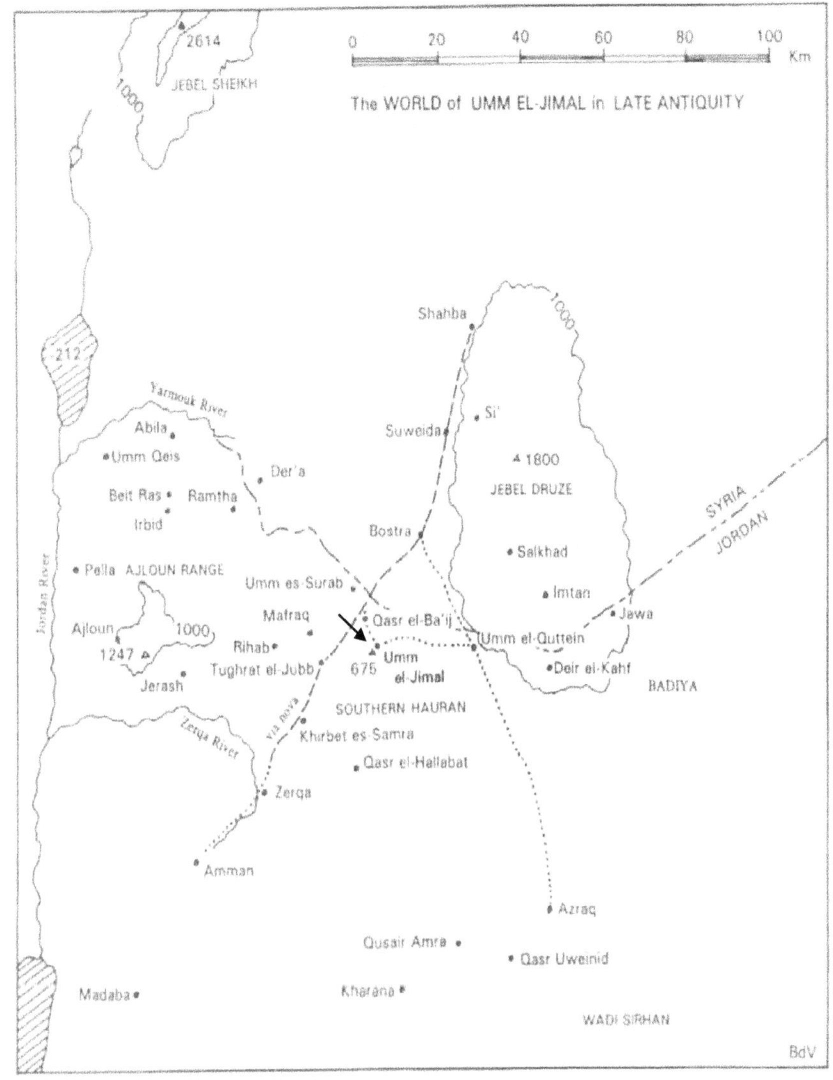

Figure 71. Map of the world of Umm el-Jimāl in Late Antiquity (from De Vries, *Umm el-Jimal*, fig. 43). This author has added an arrow to indicate Umm el-Jimāl.

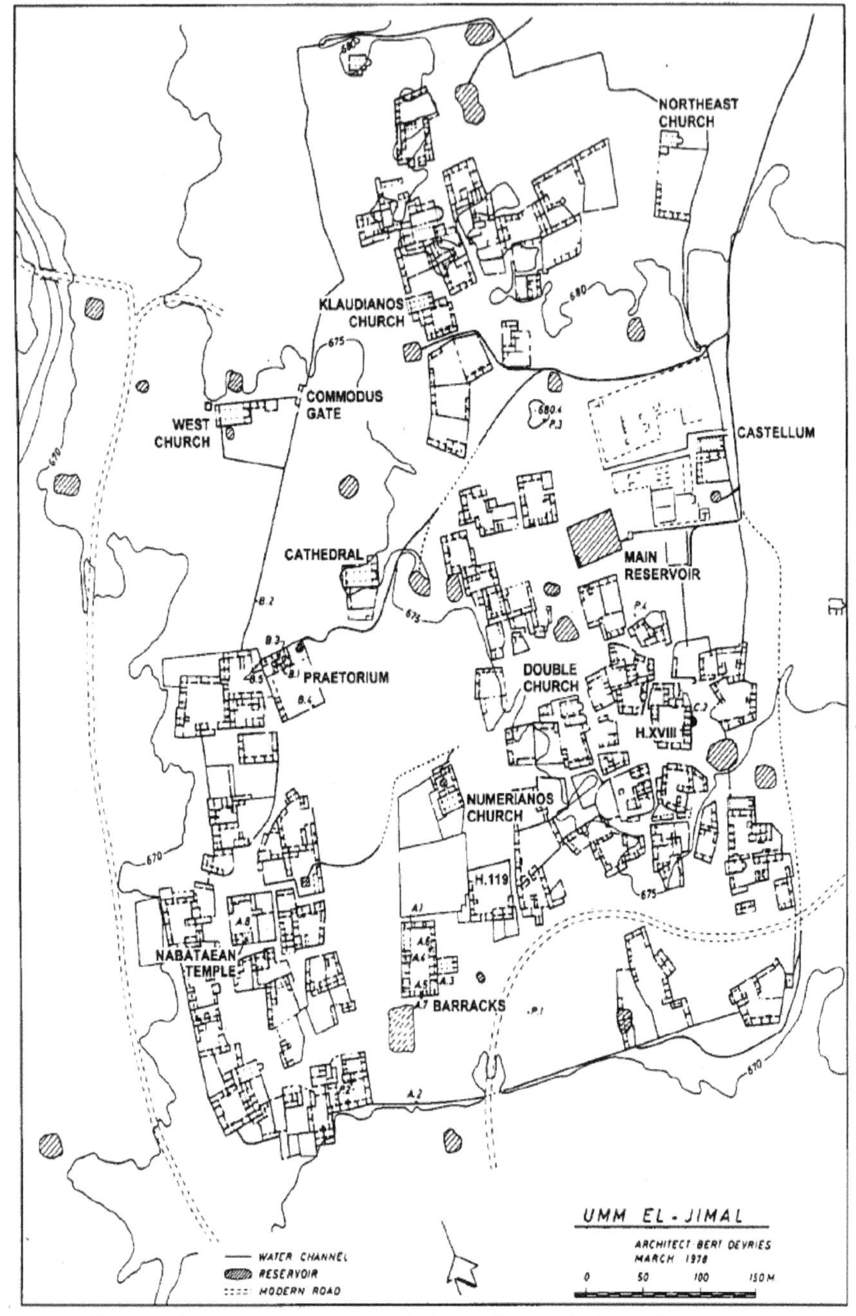

Figure 72. Plan of Late Antique Umm el-Jimāl (De Vries, "Continuity and Change," fig. 2).

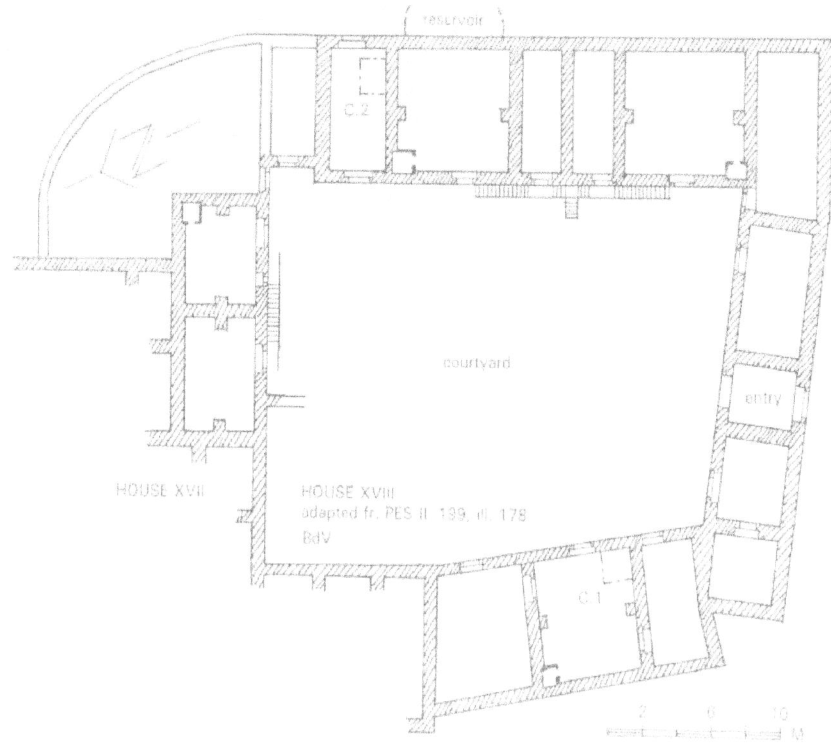

Figure 73. Plan of House XVIII showing locations of trenches C.1, C.2 (from Brown, "Large Residence," fig. 139). This author has added a compass on the bottom right-hand corner of the figure to more clearly indicate direction.

Figure 74. Cantilevered stairs in northern façade of the courtyard (from Brown, "Large Residence," fig. 140).

Figure 75. Façade of the eastern complex, inside the courtyard (from Brown, "Large Residence," fig. 141).

Figure 76. Façade of western complex, inside the courtyard (from Brown, "Large Residence," fig. 142).

Figure 77. Façade of southern side of courtyard with entrance in the center (from Brown, "Large Residence," fig. 143).

Figure 78. Method of corbelling (from De Vries, "Umm el-Jimal Project, 1972-1977," fig. 2).

Figure 79. Stairs at the north-western corner of courtyard (from De Vries, "Umm el-Jimal Project, 1972-1977," fig. 3).

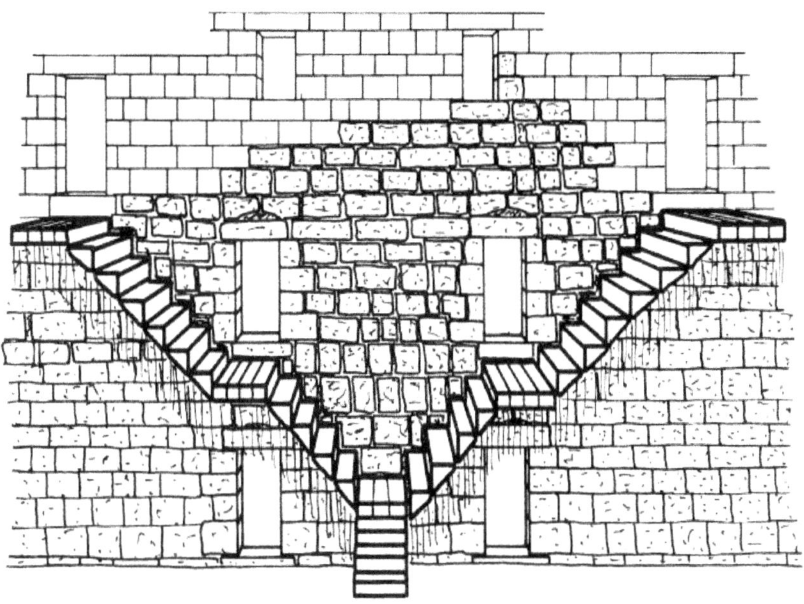

Figure 80. Reconstruction of stairs in the eastern wall of courtyard (from De Vries, "Umm el-Jimal Project, 1972-1977," fig. 4).

Figure 81. Double window of House XVIII, western face (from De Vries, *Umm el-Jimal*, fig. 66).

Figure 82. Basalt door in eastern exterior wall (from Brown, "Large Residence," fig. 144).

Figure 83. Doorway into side room on western side of courtyard in House XVIII with device to relieve lintel (from De Vries, *Umm el-Jimal*, fig. 77).

Figure 84. Cistern entrance in corner below floor corbels (from Brown, "Large Residence," fig. 150).

Figure 85. Corbelled cistern roof viewed from below (from Brown, "Large Residence," fig. 152).

Figure 86. Cobble and plaster floor (from Brown, "Large Residence," fig. 146).

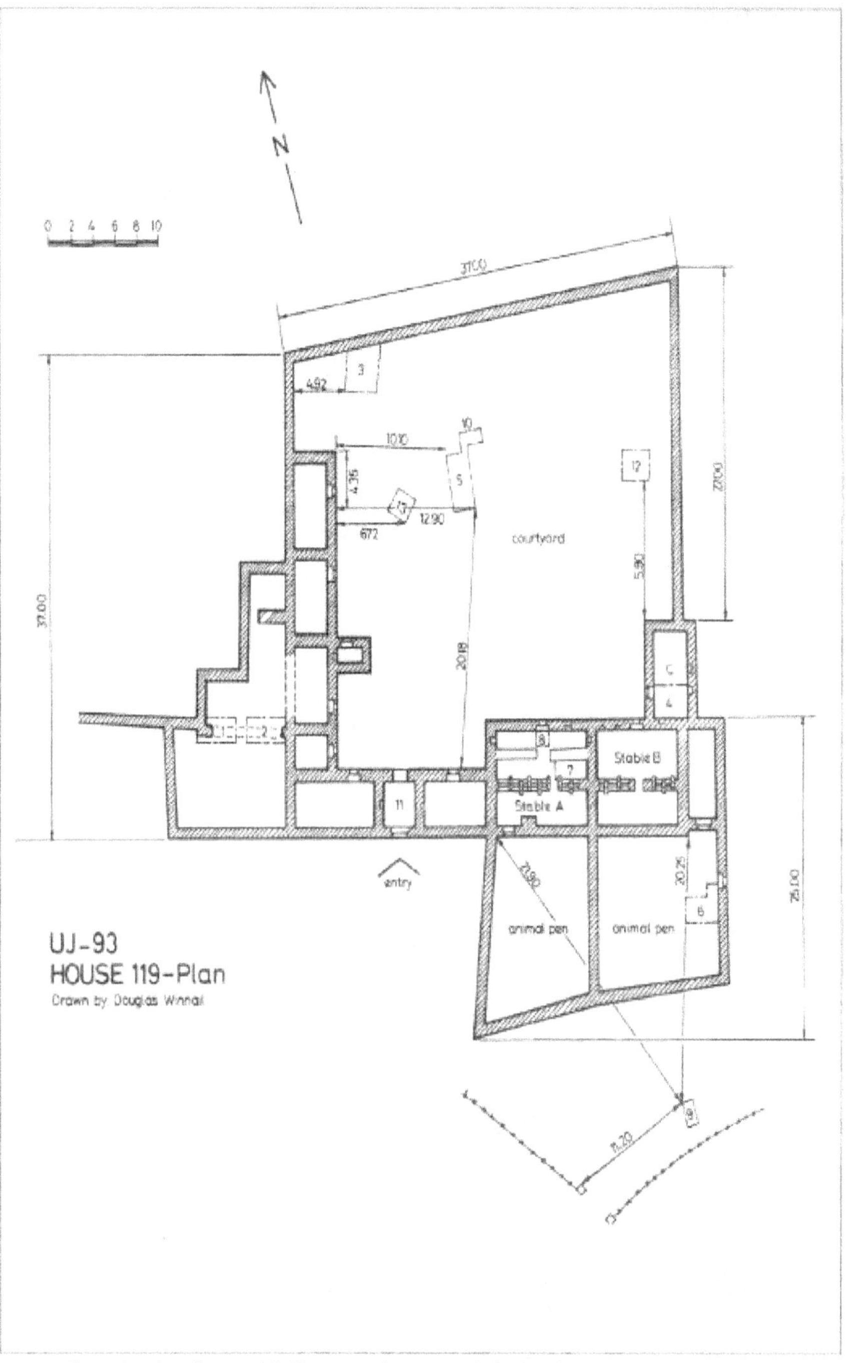

Figure 87. Plan of House 119 (from De Vries, "Umm el-Jimal Project, 1993 and 1994," fig. 3).

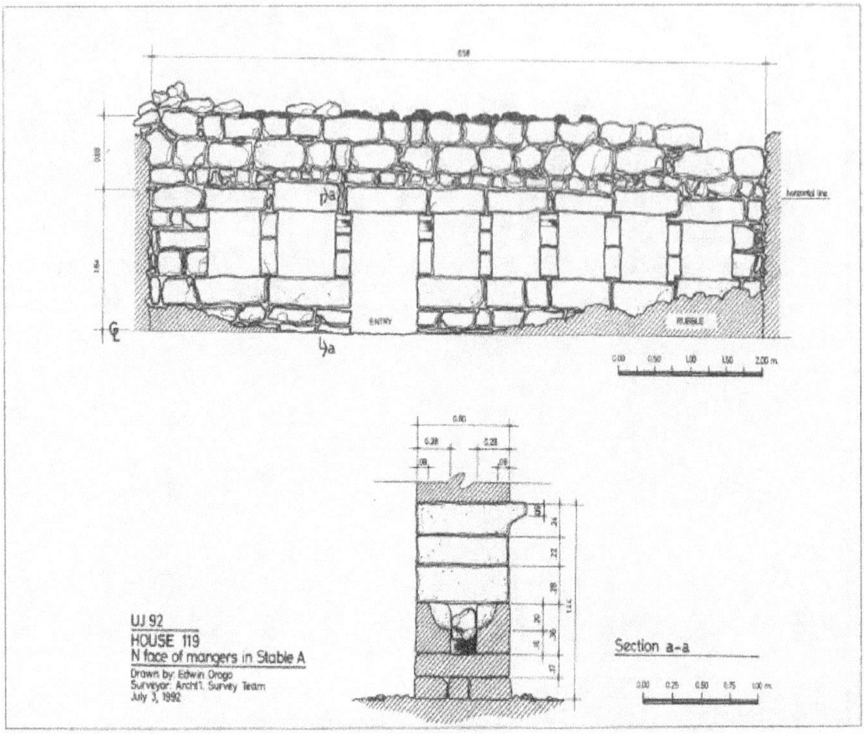

Figure 88. North elevation and sections of mangers in Stable A (from De Vries, "Umm el-Jimal Project, 1993 and 1994," fig. 5).

Figure 89. Doorway and manger in Stable A (from De Vries, "Umm el-Jimal Project, 1993 and 1994," fig. 6).

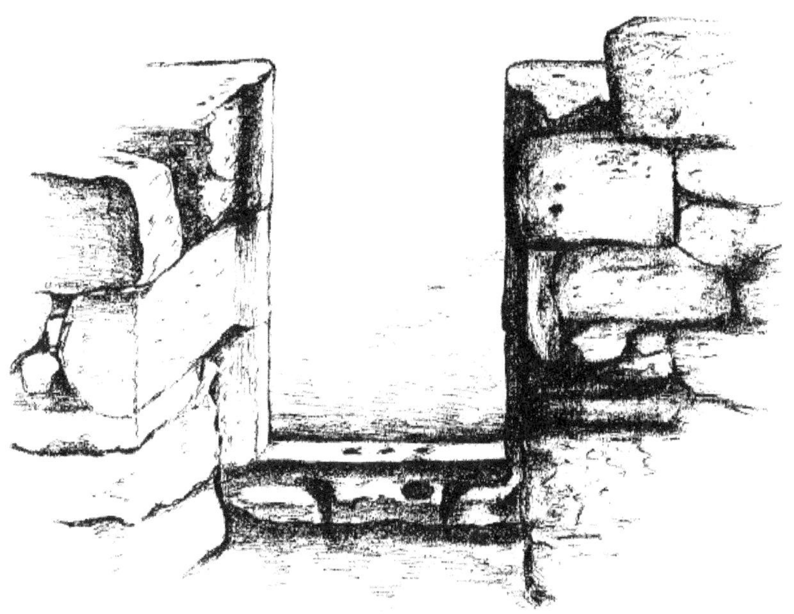

Figure 90. Doorstep of entry into Stable A (from De Vries, *Umm el-Jimal*, fig. 72).

Figure 91. View toward south wall of Room C in House 119 with flagstone paving and cement flooring in foreground and under meter stick (from De Vries, "Umm el-Jimal Project, 1993 and 1994," fig. 8).

Figure 92. Jarash lamp fragments no. 1 (from Lapp, "Byzantine and Early Islamic Oil Lamp Fragments," fig. 1).

Figure 93. Jarash lamp fragments nos. 2, 3 and 4 (from Lapp, "Byzantine and Early Islamic Oil Lamp Fragments," fig. 2).

Figure 94. Late Byzantine to early Islamic Lamps (from Kehrberg, "Selected Lamps and Pottery," fig. 5).

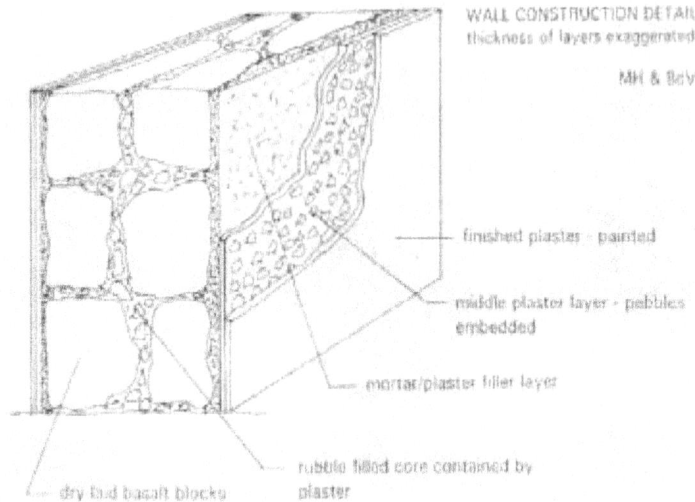

Figure 95. Schematic rendering of wall construction (from De Vries, *Umm el-Jimal*, fig. 64).

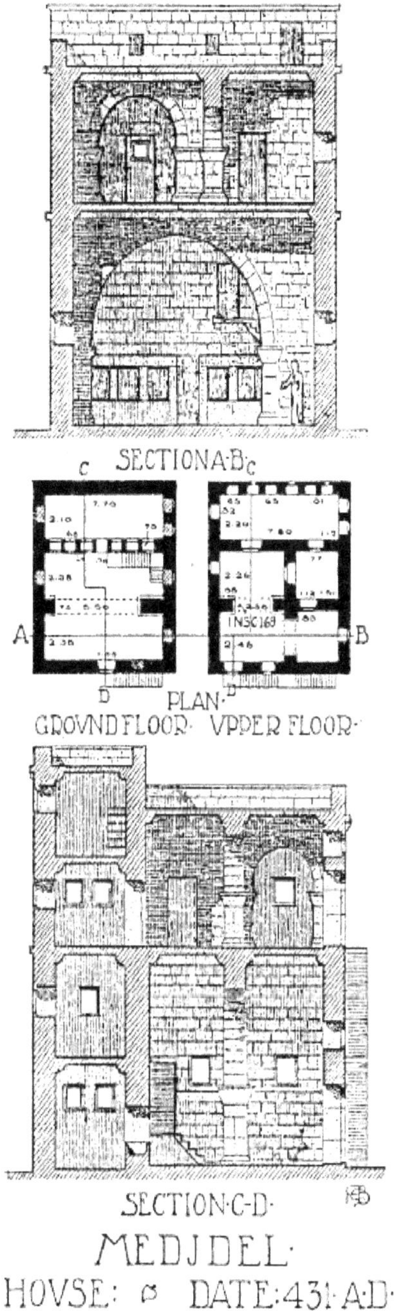

Figure 96. House at Il Medjdel, Syria: plan and elevation (from Ellis, *Roman Housing*, fig. 17).

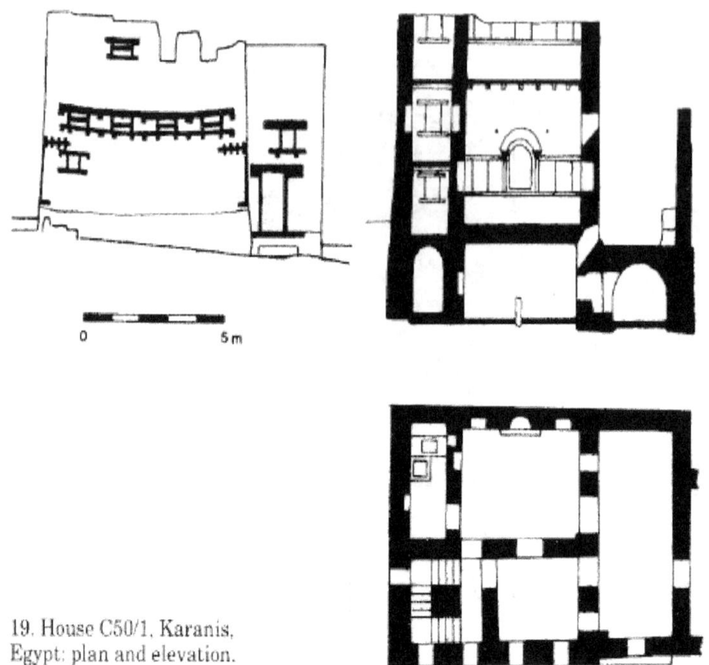

Figure 97. House at Karanis, Egypt: plan and elevation (from Ellis, *Roman Housing*, fig. 19).

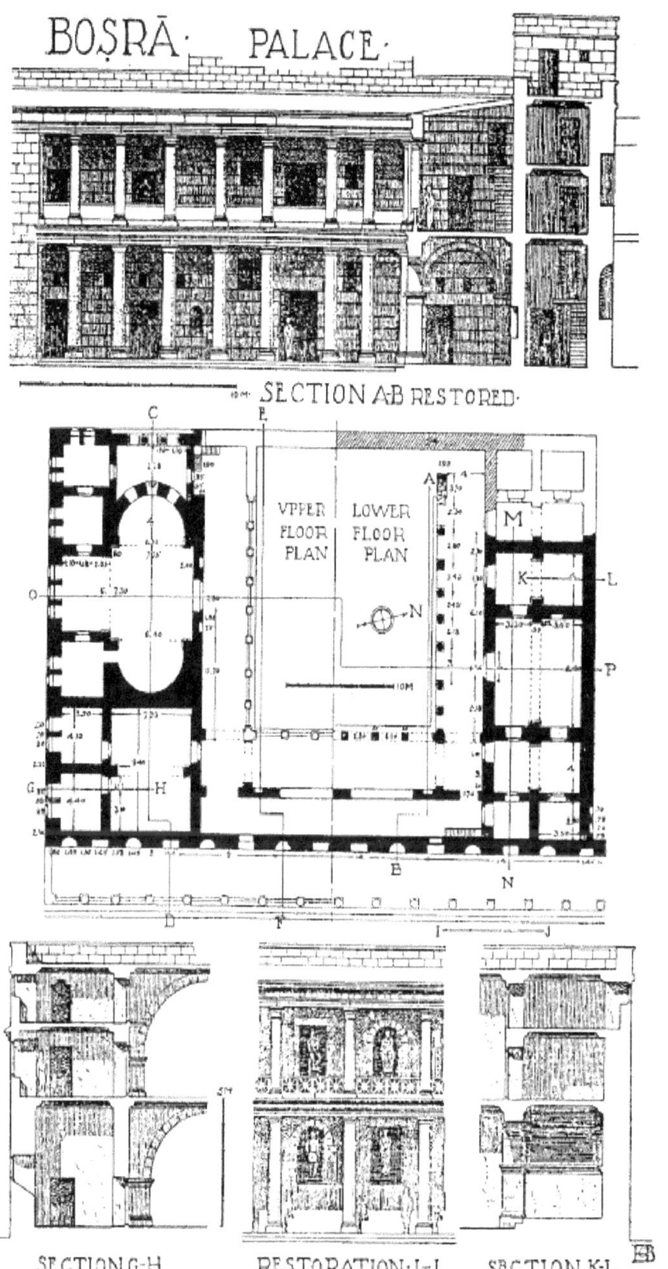

Figure 98. „Palace" at Boṣrā, Syria: plan and elevation (from Butler and Prentice, *Princeton Archaeological Expeditions*, ill. 229).

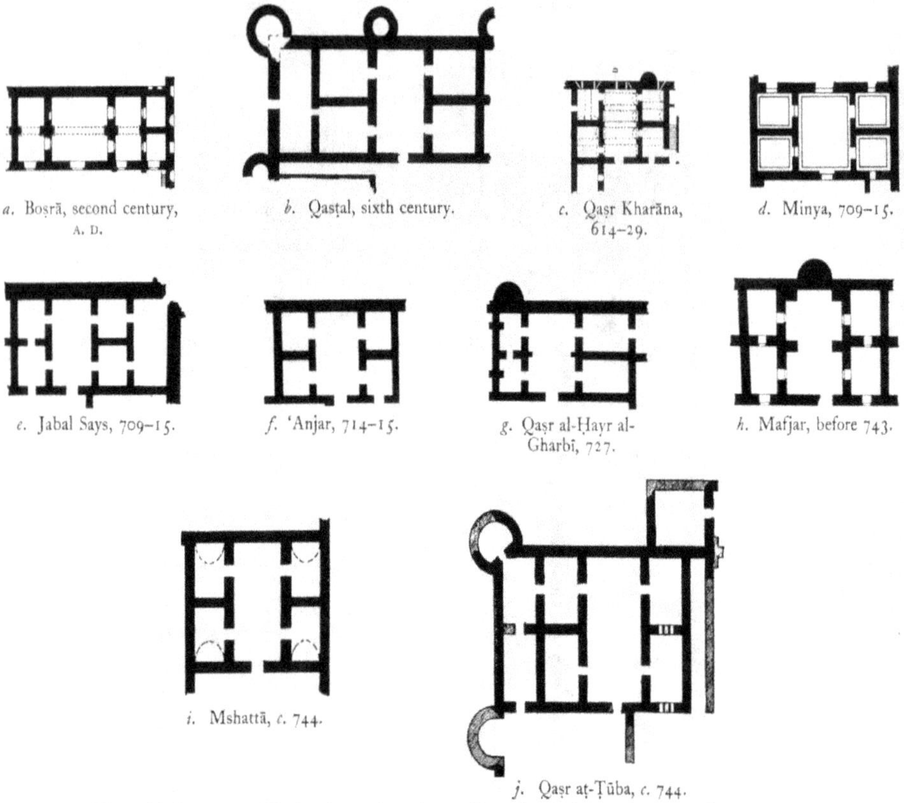

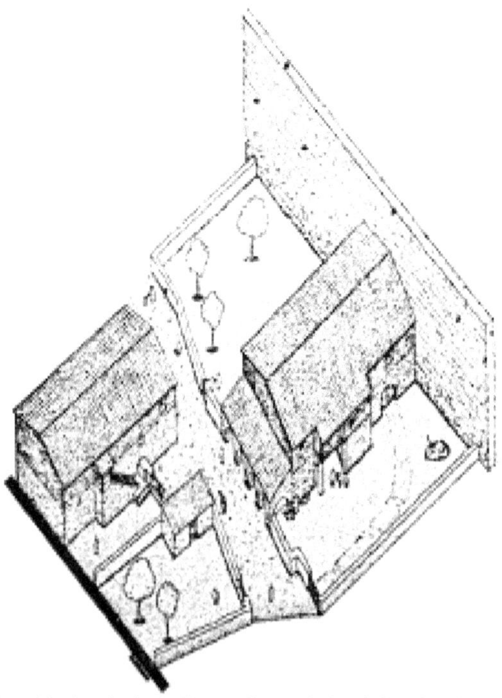

Figure 99. Sequence of Syrian *bayts* (from Creswell, *Early Muslim Architecture*, fig. 565).

Figure 100. Reconstruction of the housing in the Forum of Nerva in the ninth and tenth centuries (from Valenzani, "Residential Building," fig. 11).

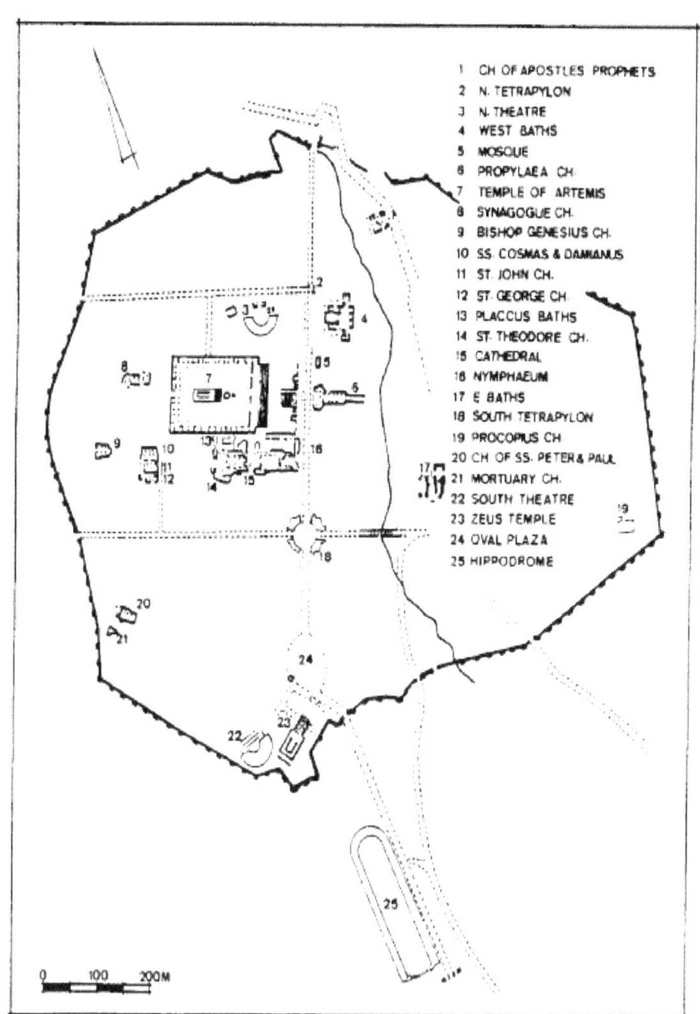

Figure 101. Jarash (from Zeyadeh, "Urban Transformation," fig. 2).

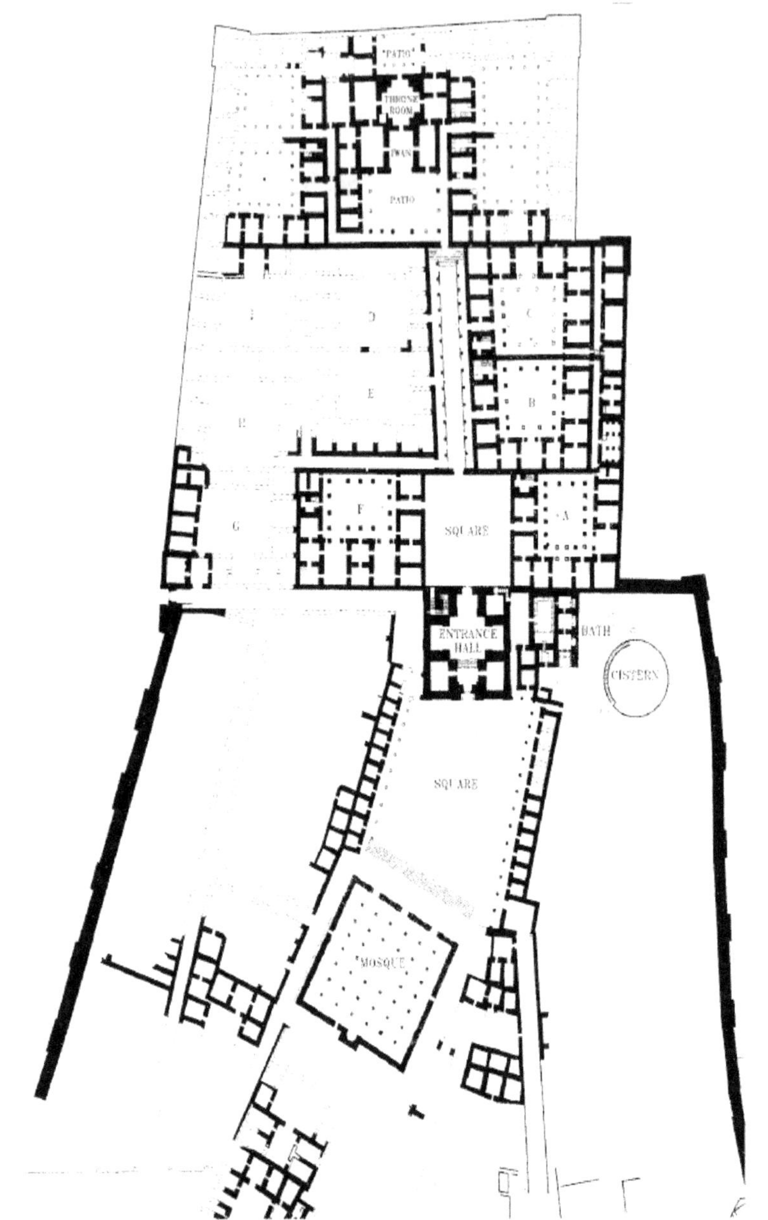

Figure 102. The central and north area of the citadel in Umayyad times (from Almagro and Arce, "Umayyad Town Planning," fig. 2).

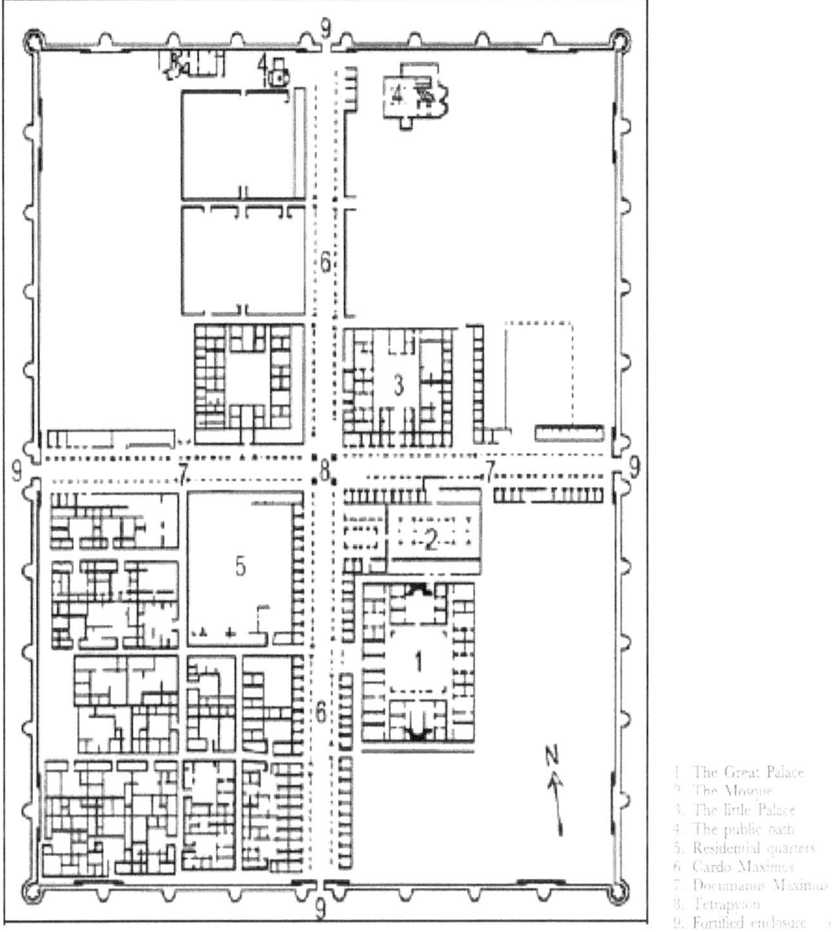

Figure 103. „Anjar, plan (from Hillenbrand, "„Anjar and Early Islamic Urbanism," fig. 1).

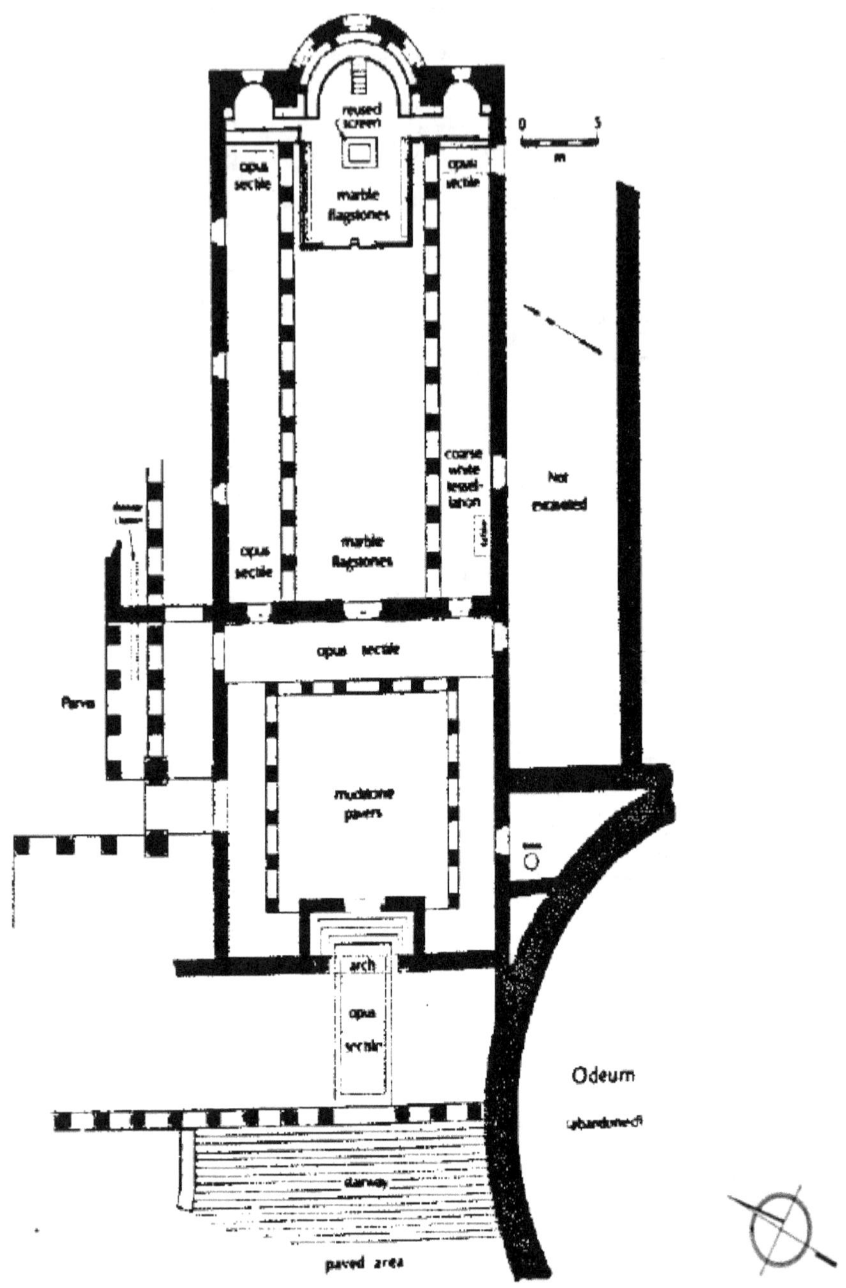

Figure 104. Civic Complex Church in the 7th century C.E. (from Walmsley, "Social and Economic Regime," fig. 5). This author has added a compass on the bottom right-hand corner of the figure to more clearly indicate direction.

Figure 105. View of the Civic Complex at Pella from the north, showing the church atrium (rear) and adjacent markets (foreground) (from Walmsley, "Economic Developments," fig. 9).

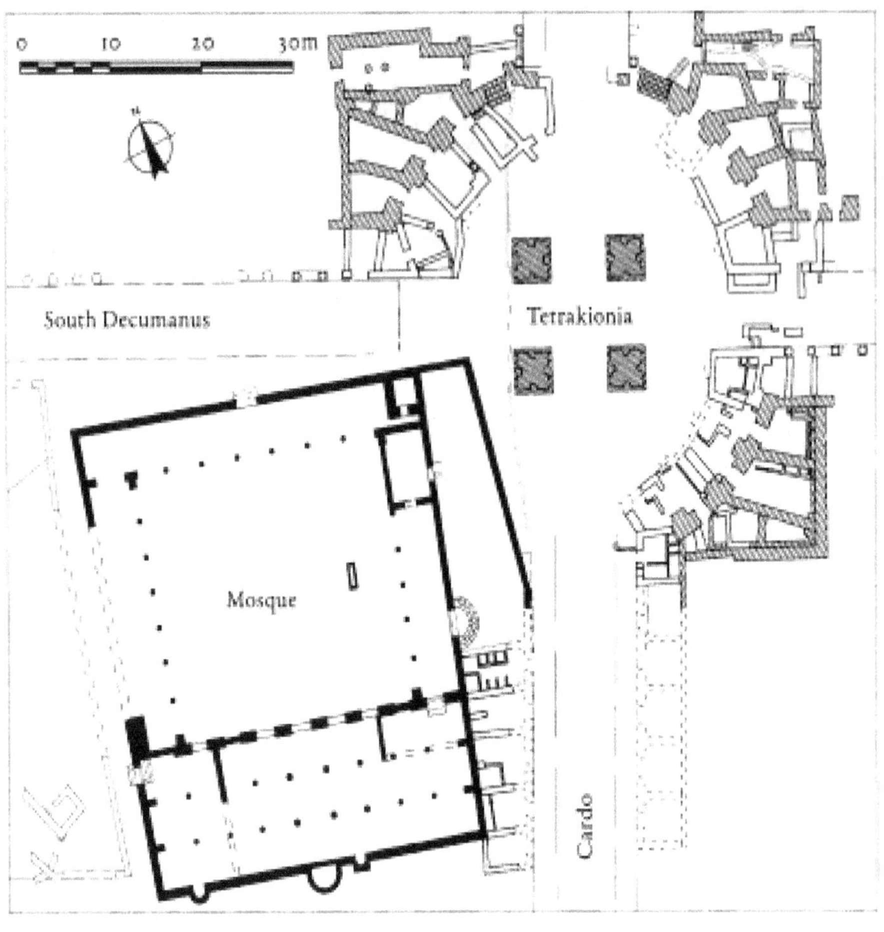

Figure 106. Plan of central Jarash in the mid-eighth century, showing the inserted mosque and related commercial structures, including new shops abutting the mosque"s east wall (from Walmsley, "Economic Developments," fig. 20).

Figure 107. Aerial photograph of Jarash taken in the late 1920s and in the possession of Walmsley (from Walmsley, "Friday Mosque," fig. 5).

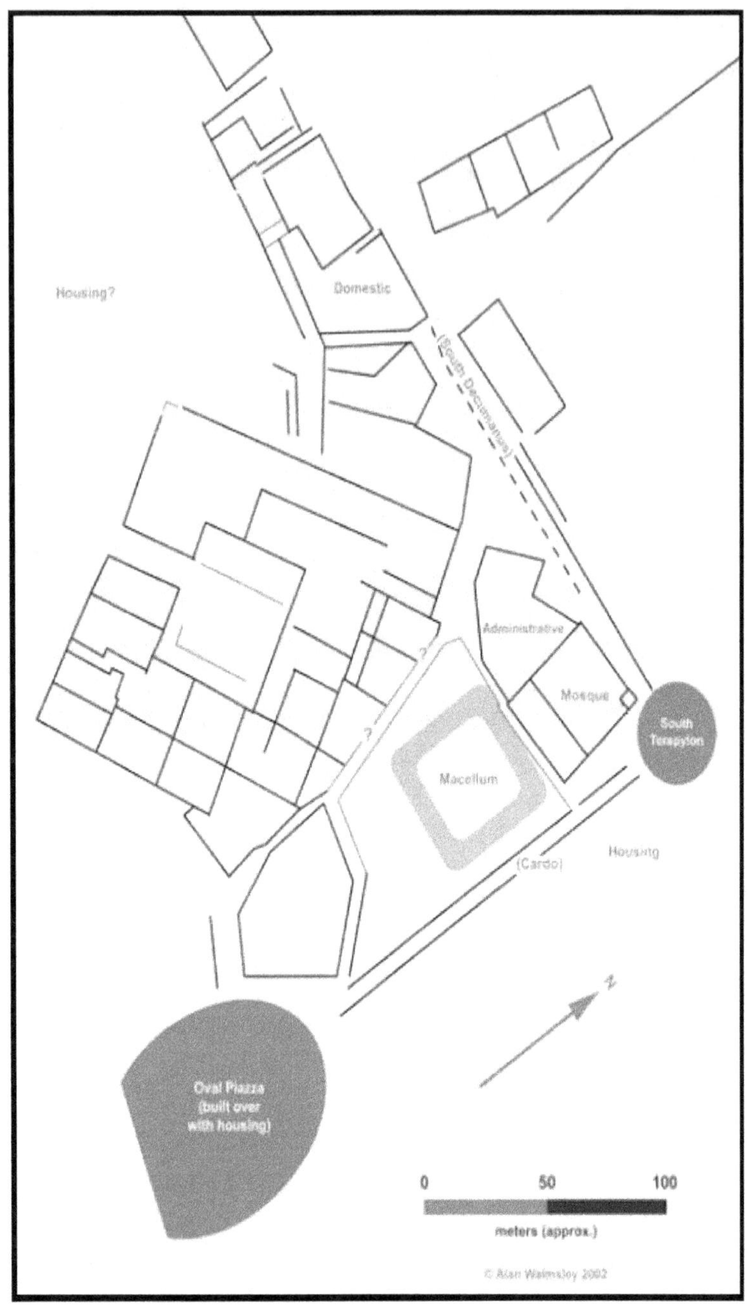

Figure 108. Preliminary schematic representation of the principal features of Islamic Jarash (from Walmsley, "Friday Mosque," fig. 7).

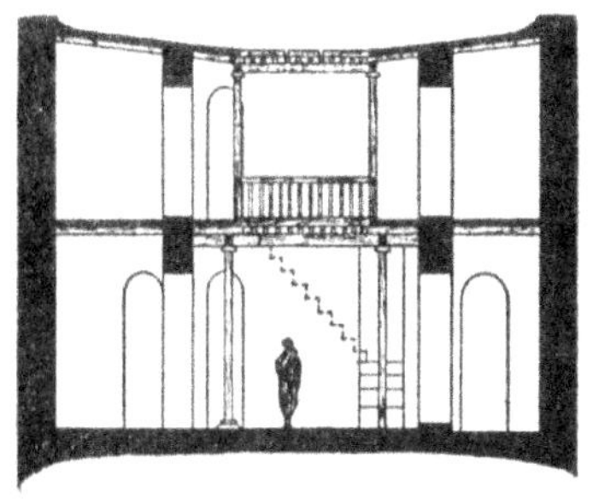

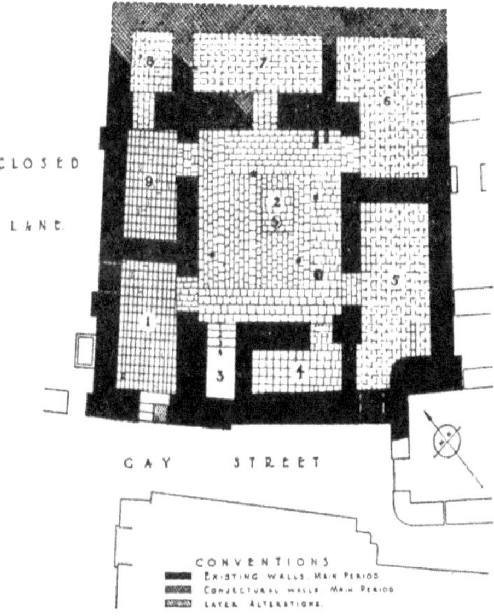

Figure 109. Plan of a private house at Ur (from Woolley, *Excavations at Ur*, fig. 13).

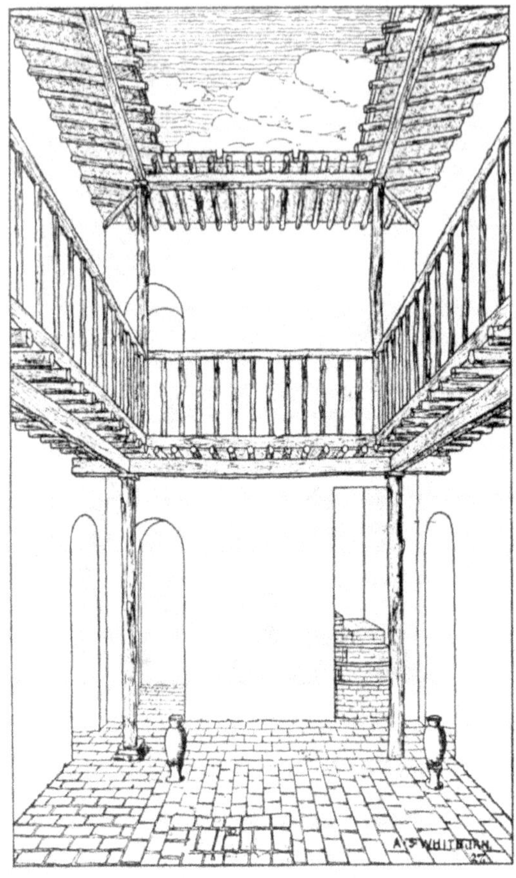

Figure 110. Reconstruction of a private house at Ur (from Woolley, *Excavations at Ur*, fig. 14).

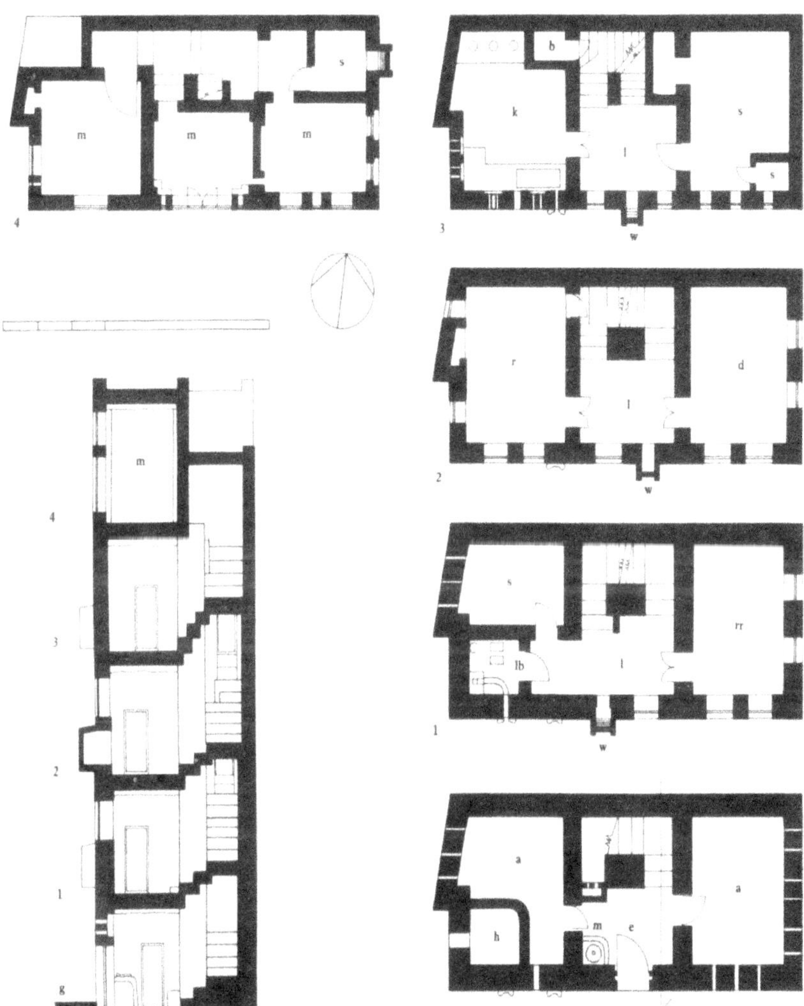

Figure 111. Plans and section of typical Islamic house in Ṣan,,āʾ (from Lewcock and Serjeant, "Houses of Ṣan,ā"," fig. 22.1).

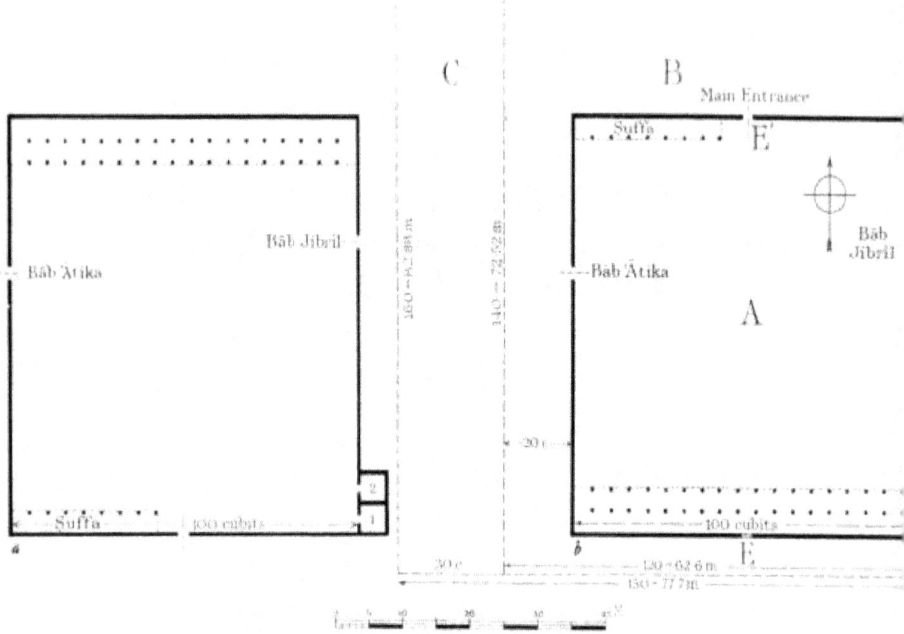

Figure 112. Prophet"s house-mosque, Medina (from Creswell, *Early Muslim Architecture*, fig. 7). (a) Before change of qibla; (b) After change of qibla.

9 788793 187799